HISTORY'S
WORST
PREDICTIONS

and the People Who Made Them

HISTORY'S
WORST
PREDICTIONS

and the People Who Made Them

Eric Chaline

CHARTWELL
BOOKS, INC.

© 2011 by Quid Publishing

This edition published in 2011 by
CHARTWELL BOOKS, INC.
A division of BOOK SALES, INC.
276 Fifth Avenue Suite 206
New York, New York 10001
USA

ISBN-13: 978-0-7858-2813-6

Printed in Singapore

Conceived, designed, and produced by
Quid Publishing
Level 4, Sheridan House
114 Western Road
Hove BN3 1DD
England
www.quidpublishing.com

All images in this book are public domain unless otherwise stated.

To Joey, because "It's a Beautiful Life."

CONTENTS

INTRODUCTION

If the past is another country, the future is another galaxy: We can revisit the former, but we cannot reach the latter by any normal human means. That, however, has not stopped humans from confidently forecasting what will happen tomorrow, next week, next year, or 1,000 years hence. Prediction began in the divinatory practices of magic and religion at a time when our understanding of the world was so limited that any event—manmade or natural—could be understood as a sign or admonition from a higher power. Even today, when our understanding of the universe has immeasurably advanced, there is no shortage of inspired futurologists. The only difference between our modern-day seers and their predecessors two millennia ago is that instead of casting the runes or cutting up a goat to see the future, the latter back up their predictions with complex computerized models that strangely, as the ongoing financial crisis shows, are no clearer a guide to what will happen than the position of the Sun and Moon or a sheep with a peculiarly shaped liver.

Unsurprisingly, religion and millenarian prophecy are constant themes that run through the 50 chronological entries featured in this book. We begin by examining the prophetic traditions of several of the world's major cultures, including pagan Rome, whose long history was said to be foretold in a mysterious collection of secret books (pp. 10–14), and the Maya of pre-Columbian Mesoamerica, whose obsession with measuring time has recently been revived with the 2012 prophecies.

Since its foundation, Christianity has been a fecund source for individuals wishing to offer up Doomsday predictions. Initial projections indicated that the Second Coming was supposed to occur soon after Jesus' resurrection—or certainly within the lifetime of many who had seen him (pp. 15–19). In later centuries, aspiring prophets employed entirely erroneous formulae to calculate to the nearest year the date of Christ's return. Such dates, it seems, tend toward round numbers, as the years 500, 1000 (pp. 25–8), and, of course, Y2K (pp. 231–5) have all been given as the date for the End of Time, the Apocalypse, the Last Trump, the Rapture (pp. 214–20), and Armageddon.

Prophets have not always been motivated by religion—for example the astrologers Nostradamus (pp. 41–7) and Johannes Stöffler (pp. 33–6). Similarly, the end of civilization might not be brought about by divine intervention but by a natural event, such as an ice age (pp. 199–203), a collision with a stray planet, asteroid, or comet, or a pandemic (pp. 241–6), or possibly a manmade one: overpopulation (pp. 53–7), nuclear war (pp. 183–7), or the exhaustion of our natural resources (pp. 164–8).

Quite apart from the much-anticipated and oft-delayed end of the world, there is no single area of human endeavor—technology, economics, politics, social and cultural trends, and military matters—that has not been subject to the most outrageously, absurdly flawed predictions. Political leaders and theorists, for example, have boasted that their empires would endure for 1,000 years (pp. 140–4), overtake the rest of the world within a decade (pp. 173–7), or gleefully forecast the demise of their ideological enemies (pp. 130–4); the same war has been confidently deemed impossible (pp. 135–9), avoidable (pp. 111–15), or as good as won (by the losing side, of course) (pp. 145–8); every technological innovation from the railroads (pp. 62–5) to the personal computer (pp. 204–8) has been derided as a flop, a fad, or a pointless waste of money; conversely, such inventions as the atomic vacuum cleaner (pp. 159–63) and the robot-servant in every home (pp. 188–93) have conspicuously failed to materialize; and last but not least, cultural commentators and critics have managed not only to slam the most successful artists of their generation (pp. 178–82), but also to reject the technological age's most influential mass media: radio (pp. 84–7), movies (pp. 116–20), and television (pp. 149–53).

PREDICTION

Millenarian

Technology

Prophecy

Politics

Military

Natural Disaster

Culture

Economics

Doomsday

READING THE FUTURE: THE SIBYLLINE BOOKS

Main culprits: The sibyls

What was predicted: The future course of Roman history

What actually happened: The Western Roman Empire effectively came to an unpredicted end when Rome was besieged and sacked (but not destroyed) by the barbarians in 410 CE

The Sibyl, speaking with inspired mouth, without a smile, without ornament, and without perfume, penetrates through centuries by the power of the gods.

Heraclitus of Ephesus (c. 535–c. 475 BCE)

The Greeks were known in Antiquity for their belief in divination. Although many ancient cultures believed that natural phenomena were guides to the future, the Greeks believed that the gods had granted certain individuals the gift of prophecy. The most famous seer of Antiquity was the Pythia, the priestess of the sun god Apollo at Delphi, who, possibly under the influence of natural gaseous fumes, answered questions in ambiguous rhyming couplets. Her poetic but rather vague pronouncements misled several kings to their deaths, but even this did not detract from her reputation or limit the petitioners who flocked to Delphi throughout Antiquity.

Compared to the superstitious Greeks, one might imagine that the rational, businesslike Romans—the legionaries who marched triumphant from the Persian Gulf to Scotland, the civil servants who ran an empire larger than the modern-day European Union, and the engineers who built straight roads and aqueducts—might be the least gullible people of the ancient world. However, the Romans, despite their overwhelming success based on their advanced military technology and engineering skills, were not immune to the human need to know what the future held. For day-to-day enquiries, they employed priests who read the immediate future in the entrails of sacrificial animals and the flight of birds. But the rulers of the Roman Republic and its Empire believed that they had the ultimate insurance policy in the shape of a written guide to the future known as the Sibylline Books.

The Sibylline Books were not bound and printed tomes like those we read today. Paper and printing in Europe were still many centuries away, so it is thought that in their first incarnation, they were probably the versified utterances of a Greek-speaking prophetess known as the sibyl, which had been recorded on oak leaves. Who the sibyl was, where she came from, and even if there was more than one were all matters of dispute in Antiquity.

EXORBITANT ROYALTIES

One tradition held that the Hellespontine Sibyl in Asia Minor (now Turkey) had originally composed the books. The prophecies would then have passed into the hands of the Erythraean Sybil, near the ancient city of Troy, and from there had finally made their way to southern Italy to the Cumaean Sybil (Cumae was a Roman town near the modern Italian city of Naples). Legend had it that this sibyl had been granted a 1,000-year lifespan by the god Apollo, but because she had spurned his sexual advances, he had withheld the all-important gift of eternal youth, so she endured century after century as an aging, diminishing crone. According to the poet Ovid (43 BCE–18 CE), she became so small that she was kept in a jar until only her disembodied voice was all that remained.

In Virgil's (70–19 BCE) epic poem the *Aeneid* (late 1st century CE), the hero Aeneas, the legendary progenitor of the Romans, escapes the destruction of Troy by the Greeks and sails to Italy where he meets the Cumaean Sibyl. She helps him visit the Underworld, where his father reveals that his descendants will one day rule the world. It is this same sibyl who many centuries later sells the Sibylline Books to the Romans. She offers nine books of prophecy to the seventh and last king of Rome, the tyrannical Lucius Tarquinius Superbus (535–496 BCE). Finding the price she is asking too high, he refuses, whereupon she burns three of the books and offers the remaining six to him at the same price.

ORACLES
The Cumaean Sybil was one of many prophetesses who conveyed divine messages to mortals. Pictured here, the Greek Sybil of Delphi.

When he turns down her second offer, she burns a further three books. Tarquinius, now realizing the magnitude of his error, agrees to buy the remaining three books at the original price. He takes them back to Rome and places them in a stone chest in a crypt under the new Temple of Jupiter that he had ordered to be built on the Capitoline Hill.

Tarquinius was not to profit long from his expensive acquisition: A few years after the purchase, he was deposed and forced into exile. From that time on, until the creation of the Empire by Augustus (63 BCE–14 CE), Rome was a nominal "republic" ruled by two consuls appointed by its unelected Senate. The care of the books was entrusted to ten and later 15 senior officials, the *quindecimviri sacris faciundis*, who were tasked with keeping them safe and secret. Consulting the books was different from questioning a living oracle, such as the Pythian Sibyl at Delphi, who would give an answer to a direct question. That her answer was in verse and usually obscure is beside the point, as it definitely went with the question asked.

The Sibylline Books, however, had been composed centuries earlier, possibly in the Near East, and their Greek verses were not arranged in any particular order. Like the much later predictions of Nostradamus (see pp. 41–7), it was a question of retrofitting the prophecy to the current situation. Hence, when an invasion or plague threatened Rome, the *quindecimviri* looked through the prophecies to find the one that best corresponded to the event, interpreted what the verse meant, and then announced what it advised to do to ward off the danger. The prophecies themselves were never made public, so one imagines that the *quindecimviri*, like other oracular interpreters throughout history, had a certain amount of leeway in what they recommended. In the majority of recorded instances, the books ordered the institution of religious festivals or the introduction of foreign gods to Rome in order to cure plagues or avert disasters predicted by comets, earthquakes, and other bad omens.

In rarer cases the books were consulted for political and military reasons. When the armies of the Carthaginian general Hannibal (248–c. 183 BCE) threatened the survival of Rome itself, the Senate ordered that the books be consulted. Their recommendation was that two luckless Greeks and two Gauls should be buried alive in the market place. Despite comprehensively beating the legions at the Battle of Cannae (216 BCE), Hannibal did not succeed in taking Rome itself. This was not, however, due to divine intervention, but because he lacked the necessary supplies and manpower to take the city, and his home city of Carthage refused his appeals for reinforcements.

Around 83 BCE, the original books were damaged or lost in a fire that destroyed the Temple of Jupiter Capitolinus. In order to replace them, the Senate dispatched envoys to collect similar oracular sayings kept in temples and shrines all over the empire and bring them back to Rome. These were placed in the newly rebuilt Temple of Jupiter and again entrusted to the care of the *quindecimviri*. In 12 BCE, during the reign of Augustus, the books were examined, edited, and recopied, and then moved to a new home in gilded chests in the Temple of Apollo Patrous on the Hill of the Palatine where they remained intact and inviolate well into the Christian era.

THEIR RECOMMENDATION WAS THAT TWO LUCKLESS GREEKS AND TWO GAULS SHOULD BE BURIED ALIVE IN THE MARKET PLACE.

The last recorded imperial consultation of the books was by the Emperor Julian (c. 331–363 CE), nicknamed "the Apostate" because of his attempt to restore paganism to the now Christianized Roman Empire. He ordered that the books be consulted when preparing his invasion of the Empire of Persia (now Iran). The response was that the books favored a crossing of the border in the year 363 CE. Just as the Delphic oracle had led King Croesus of Lydia (595–c. 547 BCE) to his death in Persia centuries earlier with a similarly rosy prediction, the Sibylline Books were not at all clear about exactly who would benefit when the Romans crossed into Persian territory. In the event, it was the Persians: The Romans were defeated, and the emperor fatally wounded during the retreat. With Julian's death, Christianity was restored and paganism was increasingly persecuted and finally proscribed during the reign of the Emperor Theodosius the Great (347–395 CE).

The books managed to survive Theodosius and the destruction of many pagan temples at the hands of Christian zealots, but only by six years. In 405 CE the Magister Militum (Commander-in-Chief) of the Western Empire and effective ruler in the emperor's name, a part-barbarian called Stilicho (359–408 CE), ordered their public burning. Although he was a Christian, his motives were more likely to have been political than religious. At the time, a barbarian army threatened Rome, and it is thought that Stilicho's Roman opponents were using the books to attack his government. Although the Sibylline Books were destroyed, a collection known as the Sibylline Oracles was much quoted in late Antiquity and the Middle Ages, as they were said to foretell the coming of Jesus Christ. However, the Oracles were composed at a much later date than the Books, probably by Jews and Christians in Alexandria, Egypt, and had little or no connection with the original Sibylline Books, whose secrets have been forever consumed by the flames.

PREDICTION

Millenarian
Technology
Prophecy
Politics
Military
Natural Disaster
Culture
Economics
Doomsday

THE "FIRST" SECOND COMING: SAINTS MARK, MATTHEW, LUKE, AND PAUL

Main culprits: Saints Matthew, Mark, Luke, and Paul

What was predicted: The Second Coming of Jesus as King of Glory and the inauguration of a millennium of peace and plenty

What actually happened: We're still here

And he said unto them, Verily I say unto you, That there be some of them that stand here, which shall not taste of death, till they have seen the kingdom of God come with power.

Mark 9:1, Holy Bible, Authorized King James Version

After our initial visit to pagan Rome, we come to the very first of many—very many—predictions of Christ's return to Earth, triggering the End of Time and the establishment of the Kingdom of Heaven on Earth. In this entry, we shall look specifically at those predictions that appear in the Gospels of Mark (d. 68 CE), Matthew (fl. 1st century CE), and Luke (d. c. 84 CE), which were written after Jesus' death, and in the writings of Paul of Tarsus (c. 5 BCE–c. 67 CE), who, although he was alive at the same time as Jesus, never met him, though he famously claimed to have done so while traveling on his Road to Damascus.

On the previous page, this entry is described as being both "prophetic" and "millenarian," and this might be an appropriate time to differentiate these two related concepts, which we shall encounter over and again.

DIVINE WRIT
The prophecies about Jesus' impending return are found in the Gospels and in the writings of Paul of Tarsus.

Prophecy refers to the foretelling of the future—any future—but millenarianism, while also dealing with things to come, constrains the future by specifying the overthrow of the current social order and its replacement by something incomparably better. Here we must confuse the issue a little more by adding one specifically Christian term to the mix, "millennialism," which originates in verses 1–6 of chapter 20 of the Book of Revelation, which predicts the Millennium, or Christ's 1,000-year reign on Earth (for more on millennialism, see pp. 66–70).

The Sibylline Books (see previous entry) are prophetic because they were said to foretell Rome's future history but they were not millenarian because the pagan Romans did not have a concept of an end of time and certainly not of a last judgment. Despite their occasional ups and downs, the Romans were confident of their own superiority over the "barbarians" (i.e., everyone else), and believed that nothing could be better than being a citizen of the empire. Millenarianism, by contrast, is a philosophy that appeals to the underdog—the downtrodden mass or minority—who fervently hopes that tomorrow will be better than today but has neither the resources nor power to bring it about by normal political, economic, or military means. For the first three centuries of its existence, the Christian Church sorely needed the promise of a better world to come, as the Roman authorities persecuted it with increasing vigor.

In Christian eschatology (concerned with the four last things: death, judgment, heaven, and hell), millenarian prophecy refers to the Second Coming of Jesus Christ and all its attendant events. For visiting aliens, or any readers who haven't been paying attention for the past 2,000 years (and haven't seen Monty Python's *Life of Brian*), Jesus of Nazareth (c. 5 BCE–c. 30 CE), also known as Jesus Christ, was the founder of a breakaway Jewish sect active in ancient Judea and Galilee (modern-day Israel), which was then a province of the Roman Empire. Jesus' message of universal peace, love, brotherhood, and doing unto others as one would be done by was both revolutionary and far-reaching; it was also millenarian, as the people he preached to were oppressed by their own priests and nobles, as well as by the Roman occupiers.

During his earthly ministry, Jesus announced that he was the Son of God and the expected messiah who, according to Jewish tradition, would become the anointed king of Israel and usher in a perfect messianic age of peace and plenty. This mightily displeased the Jewish religious establishment, who arranged for Jesus' arrest and execution by the Romans. What you believe happens three days after Jesus' death depends on the brand of your religious faith or lack of it. For unbelievers, Jesus dies and his body is removed from the tomb and buried by his followers; for Christians, he rises from the dead and is taken up to heaven.

Although the established denominations, such as the Episcopal and Catholic churches, accept the prophetic nature of Christianity (i.e. that there are passages in the Old Testament that predict the coming of Christ), they are not millenarian in their outlook. They do not expect or fervently hope that the world is about to end, to be replaced by a millennium of milk and honey for all. Let's face it, when you have investment and property portfolios worth billions, you're in it for the long haul. But what were the early Christians—long before the advent of the organized churches—expecting?

What we know about Jesus' time on Earth is recorded in the New Testament, and several passages in the gospels of Mark, Matthew, and Luke, and in Paul's epistles suggest that his early followers believed that the end of the world and Jesus' return were both imminent. In Mark 8:38 to 9:1 is written:

THE GOSPEL TRUTH

> Whosoever therefore shall be ashamed of me and of my words in this adulterous and sinful generation; of him also shall the Son of man be ashamed, when he cometh in the glory of his Father with the holy angels. And he said unto them, Verily I say unto you, That there be some of them that stand here, which shall not taste of death, till they have seen the kingdom of God come with power.

This is repeated almost word for word in Matthew 16:28: "Verily, I say unto you, There be some standing here, which shall not taste of death, till they see the Son of Man coming in his kingdom." And again in Luke 9:27: "But I tell you of a truth, there be some standing here, which shall not taste of death, till they see the kingdom of God." Jesus seems to be saying that there are people who are listening to his words who will witness his return and the advent of the kingdom of God on Earth before the end of their natural lives. If we take life expectancy in ancient Palestine to be 30 to 40 years, then, Jesus is predicting his Second Coming in the early '70s CE or earlier.

In Matthew 24 and Mark 16, Jesus predicts the destruction of Jerusalem and of the Temple—an event that did take place in 70 CE after a Jewish rebellion—but he goes on to explain that this will be a prelude to the destruction of the Earth, brought on by such events as wars, famines, false prophets, the darkening of the Sun and Moon, and the fall of the stars from the heavens (Matthew 24:4–24 and Mark 13:6–25). He concludes this prophecy in Matthew (24:34) with: "This generation shall not pass, till all these things be fulfilled." And in Mark 13:29–30, "So ye in like manner, when ye shall see these things come to pass, know that it is nigh, even at the doors. Verily I say unto you, that this generation shall not pass till all these things are done." Again, "this generation" suggests that the end of the world was a matter of years away. Paul of Tarsus was also expecting Jesus' imminent return. In 1 Thessalonians 4:16–17, he writes:

> For the Lord himself shall descend from heaven with a shout, with the voice of the archangel, and with the trump of God: and the dead in Christ shall rise first: Then we which are alive and remain shall be caught up together with them in the clouds, to meet the Lord in the air: and so shall we ever be with the Lord.

IF WE TAKE LIFE EXPECTANCY IN ANCIENT PALESTINE TO BE 30 TO 40 YEARS, THEN, JESUS IS PREDICTING HIS SECOND COMING IN THE EARLY '70s CE OR EARLIER.

This passage by Paul has led to other interpretations about what will happen at the end of time, when those faithful who are still alive at the time shall be "caught up together with them in the clouds, to meet the Lord in the air," suggesting a divine airlift, or, as others have suggested, a visitation by UFOs—but more of this later (see Carried Away, pp. 214–20). What concerns us here are the predictions made in the New Testament itself about the Second Coming and its timing.

Three of the evangelists and Paul, it appears, were true millenarians in their expectation of Jesus' return to Earth within their own lifetimes. The fact that he failed to do so needs some comment or explanation. The first explanation is that because the New Testament accounts were written many years after Jesus' death, his words were somehow misquoted or misinterpreted. For Christians, especially fundamentalists, who believe the Bible to be the word of God, and therefore cannot be subject to error, this explanation is extremely problematic. Less literal Christian interpreters of scripture have explained that he was in fact only prophesying the destruction of Jerusalem by the Emperor Titus (39–81 CE) in 70 CE; or that his remarks are meant to be interpreted as revelations about what is to come in some indeterminate future time.

Christianity, however, survived its initial millenarian leanings, and as the church grew in power and influence after the 4th century CE, the promise of an immediate millennium of peace and prosperity for the elect gradually morphed into the promise of a deferred reward in the kingdom of heaven posthumously awarded to the faithful by a risen Christ—jam, not exactly tomorrow on Earth, but definitely jam sometime in the distant future. With the passing of the last of Jesus' generation, so too passed the first prophecy of his Second Coming. As we shall see, it was far from being the last.

PREDICTION

Millenarian

Technology

Prophecy

Politics

Military

Natural Disaster

Culture

Economics

Doomsday

ROUND AND ROUND: MAYA LONG COUNT AND 2012

Main culprits: Maya astronomer-priests and their latter-day interpreters

What was predicted: The end of the world on December 21 or 23, 2012

What actually happened: We'll see....

The Maya Prophecy says that the world goes through a series of cycles, each one called a "Sun" by the Maya. At the end of each Sun, the world experiences a cataclysm, civilization collapses, and a new mankind evolves. The Maya believed — and still believe — that there have been four Suns. We are now in the period of the Fifth Sun, which began in 3114 BC. The Fifth Sun is due to end in AD 2012. On 23 December, to be precise.

Maya Prophecy (2008) by Ronald Bonewitz

Our third entry takes us far away from the Old World, on our first of many visits to the New, to a civilization whose obsession with the long-range measurement of time has recently been used to set the date for the end of the world as either Friday, December 21 or Sunday, December 23, 2012. It is, of course, slightly premature to write this prediction off as one of history's "worst" predictions, but before you cancel your Christmas plans for 2012, let's examine where this prediction has come from and how credible it might be. This doomsday date, as the quote above makes abundantly clear, was predicted over a millennium ago by the mysterious Mesoamerican Maya civilization, whose highpoint, the "Classic" period, unfolded in Yucatán in what is today southeastern Mexico, Guatemala, Belize, and Honduras, from the mid-third century to the early tenth century CE.

The Maya developed several complex ways of measuring time. They used two calendars: the Haab, a solar calendar made up of 18 20-day months plus five spare days, making a total of 365 days like our own solar year; and the Tzolk'in, a ritual calendar made up of 20 13-day periods, making a total of 260 days. If you run the two calendars concurrently from a given date, it will take 52 Haab or solar years for the same day combination to repeat. This 52-year cycle is still used today by the Maya to predict astronomical phenomena, plan religious festivals, and determine the character of newborns, like our own sun-sign astrology.

To calculate dates beyond a single calendar round, the Maya employed the Long Count, which used the solar day, or K'in, as its basic unit. Counting forward from the date of creation of the current world, or "sun," given by some authorities as September 8, 3114 BCE, it was divided into: Winal = 20 K'in; Tun = 18 Winal or Haab (360 days); K'atun = 20 Tun (7,200 days); and B'ak'tun = 20 K'atun (144,000 days or just over 394 years). As the number 13 is significant in Maya cosmology, the thirteenth B'ak'tun could be interpreted as particularly important. As the previous sun ended on the last day of the previous thirteenth B'ak'tun, several Maya scholars theorized that the Maya had foreseen the end of this age of the world on the last day of the current thirteenth B'ak'tun, which falls on either December 21 or 23, 2012.

NO TIME LIKE THE PRESENT

In order to evaluate the 2012 prophecy, we must examine the culture that produced it. Who were the Maya, and what can their history teach us about their prophetic abilities or lack of them? Finally, we must also look at the claims of the New Age prophets and how they stack up against the archeological evidence.

The Maya have fascinated us since their "rediscovery" in the early nineteenth century by two explorers, American John L. Stephens (1805–52) and his British companion, Frederick Catherwood (1799–1854). To say "rediscovered" would be a bit of an exaggeration, as the Spanish knew of and had visited several abandoned Mayan cities as early as the sixteenth century. However, the publication of Stephens' *Travels in Central America, Chiapas, and Yucatán* of 1841, which documented and illustrated many Mayan ruins for the first time, caused a sensation in the U.S. and Europe.

The Classic Maya, unlike their Postclassic and colonial-era descendants, lived in the rainforests of central Guatemala, with outposts in southeastern Mexico and western Honduras. They lived in extensive "cities," though not quite on the model of ancient European cities. They had no defensive walls, for one, and the bulk of the population lived in simple huts made of perishable materials. The religious and royal elites occupied a nucleus of imposing buildings—palaces and pyramids—which acted as the focus for royal and religious ceremonies. Perhaps in memory of their original homes in the highlands, the Maya raised their temples and palaces on high platforms, giving them the appearance of pyramids. The exteriors of their buildings were covered in intricate decorations, carved in stone or molded in stucco, representing their gods and kings, and covered in hieroglyphic (picture) writing, including the complex long-count dates that recorded their construction.

In the early 1800s, a Spanish colonial official, unable to believe that Native Americans had built these complex structures, suggested that the Egyptians had made it across the Atlantic to build them. Other early candidates as potential builders have included the Mesopotamians and the lost tribes of Israel. Subsequent archeological investigations have proved beyond doubt that the Maya cities owe nothing to the Old World. For one thing, Maya pyramids are, with few exceptions, solid, steep-sided platforms topped by small temples rather than hollow tombs as in Egypt, and more damningly, there is a 2,500-year gap between Egypt's pyramid building and the rise of Classic Maya civilization. At the midpoint of the Classic period, Egypt was part of the Roman Empire and devoutly Christian—the pharaohs and their pyramids were a dim, distant memory.

In more recent times, Mayan society has been idealized as a peace-loving theocracy, intent on observing the stars, and living in harmony with the cycles of nature. So perfect was this society that the more fanciful among New Age prophets refuse to believe that the Maya had done it all quite on their own. Refugees from the (mythical) continents of Mu or Atlantis, or in other versions alien visitors, must have taught them arcane astronomical secrets.

However, the truth is that even by the standards of ancient peoples, the Maya were technologically backward. They lacked the wheel, the arch, the plow, domesticated animals, and the use of common metals such as iron or bronze. Anyone who has visited the pyramids and palaces of Tikal and Copan, with their massive walls and cramped, windowless rooms, wonders how people could have lived in them in such a warm, humid climate. The Maya shone, it is true, in astronomy and mathematics, but no more so than many of the peoples of the ancient Near East who anticipated many of their discoveries by 1,000 years or more.

© Peter Andersen | Creative Commons

COLLAPSE
The gradual Classic Maya civilization collapse in the ninth century CE did not coincide with the ending of any of their calendar cycles.

Socially and politically, the Mayan world was far from a Utopian New Age paradise. Its numerous city-states were engaged in constant warfare over increasingly scarce resources, and over the scarcest resource of all: the lifeblood of royal captives, whom they sacrificed to nourish their gods. Far from being models of ecological probity, the Maya caused their own downfall through their relentless exploitation of the environment. As land, food, and water ran out, the Maya elites fought ever more destructive wars, until, as annihilation loomed for all, their long-suffering subjects slaughtered their kings and priests and abandoned their dying cities.

Like other ancient peoples whose religious reference points were the movements of deified astronomical bodies—the Sun, Moon, stars, and constellations—the Maya had a cyclical view of creation. From the Maya priest-astronomer's point of view, in say, 400 CE, just as the stars moved round the heavens with predictable reliability so did human affairs: cities rose and fell, dynasties came and went, wars were won and lost, but the world remained as unchanging as the space through which the stars moved. They calculated dates far into the past and future, including December 2012, but it was in the service of their arcane religion, and not as a prophetic warning to future generations.

A simple test of their prophetic skills would be if they had foreseen their own collapse in the ninth century or the destruction of their descendants by the Spanish conquistadors in the sixteenth. But the Maya collapse was not the sudden cataclysmic event of a day or even one year. It was a slow ecological suicide that took centuries. When the Maya abandoned their cities, it was not at the end of a significant calendar cycle but sometime between the end of the ninth and the beginning of the tenth B'ak'tun of the current age. As for the Spanish conquest, it falls somewhere in the middle of the eleventh B'ak'tun. The Long Count is not evidence that the Maya believed that the world would come to an end on a specific day at the end of the thirteenth B'ak'tun, but of the exact opposite. They calculated dates far into the future—many thousands of years beyond December 23, 2012—precisely because they were sure that their civilization would endure forever.

THE MILLENNIUM MYTH: 1000 CE

PREDICTION

Millenarian

Technology

Prophecy

Politics

Military

Natural Disaster

Culture

Economics

Doomsday

Main culprit: Johannes Trithemius

What was predicted: That there was a general panic in the year 1000 CE in expectation of the end of the world

What actually happened: Historians now agree that there was no such millennial panic

As the first thousand years of our calendar drew to an end, in every land of Europe the people expected with certainty the destruction of the world. Some squandered their substance in riotous living, others bestowed it for the salvation of their souls on churches and convents, bewailing multitudes lay by day and night about the altars, many looked with terror, yet most with a secret hope, for the conflagration of the earth and the falling of the heavens.

History of the First Crusade (1881) by H. von Sybel

When the second millennium was drawing to a close, Christian fundamentalists and New Age prophets alike were quick to cash in on the millennial anxieties of the Western world. As we shall see, there were Doomsday prophecies of a religious and astrological nature for 1999 and 2000, as well as predictions of natural and digital disaster. Several self-styled prophets were quick to inform us that the turn of the first millennium had witnessed a religious panic based on the belief that the Second Coming, long delayed, was at last at hand (see quote). No lesser figure than televangelist and self-appointed leader of the religious right Pat Robertson (b. 1930) dramatized these supposed events in his novel *The End of the Age* (1995). For a prophet of doom to remind his audience of a previous failed prophecy seems rather strange, but then Robertson is no stranger to failed prophecies as he had confidently predicted the end of the world in the fall of 1982.

As we saw earlier, Christianity began as a millenarian religion based on the belief that the end of the world was likely to happen at any moment. Although the first generation of Christians had been disappointed at the failure of Jesus to return within their own lifetimes, their children could at least point to the prophesied destruction of the Temple and Jerusalem in 70 CE—a sure sign that the end times had begun. They continued to wait.

The first three centuries of the Church were marked by several savage persecutions by the Roman authorities. Under such circumstances, Christian millenarianism remained an important facet of the faith. In the second century CE, a sect known as the Montanists, after one of their prophets, Montanus, preached that the kingdom of God on Earth was imminent and that the New Jerusalem would be established in the village of Pepuza in the Roman province of Phrygia (now Turkey). Even after the establishment of Christianity as the empire's official religion, there were outbreaks of millenarian fever—in France in 365 and 400 CE, and more widely in 500 CE.

MILLENNIUM, WHAT MILLENNIUM?

Now what of the first millennium itself? According to a few sources from the period, there were outbreaks of millennial panic in Europe from the mid-tenth century onward. While on a visit to Paris in 965, Saint Abbo of Fleury (c. 945–1004) records listening to a preacher who announced that the Antichrist would be born in the year 1000.

Three years later, a solar eclipse panicked the army of the Holy Roman Emperor Otto II (955–83). In September 989, Halley's Comet, which appears in our skies every 75 years, made one of its periodic visits, bringing with it the fear of disaster ahead. In 992, Good Friday (the day of Jesus' crucifixion) and the Feast of the Annunciation fell on the same day, heralding, it was believed by some, the birth of the Antichrist. As the century drew to a close, there were plagues, earthquakes, famines, and wars aplenty, all of which were reported as signs and portents, but in such dangerous and superstitious times, that was nothing out of the ordinary.

But as for the year 1000 itself, it seems fairly quiet. In May, the Emperor Otto III (980–1002) visited Aachen (now in Germany) to exhume the body of his great predecessor on the imperial throne, Charlemagne (c. 742–814), because, so legend has it, that Otto believed that he would rise from the grave to combat the Antichrist. However, when you examine the historical annals of the day with care, there are no reports of millennial panic in the population at large. So where does the evidence come from? An important and much quoted source is the German abbot, occultist, and historian Johannes Trithemius' (1462–1516) *Annales Hirsaugienses* (1509–1514), who wrote five centuries after the event:

> In this year a terrible comet appeared, which by its look terrified many, who feared that the last day was at hand; inasmuch as several years before it had been predicted by some, deluded by a false calculation, that the visible world would end in the year of Christ 1000.

HYPE
Abbot Trithemius, who popularized the first millennium panic, wrote five centuries after events for which he had no reliable firsthand sources.

This passage was much quoted by later popular historians, including the influential Charles Mackay (1814–89), whose bestselling *Extraordinary Popular Delusions and the Madness of Crowds* (1841) established the idea that the millennial panic had been the cause of the First Crusade (1095–99) that took place almost a century later. He wrote:

> A panic terror seized upon the weak, the credulous and the guilty, who in those days formed more than nineteen-twentieths of the population. Forsaking their homes, kindred, and occupation, they crowded to Jerusalem to await the coming of the Lord, lightened, as they imagined, of a load of sin by their weary pilgrimage.

Serious medieval historians, however, began to question this popular view as early as the late nineteenth century. The first Crusade, they argue, was not triggered by a millennial panic, as it took place almost a century (and four medieval generations) later. The real cause of the crusade was the advance of Islam in the Middle East and Anatolia (now Turkey), and the subsequent appeal for assistance from the beleaguered Byzantine Empire. More damningly, not only is there an absence of firsthand evidence from the writers of the period, but there are also a couple of very practical reasons for the year 1000 not to have impacted that much on the people of the day. Although the Anno Domini system, which is used and no doubt taken for granted, had been first used in the year 525 CE, it did not enter into common use until the late tenth century, and even then only among the educated, clerical elites. Additionally, dates were not rendered in Arabic numerals but the old Roman letter system, so the year 1000 would not have been a worrying round number but the letter "M" for *mille* ("one thousand").

While the millennium panic makes for a good story, that's all it is. At best, a very few churchmen might have been worried, but in fact there seems to have been more concern expressed around the millennium after the date of Jesus' crucifixion, which was taken to be the year 1033. For the vast bulk of Europe's population, which was illiterate and innumerate, the year, and its many portents, plagues, wars, and famines, passed like any other, no better and certainly no worse.

TWILIGHT OF THE GODS: SNORRI STURLUSON

Main culprit: Snorri Sturluson

What was predicted: Monsters lay waste to the world, kill the gods and most of humanity. Only two humans survive to repopulate the earth and inaugurate a golden age of peace and prosperity

What actually happened: The Vikings became Christians, and although their gods vanished, their world did not come to an end

The wolf Fenrir advances mouth wide open; his upper jaw reaches heaven and his lower rests on the earth. He would open it still wider had he room. Fire flashes from his eyes and nostrils. The serpent Jormungand vomits forth venom, defiling the air and sea.

Gylfaginning (1220) by Snorri Sturluson

When the Icelandic scholar and lawyer Snorri Sturluson (1179–1241) compiled the collection of Norse mythology known as *Prose Edda* in 1220, it was a link to the heroic Viking Age, which had long ago passed. The Norse, as the Vikings are more correctly known, were a warlike seafaring people who lived in Scandinavia, in an area occupied by the present-day countries of Sweden, Norway, and Denmark. They enter the annals of Western European history with a devastating raid on the unprotected island of Lindisfarne, home to a famous Christian abbey, in 793. Commenting on the attack, which had seen the brutal massacre of the monks, the enslavement of the survivors, and the pillaging of the church and abbey, the Christian scholar Alcuin of York (c. 730–804) wrote: "Never before in Britain has such terror appeared as this we have now suffered at the hands of the heathen."

The Norse had only just begun. For the next two centuries, they raided, raped, and pillaged their way across Europe from Scotland to Spain, from Russia to Constantinople (now Istanbul, Turkey), wherever their famous dragon-prowed longboats could take them. They created independent kingdoms, most famously in northeastern England, Ireland, Scotland, and in Northern France and along the river valleys of Russia, and explored and settled Iceland and Greenland, reaching the American mainland, known to them as Vinland, in around 1000 CE.

Historians still argue as to what caused this extraordinary migration of peoples who had previously been content to stay in their Scandinavian homelands. It could have been a warming of the climate, making navigation easier; a population increase that was not matched by an increase in agricultural production; or a response to growing Christian pressure from the Carolingian Empire of Charlemagne (c. 742–814). Another factor that must be taken into consideration is their religion, and in particular their belief in the apocalyptic end of the world known as Ragnarök (the doom of the gods).

SAGA
The *Prose Edda* is a collection of Norse myths compiled in the thirteenth century CE, when the Norse had been Christianized and given up their bloodthirsty ways.

Ragnarök is described in chapter 51 of the *Gylfaginning* (Tricking of Gylfi), which forms part of Snorri Sturluson's collection of Norse myth the *Prose Edda*. The *Gylfaginning* is itself based on an earlier epic poem known as the *Völuspá* (*Prophecy of the Völva*) in which a prophetess predicts the doom of the gods to their leader Odin. The prelude to Ragnarök is the "ax-age, sword-age" when war and greed overtake the earth and brother turns against brother, after which the power of the sun fails and there is a three-year winter. At this point the end-times begin, known as the "wind-age, wolf-age." The giant wolf-monster Fenrir, child of the evil fire god Loki, swallows the sun and moon; great earthquakes over-topple the mountains and uproot the trees, and free Fenrir from the magic bonds that have kept him a prisoner of the gods.

At this point another of Loki's monstrous children, the giant serpent Jormungand, is released, causing the sea to flood and breaking the moorings of the sinister ship *Naglfar*, described in the *Prose Edda* as being made from the nails of the dead. Fenrir and Jormungand lay waste to the face of the Earth, the wolf with fire and the serpent with venom. Finally two great armies meet on the plain of Vigrid: Odin leading the gods and the "glorious dead" from Valhalla, who have died in battle, against Loki, Fenrir, Jormungand, the frost giants, and the legions of the "unworthy dead" who have languished in *Hel* (the origin of our own "Hell").

The battle of Vigrid Plain is no Armageddon, where the armies of the righteous are sure to triumph over Satan's demonic hordes; it is the wholesale slaughter of both sides. Odin fights but is killed by Fenrir, who in turn falls at the hands of Odin's son Vidar; Thor attacks and kills Jormungand but succumbs to the snake's poison; Loki and the god Heimdallr kill one another. The plain is strewn with the dead from both sides. At the end of the battle almost none survive, and the earth is consumed by fire. The destruction, however, is not absolute. Two gods, Vidar and Vali, survive, as do a human couple, Lif and Lifthrasir, who have taken refuge in the branches of the world-tree Yggdrasil. The land reemerges from the waters like an Icelandic volcano rising from the seabed and is repopulated by the two survivors. A new age of peace and plenty dawns for humankind.

AX-AGE, SWORD-AGE

NORSE NIHILISM

Like many other early cultures that existed on the precarious border between survival and annihilation from natural disaster, famine, plague, or war, the Norse Vikings lived literally on the edge. Unlike the Christians, who hoped through their good deeds to win heavenly rewards, the Norse believed that only the brave who died heroically in battle would be allowed into Odin's hall of Valhalla. Like early Christianity, Norse religion has strong millenarian overtones. The significant difference between them was that the Christians expected to be saved and rewarded at the end of the world; the Norse—good and bad—were all going to be slaughtered on Vigrid Plain. Even their all-powerful gods would fail—an idea that would have struck Christians, who were convinced of the omnipotence of their god, as very strange indeed.

The psychological impact of these beliefs, however, should not be underestimated. It gave the Norse a very pessimistic, almost nihilistic view of life and the universe. As they unleashed their terror onto the settled lands of Western Europe, the Norse must have believed that they were living through the "ax-age, sword-age" of Ragnarök. They must fight and die heroically, so at least they would be on Odin's side in the final battle on the Vigrid Plain, even if it meant a second annihilation at the hands of the forces of evil.

By the time Snorri Sturluson recorded the story of Ragnarök, the Norse had been converted to Christianity and had turned their backs on their earlier warlike ways. Nevertheless, pessimism and nihilism survived as a feature of Scandinavian and Germanic culture. It could be seen in a special interest in scenes of the end of the world and the Last Judgment in Christian Norse art, and much later, in the theme of Richard Wagner's (1813–83) fourth and final opera in the Ring Cycle, *Götterdämmerung* (*Twilight of the Gods*, 1876). It has been suggested that the folk memory of Ragnarök contributed to the self-destruction of Adolf Hitler's (1889–1945) Nazi regime at the end of World War Two.

ARK OF FOOLS: JOHANNES STÖFFLER

PREDICTION

Millenarian

Technology

Prophecy

Politics

Military

Natural Disaster

Culture

Economics

Doomsday

Main culprit: Johannes Stöffler

What was predicted: The destruction of the Earth in a second Great Flood on February 20, 1524 due to a planetary alignment

What actually happened: There was a light shower that day

In the year [1524] ... most wondrous positions of the planets will occur. For in February there will be 20 small, mean, as well as great conjunctions, 16 of which will occupy a watery sign. These will signify indubitable change, variation, and alteration for almost the entire world, climes, kingdoms, provinces, estates, dignitaries, brutes, sea-creatures, and crops, such as we have rarely heard of for many centuries from historiographers, or our ancestors. Therefore lift up your heads, you Christian men.

***Almanach nova plurimis annis venturis inserentia* (1499) by**
Johannes Stöffler and Jakob Pflaum

We are used to reading our horoscopes in newspapers and magazines, and though about a third of people polled claim to have some belief in astrology, it is unlikely that many of them would base important life choices only on the position of Mars or Jupiter in a particular constellation on a particular day. In Renaissance Europe, however, things were very different, and rich and poor, layman and churchman alike consulted astrologers whenever faced by difficult decisions. Although the church had banned all pagan divination and soothsaying, branding them as black magic and witchcraft, astrology managed to escape the ban because of its spurious claim to have a scientific basis and because of its connections with the science of astronomy. Another element in its favor, especially among Renaissance scholars, was its Hellenistic pedigree, which, although pagan, gave it the added cachet of ancient knowledge.

Astrology was so respected that it attracted the best scientific minds of the day. Such was the case of the subject of this entry, one Johannes Stöffler (1452–1531). Born in the small German town of Blauberen, Stöffler, like most other scholars of the day, took holy orders after completing his studies. The care of his parishioners, however, was only one of his many avocations. A true "Renaissance man," he was also an astronomer, a builder of astronomical instruments and clocks, a mathematician, and, of course, an astrologer. His work attracted princely attention, and the Duke of Württemberg appointed him to the Chair of Mathematics at the University of Tubingen in 1507. During a long and distinguished career, Stöffler made contributions to astronomical knowledge, and the reform of the calendar that we still use today was in part based on his astronomical work. He should have been remembered as a serious mathematician and astronomer, had it not been for a prediction that he made on the eve of the sixteenth century.

STORMY WEATHER

In 1499, he compiled the *Almanach nova plurimis annis venturis inserentia* with the astronomer Jakob Pflaum (fl. early 15th century), which listed the positions of the Sun, Moon, and planets for several decades to come, accompanied by astrological predictions for each year. It is one of the predictions he made in the *Almanach* that concerns us here. For 1524, still a quarter of a century in the future, the 47-year-old Stöffler predicted the occurrence of "indubitable change, variation, and alteration for almost the entire world, climes, kingdoms, provinces, estates, dignitaries, brutes, sea-creatures, and crops, such as we have rarely heard of for many centuries from historiographers, or our ancestors." These far-reaching changes, variations, and alterations were to be brought about by "20 small, mean, as well as great conjunctions, 16 of which will occupy a watery sign."

What does this mean exactly? In astrology, the heavens are divided into the 12 signs of the Zodiac, which each correspond to different groups of stars known as the "constellations," such as Leo, the lion, and Libra, the scales, which are also the signs under which individuals are born, depending on the position of the Sun at the time of their birth. The 12 signs are divided into four groups of three, each assigned to one of the ancient components of matter: fire, earth, water, and air. When casting an astrological chart—for an individual, a country, or a specific day—astrologers use an almanac, which lists the positions of the Sun, Moon, and planets within the 12 signs for any given date. Astrologers then work out the "aspects" of the celestial bodies in the chart because they believe that the relationships between the planets are just as important as their positions within each sign.

What Stöffler calculated for the year 1524 was a series of "conjunctions," or alignments, for the planets, culminating in a major conjunction of four planets (actually five but Uranus had not been discovered), in the water sign Pisces (the fish) for February 20, 1524. His conclusions were that "change, variation, and alteration" would overtake the entire world, and though he was not specific as to the exact nature of the change in the *Almanach*, the fact that the conjunction was to take place in Pisces suggested that the element water would play a major role. It was a short step from there for pamphleteers (the tabloids of their day) to sensationalize the discovery and claim that the world would be swept away in a second Great Flood.

SHOWER
Astrological predictions for the year 1524 predicted a second Great Flood. In the event, all that occurred was a light shower.

Other astrologers and prophets joined the 1524 bandwagon (not dissimilar to the 2012 one we are experiencing now), and as the fateful date approached, the more gullible elements among the European population were seriously disturbed. It is said that people in London prepared themselves by moving to higher ground, and provisioning the upper floors of their houses, though all that would have achieved in the event of a true biblical flood would have been a better view of the disaster, and a slight delay in one's own drowning. A German nobleman, Count Iggleheim, had the inspired idea of imitating Noah by building a three-story ark on the river Rhine for himself and his family. Whether he included a menagerie of animals two by two is not recorded.

What we know about 1524 is that it was an unusually dry year. However, on the appointed day the clouds temporarily obscured the sun and produced a light shower. This was enough to cause an outcry among the German mob that had come to see Iggleheim's ark. Furious that the rich, as usual, would be spared god's wrath, the mob stoned the count to death. Stöffler, who had done nothing to correct the more outlandish rumors of global deluge and was no doubt enjoying the limelight, went back to his charts and recalculated the end of the world for 1528, but by then no one was particularly interested. Like most other astrologers, Stöffler was not very good at predicting his own fate. When plague broke out in Tubingen in 1531, he hoped to avoid it by returning to Blauberen. Unfortunately, the plague, which was no respecter of horoscopes, swept through the entire region, and carried off Stöffler and thousands of other citizens.

THE YORKSHIRE SYBIL: URSULA SOUTHEIL

PREDICTION

Millenarian

Technology

Prophecy

Politics

Military

Natural Disaster

Culture

Economics

Doomsday

Main culprit: Ursula Southeil

What was predicted: The end of the world (cause unspecified) in 1881

What actually happened: No major manmade or natural disasters afflicted humanity in what was an unusually peaceful year by the standards of the late nineteenth century

Carriages without horses shall go,

And accidents fill the world with woe.

Around the world thoughts shall fly

In the twinkling of an eye.

The world upside down shall be

And gold be found at the root of a tree.

The Prophecies of Mother Shipton (1641)

Of all the weird and wonderful individuals featured in this book, Ursula Southeil (c. 1488–1561), better known to history as Mother Shipton, is perhaps the most mysterious. She hailed from the picturesque but remote market town of Knaresborough in the county of Yorkshire in northeast England. She was born at a time when printing technology was still in its infancy, which means that all we know about her comes from oral traditions written down and published years, sometimes centuries, after her death. The task of separating solid fact from fantastic anecdote and total fabrication has defeated many researchers from the seventeenth century onward.

What is certain is that Mother Shipton holds a place in the British occult tradition that matches Nostradamus' (1503–66; see next entry) fame in the rest of the world. What she shares with the French prophet is the habit of making her predictions in striking but extremely obscure verses that can be interpreted in different ways. Unlike Nostradamus, whose prophecies range far and wide in time and place, Mother Shipton is a particularly English prophetess, and her verses deal only with events in England, from the reign of Henry VIII (1491–1547) to possibly the late nineteenth century or, according to several Mother Shipton aficionados, to our own time.

© Chris | Creative Commons

PETRIFYING
The mysterious cave whose waters petrify any objects left in them is said to be the birthplace of the English Sybil, Ursula Southeil.

Ursula Southeil was not a fortunate baby. First there were the circumstances of her birth: She was the illegitimate daughter of Agatha Southeil and an unnamed father, and her mother either died in childbirth or gave her daughter away and retired to a convent soon after Ursula's birth. Second was her appearance, which was said to be particularly unattractive. In representations of her as an old woman, she is shown as the archetypal witch, with a hooked nose, staring goggle eyes, and a hunchback. According to legend, Agatha gave birth in Knaresborough's petrifying cave near the River Nidd, now known as "Mother Shipton's Cave." Any object left in the waters of the cave is quickly petrified. Once thought to be magic, the process is now understood to be due to calcification in the unusually mineral-rich waters.

The circumstances of Ursula's birth gave rise to tales that she was the "Devil's daughter." Nevertheless, she was taken in by a foster mother, who had her baptized and tried to raise the unusual child as best she could. One story relates that the infant Ursula went missing from her cot and was nowhere to be found. A thorough search of the house revealed that she was sitting naked on a metal hook high inside the chimney, smiling and looking very pleased with herself. Despite her appearance and the paranormal events that had marked her childhood, Ursula found a husband, a carpenter by the name of Toby Shipton, and settled down to married life.

It was not long before her neighbors came to her to ask for help when their property had been lost or stolen—a common task of "wise women" of the day. Had she limited herself to these mundane, local matters, she would have been quickly forgotten, but when she prophesied the collapse of a church tower, and then the murder of the Mayor of York — both events taking place soon after—her fame began to spread in the county and then nationally.

Her most famous prophecies during her lifetime concerned the fates of the then young King Henry VIII, who had acceded to the throne in 1509, his powerful first minister, Cardinal Thomas Wolsey (1473–1530), and Henry's second wife Anne Boleyn (c. 1501–1536). Henry came to the throne young, handsome, charismatic, and determined to make a name for himself. When his first wife, the older and rather dour Spanish Catherine of Aragon (1485–1536), failed to give him a male heir, he decided to divorce her. The Catholic Church, however, forbade divorce and refused to grant Henry the annulment that would allow him to marry his mistress Anne Boleyn. According to the Abbot of Beverley, Ursula then pronounced the following prophecy:

> When the Cow doth ride the Bull,
> Then, Priest, beware thy Skull;
> And when the lower shrubs do fall,
> The great Trees quickly follow shall.
> The Mitred Peacock's lofty Pride
> Shall to his Master be a guide,
> And one great Court to pass shall bring
> What was never done by any king.

"WHEN THE COW DOTH RIDE THE BULL"

The Poor shall grieve, to see that day,
And who did feast, must fast and pray.
Fate so decreed their overthrow
Riches brought Pride, and Pride brought woe.

The "Cow" and "Bull" represent the king and Anne Boleyn (from heraldic animals in their coats of arms); the "Mitred Peacock" is Wolsey, who, although a churchman, was well known for his pride and love of luxury. Henry, assisted by Wolsey, begins the dissolution of the monasteries: the fall of "lower shrubs" and the "great trees," which leads, with Henry's divorce of Catherine, to the break with Rome and the establishment of the Church of England in 1532 — "What was never done by any king." Wolsey, however, fell foul of his master, and was disgraced in 1529. He was particularly upset by Ursula's prophecy that he would never see the city of York, of which he was archbishop but had never visited. Determined to prove her wrong, he set out for his northern diocese but was forced to stop a few miles from the city by an arrest warrant from the king. He died shortly after during the return trip to London.

So far Ursula's prophetic abilities might seem to place her in the best rather than the worst predictions category. However, because her prophetic utterances were published 80 years after her death, on the eve of the English Civil War, one could suspect that many of them might have been tailored or invented to fit the political needs of the time: a rebellion against a tyrannical Catholic monarch who was determined to rule without his parliament.

One of her most often quoted prophecies concerning modern times ends: "The world to an end shall come/In eighteen hundred and eighty-one." While she is absolutely correct about, among other things, trains or cars, and the telegraph, telephone, or radio, her dooms-date has passed and did so with remarkably little incident. However, we are not certain that Ursula Southeil, a.k.a. Mother Shipton, a.k.a. the Yorkshire Sybil, ever made any of the predictions she is credited with, or if they were not later fabrications made for profit or propaganda. Her predictions are not the worst because they are incorrect but rather because they might be wholly fabricated, after the events described, by others trying to cash in on her name.

PLAGIARIST PROPHET: NOSTRADAMUS

PREDICTION

Millenarian

Technology

Prophecy

Politics

Military

Natural Disaster

Culture

Economics

Doomsday

Main culprit: Michel de Nostredame

What was predicted: Nostradamus' prophecies have been used retrospectively to predict everything from the Great Fire of London to the end of the world in 1999

What actually happened: No historical event has ever been predicted before taking place by using Nostradamus' prophecies

Beasts ferocious from hunger will swim across rivers:

The greater part of the region will be against the Hister, the great one will cause it to be dragged in an iron cage, when the German child will observe nothing.

The Prophecies, Quatrain 24 of Century II, said to predict the rise of Adolf Hitler

We have reached the man, who, for true believers, represents the pinnacle of prophecy and the ultimate proof of its existence. Other, lesser prophets may be discredited or proved wrong, but what about Michel de Nostredame (1503–66), better known to us as Nostradamus? He single-handedly predicted every major event in world history from his own time until Armageddon—it's there in black and white for all to read in the 1,000 or so rhyming verses of *Les Propheties* (*The Prophecies*). Nostradamus (even the name could not have been better chosen as it speaks to us of hidden, dangerous occult knowledge and power) was a celebrity of his day, who attracted the attention of the French king and queen. Like one of our latter-day celebrities, his biography is obscured by exaggerations and inventions, some of which he may have created or encouraged himself, and others he merely failed to deny. In the prediction business, it pays to advertise, and his more fervent admirers over the last 500 years have done such a good PR job that the Nostradamus legend is now accepted by many as an accurate biography.

NOSTRADAMUS' BIOGRAPHY IS OBSCURED BY EXAGGERATIONS AND INVENTIONS, SOME OF WHICH HE MAY HAVE CREATED OR ENCOURAGED HIMSELF.

In looking at his life, we shall try to limit ourselves to those facts that can be ascertained from the historical record. Michel de Nostredame was born to a well-to-do merchant family in the small town of Saint-Rémy-de-Provence, near the city of Arles in southern France. The young Michel owes his name and his religion to his paternal grandfather, who converted from Judaism to Catholicism and adopted the name Pierre de Nostredame (*Notre Dame* in today's French, or "Our Lady") in around 1455. Jews did not have an easy time in late medieval Europe. Their civil rights were severely constrained, and the Church and civilian authorities and their Christian neighbors periodically persecuted them. During the reign of Louis XI (1423–83) and his successors, many French Jews were forced to choose between exile and conversion. One tradition holds that the three-year-old Michel was taught mathematics and medicine by his maternal grandfather, Jean de Saint-Rémy, but this seems unlikely, as Jean is thought to have died in 1504 when the future prophet was only one year old.

In 1518, at the age of 15, Michel went to Avignon, one-time seat of the papacy, to study for his baccalaureate at the town's illustrious university. He followed the standard curriculum of grammar, rhetoric, and logic, but his fellow students are said to have nicknamed him "the young astrologer" because of his interest in astrology and astronomical phenomena. An outbreak of bubonic plague forced him to abandon his studies and leave the city. According to his own, much later account, he spent the next eight years in the countryside studying herbal medicine and working as an apothecary.

In an age when medical knowledge was extremely primitive, and qualified doctors were far and few between, village apothecaries filled the dual roles of doctor and pharmacist. They had no formal medical training or qualifications and learned their skills on the job. This lowly status did not satisfy Michel, who in 1529 decided to study for a doctorate in medicine at the University of Montpellier. Unfortunately, he was soon expelled for engaging in a "manual trade"—his work as an apothecary—which was expressly forbidden to students by the university statutes. There are no records of Michel attending any other educational institution; therefore, he never earned the title of doctor that he was accorded by his publishers and admirers.

For the next 17 years, Michel traveled throughout France and Italy, meeting the leading scientists, doctors, and intellectuals of the day, and engaging in his self-taught professions of apothecary and healer. In the early 1530s he settled in the town of Agen, where he married for the first time and had two children, but his wife and children died in one of the many murderous outbreaks of the plague that afflicted Europe during the sixteenth century.

At this time he owed his fame not to his prophetic abilities but to the herbal *boules de senteur* (odoriferous pills) and other herbal remedies that he made to prevent and treat the plague, which was then thought to be spread by "bad evil-smelling air." During the 1540s, he was much in demand for his medical skills, and he was called to the cities of Marseille, Aix-en-Provence, and Arles to deal with outbreaks of the deadly disease. In 1547, he settled in the nearby Salon-de-Provence, where he married for the second time—on this occasion with a rich widow called Anne Ponsarde.

Approaching his 50s and relieved of any financial worries because of his wife's wealth, Michel de Nostredame decided on a change of career. In 1550 he published the first of many almanacs, containing

"BOULES DE SENTEURS" AND OTHER MAGIC BULLETS

ever preserved from a state of inferiority and consequently falling into a very low class among the European States.

Even after the outbreak of hostilities and the subsequent Declaration of Independence in 1776, George urged his ministers to fight on and confidently predicted a British victory. The defeat of Great Britain by a handful of provincial colonists was impossible in his eyes. When defeat came, he was the first to blame himself, and he railed that the empire might be better off without the "knavery" of the Americans. However, his anger was short-lived and when John Adams (1725–1836) presented his credentials to the king as the United States' first ambassador to Great Britain in 1785, George III, inaugurating the "special relationship" between the two countries, said: "I was the last person to consent to the separation, but I will be the first to accept the friendship of the United States as an independent power."

George III has often been portrayed as a bloodthirsty tyrant hell-bent on oppressing his American subjects. He was, however, a typical English gentleman of his day, conservative and well intentioned, but who was not equipped to deal with the sweeping political and social changes that marked his reign. He was not the first, and, as we shall see, certainly not the last political and military leader to predict certain victory in war only to suffer the most comprehensive and ignominious defeat.

OVERCROWDED EARTH: THOMAS MALTHUS

PREDICTION

Millenarian

Technology

Prophecy

Politics

Military

Natural Disaster

Culture

Economics

Doomsday

Main culprit: Thomas Malthus

What was predicted: A cycle of poverty and deprivation due to overpopulation

What actually happened: The population has increased many times over since Malthus' day and living standards and life expectancy have continued to improve

The power of population is so superior to the power of the earth to produce subsistence for man, that premature death must in some shape or other visit the human race. The vices of mankind are active and able ministers of depopulation. They are the precursors in the great army of destruction, and often finish the dreadful work themselves. But should they fail in this war of extermination, sickly seasons, epidemics, pestilence, and plague advance in terrific array, and sweep off their thousands and tens of thousands. Should success be still incomplete, gigantic inevitable famine stalks in the rear, and with one mighty blow levels the population with the food of the world.

Essay on the Principle of Population (1798)
by Thomas Malthus

Population has always been a major preoccupation of statesmen and social commentators, though for most of history it has been the decline in population that worried them most. Looking back to a few notable historical examples, it was a fall in population that contributed to the collapse of the Western Roman Empire in the fifth century CE; the Black Death that struck Europe between 1348 and 1350 killed between an estimated one- and two-thirds of the population; and the arrival of Old World diseases in the New World in the sixteenth century was responsible for the decimation of up to 90 percent of the Native American population.

EVEN WITH DISASTERS OF THIS MAGNITUDE, SINCE THE YEAR 1000 CE, THE TREND FOR WORLD POPULATION GROWTH HAS ALWAYS BEEN EVER UPWARD.

Even with disasters of this magnitude, since the year 1000 CE, the trend for world population growth has always been ever upward. The first major population milestone—one billion humans to live on planet Earth—is thought to have occurred in the first decade of the nineteenth century, and although the people of the day would not have been aware of it, it is precisely at this time that economists started to question the sustainability of an ever-increasing population.

The population of the United Kingdom for the first decades of the eighteenth century is estimated as being stable at around six million, but the first British census conducted in 1801 recorded 10.5 million in England, Wales, and Scotland, and another 5.5 million in Ireland. This sudden growth spurt was reproduced in the rest of Europe, whose population doubled in the eighteenth century from 50 to 100 million, and had doubled again to 200 million by the end of the nineteenth century. The immediate cause of this increase was the decline in infant mortality for children aged 0–5 from almost 75 percent at the beginning of the eighteenth century, to just over 30 percent 100 years later. This marked amelioration in infant survival had much more complex socio-economic causes: industrialization and urbanization, which improved overall living standards, and advances in medicine and sanitation that reduced the impact of epidemic diseases.

The socio-economic transformations that caused the sudden increase in Europe's population were particularly marked in Britain, which was the first country in the region to experience large-scale industrialization and urbanization, beginning in the 1760s. It is not surprising, therefore, that it was an Englishman, the Reverend Thomas Malthus (1766–1834),

who first raised the specter of overpopulation and its potentially catastrophic effects on the world in *An Essay on the Principle of Population*. The work was so popular that he had to revise it five times between 1798 and 1826.

Malthus had the perfect British intellectual pedigree. Born into a well-to-do country family, he attended private schools before graduating from Jesus College, Cambridge, where he studied Latin and Greek, and excelled in Mathematics. He was elected a fellow of the college in 1791. In 1798, having entered holy orders, he became curate of a small village parish in Surrey just outside London. He married in 1804, and the following year was appointed Professor of History and Political Economy at the East India Company College, where his students nicknamed him "Pop" or "Population" Malthus because of his fame in the field of population studies. In 1818, Malthus earned the ultimate accolade by being elected a Fellow of the prestigious Royal Society. He was extremely influential during his lifetime, causing changes in the British government's welfare policies, and he made his mark on a generation of economists and scientists, including no lesser a figure than the father of evolutionary science, Charles Darwin (1809–82), who quoted Malthus' work in his *On the Origin of Species* (1859).

Although I'll probably be accused of gross oversimplification, the basic outline of the theory Malthus expounded in *Principle of Population* is as follows. Population is governed by man's ability to produce the necessities of life (for Malthus, primarily food, but the same can be applied to housing, oil, energy, consumer goods, and so on). When food and goods are plentiful, humans breed (because we enjoy sex and cannot control our "passions"), and population inexorably rises until it outstrips the available resources. At this point, what Malthus calls the "positive" checks of famine, disease, and war kick in and lead to population decline (i.e., the surplus human population is wiped out). When the population has dropped below a certain level, the available resources are once again sufficient to feed, clothe, and house the workforce, who, because of the law of supply and demand, are also earning higher wages at this point. This sets off the whole cycle of "loose living" (in Malthus' words, "vice") among

"POPULATION" MALTHUS

"POP" MALTHUS
Malthus' chilling theories on population growth made the British government change its welfare policies and worsened the lot of the poor.

the lower orders, who being completely improvident, start reproducing uncontrollably, leading to a further cycle of population growth and decline, and so on.

Malthus believed that humanity was caught in a "population trap" (later named the "Malthusian trap" in his honor), which condemned it to repeat the vicious cycle of population growth in times of plenty, followed by steep population decline as resources became scarce. Although the population of the United Kingdom in Malthus' day was around 15 million—one-fifth of what it is today—he was already warning that the country's population had reached dangerously unsustainable levels. He predicted not the extinction of the human species, but an endless cycle of misery, suffering, and death in the centuries to come.

His idea won widespread recognition in the intellectual and ruling circles of the day, and his work was directly responsible for two areas of legislation that did untold harm to the living conditions and life expectancy of the working population of Britain. The first concerned the very basic welfare system established by the Poor Laws, which dated back to the early seventeenth century, and provided for the most basic relief of the poor and unemployed. When the government proposed a measure to extend poor relief, Malthus, although he was a clergyman and might have been expected to support the extension of charity, opposed it vigorously on the grounds that it would increase agricultural prices, and that it would only "create the poor which they maintain." He went further and argued that poor relief should be abolished altogether and that poor relief should be left to the dubious charity of the wealthy. The second measure was his support for the Corn Laws, passed to maintain an artificially high price for locally grown corn. This caused price hikes for bread, then the working class' staple food, and led to profiteering, food shortages, famine, and serious civil unrest.

Now, since 1798, the world has experienced no end of plagues, famines, wars, and revolutions that have slaughtered untold millions. Yet despite this carnage, the world population has continued to grow, and, just as importantly, average lifespans and quality of life has also continued to improve. The world has not fallen into the Malthusian trap, and for the two reasons that Malthus himself ridiculed and dismissed as impossible in the *Principle of Population*. The first is that humans can be taught to

control their "passions" and breed less in the good times. It has been shown that increased affluence and education cause a decrease in the birthrate, as can be seen in the developed world, where affluence coupled with effective contraception has stabilized the population. The second, which has allowed increased living standards and prolonged human life everywhere, is the extraordinary progress in technology, medicine, and agriculture that has been achieved in the past four decades.

Despite a population of almost seven billion and growing, and the repeated warnings of latter-day Malthusians such as Paul Ehrlich, who predicted in his 1968 bestseller, *The Population Bomb*, that there would be mass starvation due to overpopulation by the 1980s at the latest, life expectancy and living standards continue to rise, and the Malthusian trap and long-awaited Malthusian population "catastrophe" have yet to materialize.

UN POPULATION ESTIMATES

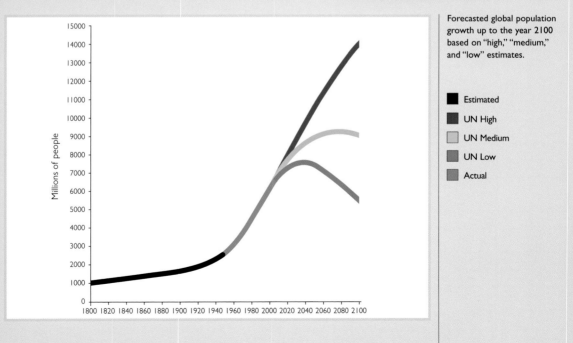

Forecasted global population growth up to the year 2100 based on "high," "medium," and "low" estimates.

■ Estimated

■ UN High

☐ UN Medium

■ UN Low

■ Actual

PREDICTION

Millenarian

Technology

Prophecy

Politics

Military

Natural disaster

Culture

Economics

Doomsday

MARCHING ON: JOSEPH SMITH, JR.

Main culprit: Joseph Smith, Jr.

What was predicted: Smith predicted the end of the world and the Second Coming when he turned 85 in 1890

What actually happened: Unfortunately, Smith died at the age of 39, murdered by a mob in Carthage, IL

I was once praying very earnestly to know the time of the coming of the Son of Man, when I heard a voice repeat the following:

Joseph, my son, if thou livest until thou art eighty-five years old, thou shalt see the face of the Son of Man; therefore let this suffice, and trouble me no more on this matter.

Doctrine and Covenants (1835) by Joseph Smith, Jr.

We return to the New World and to Christian millenarian prophecy, in the person of Joseph Smith, Jr. (1805–44), the founder of the Church of Jesus Christ of Latter-day Saints, also known as the Mormon Church. Smith's short but adventurous life began on the eastern seaboard, in Vermont, New England. When he was 11 or 12, his parents moved to Palmyra, New York, a part of New England noted for its religious sectarianism in the nineteenth century. His biographers agree that Joseph and his family were involved in the revivalist movement active in the region. He himself claimed to have had his first divinely inspired vision at the age of 15. As a profitable sideline, the young Joseph also advertised his talents as a treasure finder. Without too much success, however, as it earned him an indictment for fraud in 1826.

In 1823, combining his treasure-seeking abilities with his interest in revivalist Christianity, Smith reported a visitation of the Angel Moroni, who revealed to him the hiding place of golden plates, written in "reformed Egyptian," purporting to record the history of pre-Columbian America up to the fifth century CE. The angel also thoughtfully provided "seer stones" mounted into silver spectacles with which Smith would be able to understand the plates. The translation, which took seven years and was interrupted by many a mishap, was finally published in 1830 as the *Book of Mormon*, which became the founding text of the Church of Jesus Christ of Latter-day Saints.

In brief, the *Book of Mormon* describes the colonization of the Americas by refugees from Israel in the seventh century BCE and their subsequent history up to the fifth century CE. Jesus Christ visited the continent soon after his resurrection to convert its people. One group, the Nephites, who were Caucasian in appearance, kept the faith, but the dark-skinned Lamanites became pagan, and ultimately wiped out their Christian brethren. In this way, Smith explained the absence of Christianity and Caucasians in the Americas when the Spanish arrived in the fifteenth century, and the presence of pagan Native Americans, including the Maya. However, the story gave Americans a direct link to the Old and New Testaments that not only pre-dated the established churches of the Old World but also recast America as a second Promised Land.

Smith spent the remaining 14 years of his life attempting to build a new Zion on American soil in preparation for the Second Coming. Those years were, to say the least, full of incident. He and his followers were first expelled from New York, subsequently settling in Ohio (1831–38), then Missouri (1838–39), and finally Illinois (1839–44). These complex political and religious persecutions, worthy of a book of the Old Testament, were sometimes triggered by other settlers who felt threatened by the Mormons, and sometimes by conflicts within the Church itself. During his wilderness years, Smith made powerful enemies at both state and federal level. He died at the hands of an enraged mob after an unsuccessful attempt to close down a newspaper that had attacked him and his beliefs, in particular his espousal of the doctrine of polygamy.

FOUR SCORE YEARS AND FIVE

Smith made several prophetic utterances during his ministry, and I am indebted to the Institute for Religious Studies for its list of Smith's failed prophecies. We shall gloss over the failure to find a promised treasure in Salem, MA, and concentrate on the major prophecies that deal with the future of the Church, the U.S., and the world as a whole. The first of these concerns the construction of a temple in Zion, Missouri: "Verily, this is the word of the Lord, that the city New Jerusalem shall be built by the gathering of the saints, beginning at this place, even the place of the temple, which temple shall be reared in this generation." Unfortunately, Smith and his followers were ejected from Missouri and the temple was never built.

Several predict the fate of the United States, specifically its Congress, government, and its "wicked" people:

> And now I am prepared to say by the authority of Jesus Christ,
> that not many years shall pass away before the United States
> shall present such a scene of bloodshed as has not a parallel in
> the history of our nation; pestilence, hail, famine, and earthquake
> will sweep the wicked of this generation from off the face of the
> land, to open and prepare the way for the return of the lost tribes
> of Israel from the north country.

When Smith petitioned Congress for help against his enemies, he warned, "If Congress will not hear our petition and grant us protection, they shall be broken up as a government, and God shall damn them,

and there shall be nothing left of them." And again, one year before his death, he thundered that, "Unless the United States redress the wrongs committed upon the Saints in the state of Missouri and punish the crimes committed by her officers that in a few years the government will be utterly overthrown and wasted." Needless to say, Congress and the federal government did not accede to Smith's demands but somehow managed to escape divine retribution.

Last but not least was his predicted date for the end of the world and the advent of the Kingdom on Earth. As we shall see later, it is always wise for a prophet to place this far ahead in the future to avoid any possible embarrassment when the heavens do not burn and the seas do not boil. Smith wisely deferred his Doomsday until his 85th year (see quote), which would have been 1890, though another prediction, made in 1835, suggested that the end would take place a year later in 1891: "It was the will of God that they should be ordained to the ministry and go forth to prune the vineyard for the last time, for the coming of the Lord, which was nigh—even fifty-six years should wind up the scene."

Either way, those two years passed without so much of a whiff of brimstone in the air. Smith avoided all embarrassment, however, by having expired 46 years earlier while trying to escape a lynch mob in Carthage, IL. By the 1890s, the Mormon Church had established itself in its current home of Salt Lake City, Utah, and, like many Christian movements before and since, quietly disposed of its millenarian roots, relegating the Second Coming to an indeterminate future to concentrate on converts and real estate.

DEAD WRONG
Joseph Smith predicted that the second coming of Christ would occur in his 85th year, but he himself died at the age of 39.

HIGH-SPEED DEATH: DIONYSIUS LARDNER

Main culprit: Dionysius Lardner

What was predicted: That train passengers would suffocate when reaching speeds of 120 mph

What actually happened: The current record for a conventional passenger train is in the region of 275 mph

Rail travel at high speed is not possible, because passengers, unable to breathe, would die of asphyxia.

Dr. Dionysius Lardner (1793–1859)

With this 12th entry, we come to a new type of prediction: the "it'll never work, get off the ground, sell, or be of any practical use!" which, as we shall see, has been applied to every major technological development since the beginning of the Industrial Revolution (and probably since the invention of the wheel—very nice but what good is it?). Of course, in certain cases, the nay-sayers were absolutely right, as such wonders as the steam-powered airship and omnibus, the atmospheric railway, and the flying car amply demonstrate. But in this case, the invention in question—the passenger train—is one that has transformed the world in ways that even its most ardent supporters and bitterest critics alike could never have imagined.

The age of the passenger train began modestly in northeast England in 1825 with the 26-mile (40-km) Stockton and Darlington Railway (S&DR). The inaugural train, carrying 600 passengers in converted coal wagons, traveled at a sedate 6–7 mph (9–11 kph)—still faster than walking pace and much smoother than the kidney-jolting stagecoaches of the day. The success of the S&DR encouraged engineers and entrepreneurs to plan a network of freight and passenger lines between the cities of the industrial North and Midlands, starting with the first modern railway with timetables and purpose-designed engines and rolling stock, the Liverpool and Manchester Railway, which opened in 1830.

Regrettably, the opening of the Liverpool and Manchester line was also the occasion of the first widely recorded rail fatality: William Huskisson (1770–1830), a member of the British parliament and minister of the crown, who stepped out onto the tracks into the path of an incoming steam engine. However, not even this high-profile death could slow the development of rail transport in the UK. Investment in railroads in the 1840s, known in England as "railway mania," was the dotcom bubble of its day. In two years between 1844 and 1846, 6,220 miles (10,010 km) of railway were built, which amounted to over half the mileage of the current UK network of 11,000 miles (18,000 km).

The growth of rail was not universally welcomed, however. The French scientist François Arago (1786–1853) deplored that rail transport for the army would result in the "emasculation" of the troops deprived of the "joy of marching" (one can imagine what footsore Gallic infantrymen

thought of Mr Arago's joy of marching!). In New York, future president of the Union Martin Van Buren (1782–1862) warned the president of the day that the railroads would bankrupt the canals, and that trains traveling at the "enormous speed of 15 miles per hour" would endanger the "life and limb of passengers, roar and snort their way through the countryside, setting fire to crops, scaring the livestock and frightening women and children." He concluded with the pious: "The Almighty certainly never intended that people should travel at such breakneck speed."

TAKE YOUR BREATH AWAY

Divine planning aside, there were many who worried that train travel might be injurious to human health. A committee of German doctors predicted unspecified "brain problems" for rail passengers and recommended that train tracks be enclosed with high fencing to prevent vertigo among onlookers. But it was the Irish mathematician and astronomer Dionysius Lardner (1793–1859) whose dire warnings most alarmed the general public. In the 1830s, the great civil engineer Isambard Kingdom Brunel (1806–59) was building his Great Western Railway (GWR), linking London to the west and southwest of England. One of the engineering marvels of the line is the GWR's Box Tunnel between the cities of Bath and Chippenham. The tunnel runs perfectly straight for its 1.83 miles (2.937 km) length and has a gradient of 1/100.

Lardner warned that if the brakes failed when the train was going through the tunnel, the steep gradient would accelerate it and its passengers to a velocity of 120 mph (192 km/h), which in the age of the horse-driven buggy was a mind-boggling speed. The lungs of humans traveling at this speed would become compressed, and they would die of asphyxia—the acceleration would literally take their breath away. Although the warning is patently absurd, as we routinely travel many hundred miles per hour by airplane, the less science-savvy travelers of the day were more likely to give credence to Lardner because of his eminent position as Professor of Natural Philosophy and Astronomy at the capital's most prestigious educational institution, University College London.

Although he is not credited with any major scientific discoveries of his own, Lardner was an able expounder of scientific and mathematical

principles. The Carl Sagan of his day, he was best known for a part work, the 133-volume *Cabinet Cyclopaedia* (1829–46), which aimed to bring the latest scientific, technical, and philosophical knowledge to a popular audience. The Box Tunnel controversy was not the only time he clashed with the great Brunel. When the latter proposed to build the first transatlantic steamship, the SS *Great Western* (launched in 1838), Lardner described the project as "perfectly chimerical," and opined that Brunel might as well have projected a journey from New York to the Moon. He predicted that the steamship would run out of fuel part-way through the crossing. Once again, he was proved conclusively wrong when the *Great Western* sailed into New York with 200 tons of coal to spare.

No stranger to scientific controversy, Lardner also had a scandalous private life, which was to prove his ultimate downfall. Married and divorced in Ireland, he fathered an illegitimate child with his mistress while in Dublin. In 1840, after moving to London, he met and fell in love with the wife of an army captain. The couple ran away together to Paris, where the enraged husband pursued them, beat Lardner up, but failed to win his wife back. Lardner was able to marry her in 1846, but the scandal had put an end to his career in England. He lived the rest of his life in Europe, living from his publishing income and lucrative lecture tours in the U.S. He died in Naples, Italy, at the age of 66.

DEATH TRAIN
Lardner's fanciful predictions of death from asphyxia from high-speed train travel alarmed the public of his day.

PREDICTION

Millenarian

Technology

Prophecy

Politics

Military

Natural Disaster

Culture

Economics

Doomsday

BORN-AGAIN RATIONALIST: WILLIAM MILLER

Main culprit: William Miller

What was predicted: The end of the world and the Advent (Second Coming) of Christ between March 21, 1843 and March 21, 1844

What actually happened: When the end did not come, the Millerites dispersed, many abandoning their beliefs altogether, while others regrouped into various Adventist churches

And both together make 2520 years, beginning before Christ 677, which taken out of 2520, leaves 1843 after Christ, when captive Zion will go free from all bondage, even from death, and the last enemy conquered, the remnant of all nations saved, the New Jerusalem completed, the saints glorified.

Views of the Prophecies and Prophetic Chronology (1842)
by William Miller

In the entry on the Maya calendar, we saw how its later interpreters used it to calculate the end of the world in December 2012. There is something mesmerizing about numbers. Numbers, unlike words, cannot be made to lie: $2 + 2 = 4$ and cannot equal 3 or 5, however much you twist them. And prophecies based on numbers and arcane calculations, like those generated by the Maya Long Count, also have an aura of scientific accuracy and authority. Numbers, facts, and science are, after all, inseparable. But the purposes to which calculations and numbers are applied are not immune from human invention and distortion. In this entry, we examine the calculation that led William Miller (1782–1849) to believe that the end of the world would fall some time between March 21, 1843, and March 21, 1844.

Miller was born in Pittsfield, MA, the son of a veteran of the American War of Independence. Married at the age of 21, he moved to Poultney, VT, and settled down to become a farmer. He joined the state militia, earning his commission as a lieutenant in 1810. He served with distinction in the War of 1812, which pitted the U.S. against the British Empire, finishing with the rank of Captain. He later moved his family to Low Hampton on the border of Vermont and New York State.

With this biography, and compared to Joseph Smith who had been steeped in the New England revivalist movement, Miller seems an unlikely candidate as the leader of a fundamentalist, millenarian religious movement. Granted he had been raised a Baptist, but he had traded in his Christian faith around 1810 for Deism and Freemasonry, both products of the eighteenth century's Age of Enlightenment. These two beliefs stripped the belief in God from its faith-based historical and supernatural dimensions, replacing them with the tenets of reason that proved the existence of a "Supreme Being"—a sort of divine engineer who had created the world but did not interfere in its day-to-day affairs. However, once he returned from his military service, Miller seems to have become troubled about what would happen to him after his death. Several of his biographers have speculated that the death of close family members and his own near-death experiences during the war precipitated an existential crisis that made him rethink his religious views. He returned to the Baptist Church of his childhood, but did not abandon his ties with Deism and Freemasonry until 1831.

Miller spent many years trying to reconcile his contrasting beliefs in a religion based on reason and his Baptist faith based on scriptural revelation. Although he recorded a strong emotional experience while reading the sermon one Sunday at church in Low Hampton, which can be described as his being "born again," he could not quite rid himself of the rationalism of his own earlier beliefs. His answer was to begin a meticulous and systematic verse-by-verse study of the Bible through which he hoped to bridge the gap between reason and faith. The attempt was bound to end in failure but produced an interesting result: his sincere conviction that the date of the end of the world and the Second Coming had been revealed in the Bible.

At this point we shall make a brief aside to examine the varieties of millennial predictions found in Christian eschatology (the last four things, remember: death, judgment, heaven, and hell). Millennialism comes in three distinct flavors: pre-, post-, and a-. The first states that the Second Coming of Jesus Christ will occur before the millennium, with the Last Judgment coming at the end of his 1,000-year reign. At the other end of the spectrum, the postmillennialists believe that the Second Coming will occur after Satan is defeated, and the Kingdom of God has been established on Earth for 1,000 years. Many in this group believe that we have already lived through most of the millennium and entered the end times and that the Second Coming and Last Judgment are at hand. The Amillennialists reject the idea of a temporal millennium altogether, seeing it as a symbolic rather than literal event.

COUNTDOWN TO ARMAGEDDON

Miller, having rejected postmillennialism, created his own chronology for the Second Coming or Advent of Jesus Christ. The calculation is fairly abstruse, combining number crunching with Old and New Testament scriptural prophecy, and I will summarize it below as best I can. Those interested in Miller's complete exposition can find it in Lecture III of his *Evidence from Scripture and History of the Second Coming of Christ, about the Year 1843: Exhibited in a Course of Lectures*, first published in 1834.

The Bible is big on numbers: the Ten Commandments; the seven cows of Joseph's dream; the 40 years in the wilderness—there is even a book of the Old Testament called "Numbers." Miller decided that three biblical numbers were particularly significant: the numbers seven,

70, and 2,300, which he found in the following verses from the Book of Daniel:

> And he said unto me, Unto two thousand and three hundred days; then shall the sanctuary be cleansed. (8:14)

> Seventy weeks are determined upon thy people and upon thy holy city, to finish the transgression, and to make an end of sins, and to make reconciliation for iniquity, and to bring in everlasting righteousness, and to seal up the vision and prophecy, and to anoint the most Holy. (9:24)

> Know therefore and understand, that from the going forth of the commandment to restore and to build Jerusalem unto the Messiah the Prince shall be seven weeks, and threescore and two weeks: the street shall be built again, and the wall, even in troublous times. (9:25)

Miller used the one day = one year principle to determine that Daniel's 2,300 days was in fact referring to 2,300 years, and that the cleansing of the sanctuary referred not to the sanctuary of the Temple of Jerusalem but to the cleansing of the world by fire and the Second Coming. Now he needed to find out when the 2,300 years had begun to calculate the date on which the world would end. To do this he used two further verses from Daniel that referred to seven, 62, and 70 weeks from the rebuilding of Jerusalem and the coming of the Messiah.

Using the same principle of days = years, Miller chose 457 BCE as the start of the 2,300-year countdown to Armageddon. In 457, the Persian King Artaxerxes I (r. 465–24 BCE) instructed the prophet Ezra to return to Jerusalem to restore the city walls. We will put aside for the time being the fact that the Jews had started to return to Jerusalem in 538 BCE and had already built the second Temple at the time of Ezra's journey. Seventy weeks is equal to 490 days (7 x 70), which is, according to Miller, 490 years. So if you subtract 457 from 490, you get 33, the age of Christ when he was crucified, therefore the final number needed to complete Daniel's prophecy. Having worked out this figure, he subtracted 457 from 2,300 to come up with the year 1843. He never specified an exact

2 + 2 = 5
Miller employed complex formulae using numbers taken from the Bible to calculate the date of the end of the world.

day in that year, stating that as the Persian New Year began in March, the event might take place any time between March 21, 1843, and March 21, 1844.

Although Miller had completed his calculations by 1818, he did not make them public until 1831. In the hothouse atmosphere of nineteenth-century New England millenarian Christianity, Miller's prediction had an immediate and profound impact. Estimates of the number of his followers, who became known as Millerites, vary from 50,000 to 500,000 nationwide. Needless to say, 1843 passed without incident, and the end of the world was recalculated several times and rescheduled for 1844. The final revision for October 22, 1844, resulted in the "Great Disappointment" and the effective end of the Millerite movement. Many abandoned their Christian faith and belief in prophecy altogether, while others tried to redefine their beliefs at a conference in Albany, NY, in 1845. From this meeting emerged the Adventist movement, whose main representative bodies are the small Advent Christian Church and the much larger Seventh-day Adventist Church. Miller himself remained convinced that the Second Coming was at hand, although he never produced another date for the event.

HISTORICAL IMPERATIVE: KARL MARX

PREDICTION

Millenarian

Technology

Prophecy

Politics

Military

Natural Disaster

Culture

Economics

Doomsday

Main culprit: Karl Marx

What was predicted: The collapse of capitalism and the victory of communism

What actually happened: The collapse of communism and the victory of capitalism

The development of Modern Industry, therefore, cuts from under its feet the very foundation on which the bourgeoisie produces and appropriates products. What the bourgeoisie, therefore, produces, above all, are its own gravediggers. Its fall and the victory of the proletariat are equally inevitable.

The Communist Manifesto (1848), by Karl Marx and Friedrich Engels

We move away from Christian prophecy and eschatology and travel to the opposite end of the ideological spectrum to the man who is praised or vilified as the father of revolutionary communism, Karl Marx (1818–83). Marx, who, with Friedrich Engels (1820–95), published *The Communist Manifesto* in 1848, developed a theory of history and economics that described the future course of world history and predicted the collapse of capitalism and its ultimate replacement by communism. Love him or loathe him, Marx is without doubt the nineteenth-century thinker who has had the greatest impact on the course of political history in the twentieth century, as his ideas were the basis for the communist revolutions in Russia (1917) and China (1949).

His predictions, however, have conspicuously failed to materialize (so far). Quite to the contrary, Soviet communism collapsed in 1990, and China's Maoist-communist autocracy, while still in power, has led the country into a hybrid version of communism and capitalism, which many think will ultimately lead to the democratization of the country. Marx clearly got it wrong, but was it because his ideas were completely mistaken, or was it the fault of the men and women who went aout trying to implement them in Russia and China? Because of the ideological baggage around Marx's work—either fanatically pro or anti—it is sometimes difficult to untangle what Marx actually said and believed from what his interpreters would like him to have said. Like any great thinker, he was also allowed to change his mind at different periods of his life.

Before examining Marx's works and predictions, we should look at the intellectual and social background of his times. Marx was born in Trier in the Kingdom of Prussia in 1818, some 53 years before the unification of Germany. Until 1871, Germany was a patchwork of independent kingdoms, dukedoms, bishoprics, and principalities, which was dominated by the powerful Kingdom of Prussia. Although all these states shared the same Germanic background, they varied in culture, religion, wealth, industrial development, and political ideology. Prussia was authoritarian, militaristic, and anti-democratic, but it was also one of the richest and most industrially developed of the German states.

At the time of Marx's birth, Europe was recovering from two decades of war triggered by the French Revolution of 1789 and continued by the Emperor Napoleon I (1769–1821), who had succeeded in conquering half of the continent, until he himself had been defeated at the Battle of Waterloo in 1815 by an alliance led by Prussia and Britain. Napoleon's conquests, although the emperor was himself an autocrat, had disseminated the liberal ideals of the Age of Enlightenment and French Revolution as far as Russia. With Napoleon's defeat, the old monarchical autocracies he had displaced or reformed were restored, and revolutionary activity on the French model severely repressed.

Marx's father was a converted Jew, who had abandoned his religion to further his career in law at a time when Jews were discriminated against by the Prussian state. The Marx family was politically liberal and inculcated its values into their son as he grew up. Little is known of his education until he entered high school in Trier in 1830, from where he went to the University of Bonn and later Berlin to study law. Marx, however, was always much more interested in philosophy and literature and did poorly in his studies. He cited the Enlightenment philosophers Voltaire (1694–1778) and Kant (1724–1804) among his early influences. For a time he was part of a radical student group known as the "Young Hegelians," which promoted the political ideas of the philosopher Georg Hegel (1770–1831). Marx's radical views would have disbarred him from working in the conservative Prussian legal or academic establishments, and after completing his doctorate in philosophy in 1841, he chose to become a political writer and journalist.

In response to Prussia's strict censorship laws, Marx with other German intellectuals moved to Paris, France, but he was expelled in 1845 and moved to Brussels, Belgium, where he and Engels wrote *The Communist Manifesto*. His support for the revolutions that erupted all over Europe in 1848 resulted in his being expelled from Belgium, from where he finally made his way to England, settling in a poor district of the British capital. He remained in London for the rest of his life, dividing his time between organizing the fledgling communist movement and writing his weighty (in both senses of the word) three-volume analysis of the capitalist system and its downfall, *Das Kapital* (*Capital*), whose first volume was published in 1867, with

MARX WAS ALWAYS MUCH MORE INTERESTED IN PHILOSOPHY AND LITERATURE AND DID POORLY IN HIS STUDIES.

volumes two and three published posthumously in the years 1885 and 1894 respectively.

DICKENSIAN VALUES

When he lived in exile in France, Belgium, and England, Marx, who was from a privileged middle-class background, was for the first time exposed to the squalor of working-class life in the first half of the nineteenth century. Anyone familiar with the books of Marx's contemporary, the novelist, advocate of social reform, and philanthropist Charles Dickens (1812–70) will know how terrible life could be for working men and women in England during the early Victorian period. What Marx witnessed first hand was raw, exploitative capitalism that thankfully has long been eradicated in the developed world. Migrants moving from the countryside into Europe's first industrial cities lived in slums and had to take any job offered to them at subsistence wages. There was only the most basic social provision—workhouses that were more like prisons than charitable hospices—no health care, and no labor unions or political parties to protect workers' rights. With little regulation by the state, capitalist enterprise was subject to extreme cycles of boom and bust. In the good times, employees prospered to a degree, but in the bad, they were summarily dismissed and condemned to destitution.

It should come as no surprise that Marx based his analysis of nineteenth-century capitalism on the exploitation of workers by bourgeois entrepreneurs. The profitability of capitalism and its ultimate downfall could be explained, he believed, by his version of the labor theory of value. According to Marx, the capitalist mode of production developed when labor became a commodity—when men and women left the land where they produced their own food and moved into cities where they sold their labor-power in exchange for wages.

The distinctive feature of industrial capitalism as opposed to the earlier mercantile capitalism was its exploitation of "surplus labor value," which is the difference between what it costs to keep a worker alive and what he or she can produce. Capitalism, Marx admitted, could produce enormous economic growth because entrepreneurs reinvested their profits in new technology and plant. This, however, created the seeds of the system's ultimate downfall. If profits were earned from the surplus value of the labor of exploited workers, the rate of profit would fall as entrepreneurs invested in new technology. The result would be cyclical periods of growth, when labor became cheap, and recessions as profits fell and whole industrial sectors became unprofitable and were eliminated. At some point, these recessionary crises would become so destructive and the conditions of the proletariat so impoverished that revolution would become a historical certainty, especially in highly urbanized and industrialized countries such as Britain and the U.S.

What actually happened during the twentieth century was the exact opposite. The U.S. and the major European countries underwent a process of gradual social and political reform, leading to improvements in the living conditions of the working classes who became integrated into the liberal-democratic capitalist system. The countries that did turn to communism, Russia and China, were among the least economically and industrially developed in the world, with largely agrarian economies and social systems very different from the ones described by Marx in *Das Kapital*.

Although (non-Marxist) economists agree that his labor theory of value is deeply flawed and does not describe the complexity of capitalism in his day or ours, many admit that his views on the class struggle and the cycles of boom and bust still have contemporary relevance. Marxist-Leninism and Marxist-Maoism may have failed in Russia and China, but that does not mean that Marx and his predictions for the transformation of capitalism into a more communitarian and egalitarian economic system may not one day be proved right.

© Bernd Untiedt | Creative Commons

WALL STREET
The New York Stock Exchange (NYSE) in Lower Manhattan.

"WHO WOULD WANT TO USE IT?": RUTHERFORD B. HAYES

Main culprit: Rutherford B. Hayes

What was predicted: The failure of the telephone

What actually happened: 4.6 billion cell phones and counting

It's a great invention but who would want to use it anyway?

President Rutherford B. Hayes, after seeing a demonstration of the telephone in 1876

The dire prediction about the dangers of traveling by train featured on pages 62–5 dates back to the early part of the Industrial Revolution, while the invention that concerns us here dates from the latter half. The Second Industrial Revolution, as the period is also known, witnessed the development of many of the innovations that shaped our daily lives in the twentieth century: electric lighting, radio, the internal combustion engine, and, of course, the telephone. Like other inventions of the day, the telephone is usually credited to one inventor—in this case, the scientist, engineer, and inventor Alexander Graham Bell (1847–1922). Bell, however, was only one link in a long chain that brought telephony to the world. In the early years of the telephone, he had to fight several legal actions to defend his patent, and there are dark stories that he stole an important component from a competitor, Elisha Gray (1835–1901), and that the officer at the patent office was either bribed or coerced to grant Bell the patent over Gray.

What is beyond dispute is that Bell was the first to patent a commercially practical telephone in the U.S. in 1876, establishing the preeminence in the field that is still evidenced today by the telephone franchises and companies that still bear the Bell name and logo. The reader would not recognize the instrument that Bell first experimented with as a telephone. It looks more like an old-style hairdryer, with its single opening through which the user had to speak and listen, moving the device between ear and mouth. Worse still, because of the poor sound transmission of the instrument, people had to shout to be heard (no change there then from the users of today's cell phones).

The first recorded telephone communication, which took place on March 10, 1876, between Bell and a colleague, consisted of: "Mr. Watson, come here! I want to see you!" The fact that Bell's interlocutor was in the next room and could probably hear him without the phone is beside the point. In August, Bell made a call from his home to a telegraph office 5 miles (8 km) away along a makeshift telephone wire strung on telegraph poles, trees, and fences. Further successful public demonstrations followed, assuring the future of the invention.

Bell's demonstration of the telephone at the Philadelphia Centennial Exposition launched the invention onto the world stage. Many in the U.S. and overseas were enthusiastic, including Britain's Queen Victoria

(1819–1901), who considered it an extraordinary invention. However, not everyone was convinced. When Bell and his associates offered to sell their patent outright to the Western Union telegraph company for the sum of $100,000, its president refused. An internal Western Union memo dated 1876 stated: "This 'telephone' has too many shortcomings to be seriously considered as a means of communication. The device is inherently of no value to us."

"RUTHERFRAUD" B. HAYES

Another telephone skeptic was President Rutherford B. Hayes (1822–93; U.S. president from 1877 to 1881). Hayes, who served twice as the governor of Ohio, had fought in the Civil War (1861–65), leaving the army with the rank of Major General and a distinguished military record. He stood as the Republican candidate for the presidency in what has been called the most contested election of American history. Although Hayes is thought to have lost the popular vote by 250,000, he won a majority in the college of electors by striking a deal with southern Democrats, promising to withdraw the Union troops still occupying the South after the Civil War. However, the whole election had been so mired in corruption and intimidation that he was sworn in in private in the White House for fear of disturbances from supporters of his Democratic opponent, before his second public swearing in on the portico of the Capitol. Throughout his presidency his opponents referred to him as "Rutherfraud" B. Hayes.

Bell demonstrated the telephone to Hayes in 1876, then still the Republican hopeful. He, at least, recognized that it was a great invention (see quote) but questioned why anyone would want to use it. With 130 years' hindsight, it is easy to laugh at this lack of foresight. However, the telegraph provided a fast, efficient, national, and international communications network and was only itself a few decades old. Granted the telegraph was never going to be in your home, but the hand-delivered telegram was fast enough for the needs of the day. As William Preece (1834–1913), later Engineer-in-Chief of the British General Post Office, commented dismissively: "The Americans have need of the telephone, but we do not. We have plenty of messenger boys."

The pace of life was considerably slower, labor was considerably cheaper, and there was little reason to adopt a new and untested technology, which might only bring marginal improvements over what was already available. Compared to our own phones, early devices had considerable technical limitations. In addition to the single ear-mouthpiece and sound-quality issues described above, the first telephones had no bell or signaling mechanism. A caller had to whistle or make a loud noise to signal a call was taking place. Before the first telephone exchanges and phone networks, each individual telephone needed its own line, so if you required to be connected to more than one place, you needed multiple lines and multiple telephones, and you'd have to pay for the construction of the lines themselves.

The telephone, needless to say, survived and launched a telecommunications revolution in the twentieth century, leading to the development of radio and TV (both featured in this book, see pp. 84–7 and pp. 149–53 respectively) and making the Internet accessible in every home. The fixed telephone is now fast disappearing to be replaced by the ubiquitous cell phone (4.6 billion handsets worldwide and counting), but even in our homes, we now use push-button cordless phones that have nothing in common with their nineteenth-century ancestors.

We'll leave the last word to Alexander Graham Bell, who, it seems, had himself not realized the full potential of the telephone when he patented it. Announcing the invention to an expectant world, he confidently predicted: "The telephone is such an important invention that one day every town will have one."

SKEPTIC
U.S. President Rutherford B. Hayes was among the many telephone skeptics who saw neither need nor usefulness in the new invention.

WHISTLING IN THE DARK: HENRY MORTON

Main culprit: Henry Morton

What was predicted: That Edison's lightbulb would be a flop

What actually happened: The incandescent lightbulb was probably one of the most ubiquitous objects of the twentieth century

When I examine the conclusion [on experiments with the electric lightbulb] which everyone acquainted with the subject will recognize as a conspicuous failure, trumpeted as a wonderful success, I [conclude ...] that the writer [...] must either be very ignorant, and the victim of deceit, or a conscious accomplice in what is nothing less than a fraud upon the public.

Henry Morton (1836–1902), first president of the Stevens Institute of Technology, in 1880

With the first commercially viable telephone (see previous entry), we've entered into the heyday of the Second Industrial Revolution (1820–1914), and the next several entries will concern themselves with predictions about the major technological innovations of the period. The skepticism that greeted the telephone is understandable if one remembers that it was an entirely new means of communication, during a period when letter writing and telegrams were perfectly sufficient to the needs of the population. In other words, its inventors had to persuade the public that they needed the telephone.

This was not the case for the subject of this entry, however. Compared to us, after sunset, nineteenth-century folk lived in a permanently twilit world. Gas lamps lit Victorian city streets, and many poorer domestic users depended on candles and oil lamps for lighting. Quite apart from the ever-present danger of fires and explosions because of naked flames and the types of gases in use, the quality of the lighting produced was poor. But despite the need for a safe, more effective replacement, the skepticism and derisive comments that greeted the first demonstrations of the lightbulb were just as forthright as those elicited by the telephone.

When the skeptic is a politician, such as U.S. President Rutherford B. Hayes, he or she may be forgiven, as politicians are not well known for their foresight in technical and scientific matters. The Emperor Napoleon I (1769–1821) when told about steamships exclaimed: "What, sir, would you make a ship sail against the wind and currents by lighting a bonfire under her deck? I pray you, excuse me, I have not the time to listen to such nonsense." It is much more distressing when the person making the prediction is himself a respected scientist, and in Henry Morton's (1836–1902) case, the head of an educational establishment dedicated to the advancement of science.

A BRIGHT IDEA

The incandescent electric lightbulb, unlike some inventions of the period, did not come, if you excuse the pun, like a bolt out of the blue. The first person to demonstrate it was the British chemist and inventor Humphrey Davey (1778–1829), who, in 1802, passed an electrical current through a platinum wire. The light he produced was not very bright and did not last long, but Davey had demonstrated the principle. It took another 75 years, and many attempts on the way, before Davey's interesting scientific curiosity was turned into the first fully functional lightbulb. It had taken that long because the technologies and materials needed to make it a commercial reality were only ready by the 1870s. By then several inventors and their financial backers were competing to be the first on the market with their version of the new product.

As with the telephone, although the invention of the lightbulb is credited to one man, Thomas Alva Edison (1847–1931), he was actually the first to patent his version in the U.S. in 1878 and 1879. But like Alexander Graham Bell, he was involved in protracted litigation with rivals, who claimed they had got there first or that he had infringed their patents. Edison won out and got the glory for inventing the lightbulb, for four reasons: First, he had a very good, saleable product—his carbonized bamboo filament could burn for 1,200 hours; second, he had the financial backing for his Edison Electric Light Company of financiers of the caliber and wealth of J. P. Morgan (1837–1913; he of the bank); third, he was developing the power infrastructure that could deliver electricity to domestic and business users; and fourth, he had a vision—in 1879, he said: "We will make electricity so cheap that only the rich will burn candles."

BRIGHT IDEA
Although Edison did not invent the light bulb, he won the race to patent it and to commercialize it throughout the world.

The British seemed particularly unimpressed by the news that an electric lightbulb had been perfected. In 1878, a committee of the British Parliament reported that it was "good enough for our transatlantic friends [...] but unworthy of the attention of practical or scientific men." Meanwhile the Anglo-German scientist, William Siemens (1823–83), who was no less a figure than the first President of the Society of Telegraph Engineers (which later became Britain's Institution of Electrical Engineers), declared in 1880: "Such startling announcements as these should be deprecated as being unworthy of science and mischievous to its true progress."

The British were not alone, and there was plenty of homegrown skepticism, notably from Henry Morton (1836–1902), whose impressive résumé included the posts of secretary of the Franklin Institute (1864–70), professor of chemistry at the University of Pennsylvania (1868–70), and first president of the Stevens Institute of Technology (1870–1902). For all his academic distinctions and impressive titles,

Morton was actually not a scientist. While at the University of Pennsylvania he studied law and interested himself in Egyptian archeology and book illumination rather than in the scientific advances of the day. He became a scientist by accident and prospered because he had a particular talent for showmanship.

Morton senior was an Episcopal minister who ran a school that, like many others at the time, had no formal scientific teaching provision. He asked his son to give a series of lectures on various scientific topics with experimental demonstrations for the edification of pupils, faculty, and parents. These were such a success that the aimless Morton junior found his vocation. He joined the Franklin Institute in Philadelphia (named for scientist and statesman Ben Franklin (1706–90) and whose aim was the advancement of science), later becoming the editor of its magazine. He continued to give his scientific lectures to such acclaim that he had to hire theaters and concert halls to accommodate his growing audiences. His success as a lecturer and popularizer of science earned him a professorship at the University of Pennsylvania and then the presidency of the newly founded Stevens Institute.

Unfortunately, Morton, although a relatively young man of 42 when he made his pronouncement about lightbulbs (see quote), failed to grasp either the science or the tremendous commercial possibilities of electric lighting. Perhaps it was ignorance, but this might also have been mixed with envy of Edison, who was one of the most prolific, successful, and wealthy inventors of the late nineteenth century.

TUNING OUT: LORD KELVIN

Main culprit: Lord Kelvin

What was predicted: That radio would have no practical use

What actually happened: Shock jocks…

Radio has no future.

William Thomson, 1st Baron Kelvin, c. 1897

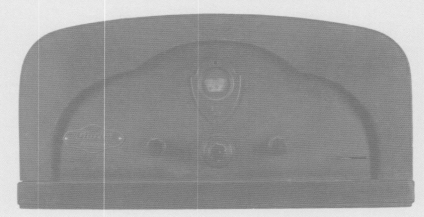

Apologies to the techonophobes among my readers, because this and the following quartet of entries deal with further notable inventions of the Second Industrial Revolution (1820–1914), which transformed human life to such an extent in the twentieth century that it is difficult for us to conceive today how or why anyone could have failed to grasp their future value and impact. But have a care, for how many of us have thought or said about some billion-dollar piece of pure research: "The Large Hadron Collider (LHC), what is it good for?" while in a decade or two we might be reading in Wikipedia that fusion, teleportation, or warp travel was developed thanks to experiments carried out at the LHC back in 2010.

Matters are significantly different, however, when the person making the prediction is him- or herself a scientist, and could be expected to act as an interpreter of scientific knowledge for the lay masses. Such is the case of the eminent Scottish mathematician, physicist, and engineer, William Thomson, 1st Baron Kelvin (or Lord Kelvin; 1824–1907), who has a particularly poor predictive record where technology is concerned, having declared that radio had no future, that X-rays were a hoax, and that heavier-than-air aircraft would never get off the ground. In all three pronouncements, he was to be proved spectacularly wrong within a decade.

Radio is another of those inventions that, like the telephone and the lightbulb, has a long and complex history and no shortage of people claiming to be its "father" (by the way, why is it always the father and not mother? Ladies, get busy!). The voice and music broadcasts that we associate with radio today come relatively late in its history—dating back to the 1920s. In the late nineteenth century, the radio was known as the "wireless telegraph." Until the invention of the telephone, the wire telegraph was the only means of long-distance communication. Messages were converted and transmitted in Morse code at one end, sent along a wired connection, decoded and typed as a telegram at the other, and delivered by hand to the recipient by a messenger boy.

By the 1860s, there were trans-oceanic cables linking the U.S. to Europe and Asia, but the system had one obvious drawback: If you were on a ship—the only means of intercontinental travel at the time—you were effectively cut off from the outside world. For a short crossing, such as the Atlantic, this might be a small matter, you might think, unless your ship was sinking and there was no way of sending out a distress call. Wireless telegraphy was the hot invention of the 1890s and engineers and scientists worldwide were involved in a race to be the first to patent a working system.

The leaders in the field, who succeeded in demonstrating experimental wireless transmissions, were the Indian Jagadish Chandra Bose (1858–1937), the Russian Alexander Popov (1859–1906), and the two inventors most commonly associated with radio in the U.S., Italian Guglielmo Marconi (1874–1937) and Serb Nikola Tesla (1856–1943). Once the principle had been demonstrated, wireless telegraphy was commercialized within a few years, with Marconi dominating the British and American markets, and the German company Telefunken taking the lead in Europe. The first application was ship-to-shore communications, and after the 1912 RMS *Titanic* disaster most large ships were equipped with wireless radio equipment.

ABSOLUTE ZERO

William Thomson is recognized as one of the scientific titans of the mid-nineteenth century. He made huge contributions to the field of physics and later won fame and fortune as an engineer. The son of a mathematics professor, Thomson studied the subject first in Belfast and Glasgow, and then went to Peterhouse, Cambridge, where he excelled in both academic subjects and sports. When he took his final exams, one of his examiners turned to his colleague and said, "You and I are just about fit to mend his pen." At the age of 22, he was appointed chair of natural philosophy (the old name for the sciences) at the University of Glasgow, where he lectured undergraduates only a few years younger than himself. Thomson soon distinguished himself in the field of physics, with discoveries in thermodynamics and electrodynamics. He helped formulate the Second Law of Thermodynamics and set the baseline temperature of absolute zero (−273° C) in 1848. The Kelvin temperature scale and its unit of measurement are named in his honor.

In his youth, Thomson was a maverick who was not afraid to upset the scientific apple cart. But that was only the beginning of his talents. In the 1850s he became interested in the proposed transatlantic telegraph cable that would link the Old and New worlds. He solved several of the practical problems connected to data-transmission rates, and then took part in the expeditions to lay the first cables across the Atlantic, which, largely thanks to his efforts, culminated in success in 1858. After science, the sea was his second love, and he continued to work on underwater telegraphy, taking part in expeditions to lay cables between France and the Americas, and along the coast of Brazil. During his career, Thomson published 600 scientific papers and filed 70 patents.

With this impressive résumé as a theoretical and practical innovator, you might expect that Thomson would be the first to embrace new ideas and discoveries, especially in the fields of physics and communications in which he himself had led the way in his youth. However, as he grew older, he became incapable of accepting new ideas. He had spent his life working within the confines of classical Newtonian physics, and assured a lecture audience in 1900 that "There is nothing new to be discovered in physics now. All that remains is more and more precise measurement." Five years later a young man by the name of Albert Einstein (1879–1955) rewrote the physics textbooks when he published the papers that included the special theory of relativity and the equation $E=mc2$. Thomson died in 1907, four years after the Wright brothers had proved beyond doubt that heavier-than-air aircraft could fly, and seven years after Marconi had opened his first radio factory.

GIANT
Lord Kelvin was a scientific and engineering titan in the field of wired telegraphy, publishing 600 papers and filing 70 patents.

PREDICTION

Millenarian

Technology

Prophecy

Politics

Military

Natural Disaster

Culture

Economics

Doomsday

NEIGH, NEIGH: THE PRESIDENT OF MICHIGAN SAVINGS BANK

Main culprit: President of Michigan Savings Bank

What was predicted: That the automobile would never replace the horse, and that an investment in Henry Ford's (1863–1947) new company would be a waste of money

What actually happened: The automobile replaced the horse within a couple of decades, and the Ford Motor Company went on to become one of the world's most successful auto makers

The horse is here to stay, but the automobile is only a novelty—a fad.

Advice given to Henry Ford's lawyer, Horace Rackam, by an unnamed president of Michigan Savings Bank, in 1903.

The automobile powered by a gasoline internal combustion engine (ICE) is yet another of those inventions that is so ubiquitous in the modern world that we find it difficult to conceive of life without it. It has become so popular that we have now entered the era of "gridlock"— huge traffic jams that periodically paralyze our great metropolitan areas. We have tried to build our way out of it, with numerous, ever wider freeways, or, as in Britain, to tax our way out of it, with London's daily £10 ($15) congestion charge. Neither strategy has so far managed to resolve matters, with dire predictions of total paralysis within decades if something is not done. We've been here before, however, in the late nineteenth century, though not with the automobile, but with another means of transport: the horse.

In the latter part of the nineteenth century, public and private transport was assured by horse-drawn vehicles—hansom cabs, horse omnibuses, carts, carriages, buggies, to name a few. By 1880, it is estimated (conservatively) that there were 150,000 horses stabled in New York City alone. Anyone who has followed a horse for any length of time will know that its "exhaust" comes out in large, brown, fragrant lumps at regular intervals. A horse produces an average of 22 pounds of manure per day. A quick calculation gives you the figure of 540,000 tons of fresh, steaming waste landing on the streets of the New York boroughs every year.

FORDISM
Henry Ford was the pioneer of assembly line mass production.

The horse-manure problem was the urban environmental crisis of its day. The streets were covered in stinking, decomposing organic waste — imagine the stench during the New York summer! The horse manure was not only unsightly and smelly but also a medium for the breeding of insects and epidemic diseases. In the early nineteenth century, farmers had been happy to use the waste as fertilizer, but by the end of the century, there was such a glut that the city and stable owners had to pay for it to be removed. And where do you put 540,000 tons of horse manure? An article in London's *The Times* in 1894 predicted that by 1930, the city would be buried under a layer of horse dung 9 feet (3 m) deep. A conference convened in New York in 1898 to deal with the manure crisis broke up a week early because the delegates failed to come up with solutions that reduced the city's reliance on the horse.

In view of our own concerns about impending social and economic disaster because of peak oil, auto gridlock, and overpopulation, we would do well to look at earlier prophets of doom and learn from their mistakes. The urban planners, city fathers, and environmentalists of the late nineteenth century made one simple error, which was to extrapolate the future from the present. If New York continued to grow at the same rate, and the equine population continued to increase to keep up with demand, they reasoned, by the early decades of the twentieth century, the streets would be three-story deep in horse manure. The reason it was not is the subject of this article: the automobile. Specifically, those made by a man whose name will forever be associated with the automobile industry: Henry Ford (1863–1947).

TO HELL ON A HANDCART

The history of the automobile begins in the late eighteenth century, with attempts to build steam-powered road vehicles. The limitations of the technology and materials meant that these attempts remained interesting but impractical curiosities. The future of the steam engine was on rail and not on road. The world had to wait until 1870 for the German-Austrian inventor Siegfried Marcus (1831–98) to create the first vehicle propelled by an internal combustion engine powered by gasoline. Marcus' "automobile" left a lot to be desired: The chassis was a handcart onto which had been bolted the gas tank and cumbersome vertical IC engine; there were no seats, dashboard, or steering mechanism. However, it was good enough to demonstrate the principle. By 1888, Karl Benz (of the Mercedes-Benz automobile company; 1844–1929) had founded the world's first auto manufacturer. We were still a long way from mass-production, and in the early years, auto production could be counted in the hundreds and not thousands.

The horse manure crisis notwithstanding, the prospect of gasoline-driven horseless carriages on America's roads caused the same kind of alarm as had greeted the arrival of the railroads 40 years earlier. A congressional committee reported on the new ICE technology:

> Instead of burning the fuel under a boiler, [gasoline] is exploded inside the cylinder of an engine. The dangers are obvious. Stores of gasoline in the hands of people interested primarily in profit would constitute a fire and explosive hazard of the first rank. Horseless carriages propelled by gasoline might attain speeds

of 14 or even 20 miles per hour. The menace to our people of vehicles of this type hurtling through our streets and along our roads and poisoning the atmosphere would call for prompt legislative action even if the military and economic implications were not so overwhelming [...] In addition, the development of this new power may displace the use of horses, which would wreck our agriculture.

Henry Ford was born to a first-generation Irish immigrant father, and a second-generation immigrant Belgian mother. His parents farmed land in Greenfield, near Detroit, Michigan. Although Henry's father wanted him to take over the family farm, the boy's true interests were in all things mechanical. At the age of 16, he left home to work as an apprentice machinist in Detroit. He came back to the family farm three years later, but left again to take up the post of engineer with Edison's Illuminating Company in 1891 (see pp. 80–3). He was promoted to Chief Engineer in 1893, and in his spare time experimented with gasoline engines. He built his first ICE vehicle, the Ford Quadricycle, in 1896.

"A CAR FOR THE GREAT MULTITUDE"

That same year, Ford met his boss, Thomas Alva Edison (1847–1931), who encouraged him to continue with his automotive experiments. Ford built an improved vehicle in 1898, which he took into production in 1899 with the Detroit Automobile Company. This proved to be a false start for Ford, but he persevered and incorporated

© Wolfgang Sauber | Creative Commons

the Ford Motor Company on June 16, 1903. The company was floated with $28,000 of capital raised from 12 investors, including a large sum from the Dodge brothers (founders of Dodge Motors), and $5,000 from his lawyer Horace Rackam (1858–1933).

MASS MARKET
The first mass-produced car, the Ford Model T, established Ford Motor Company as the world's leading automaker.

Five thousand dollars was not an inconsiderable sum in 1903, and Rackam had to borrow the money and sell off real estate holdings to raise it. In view of Ford's rocky business career so far and despite the advice of skeptics, including the president of the Michigan Savings Bank (see quote), Rackam decided to take the risk and bought 50 of the total 890 shares of Ford Motor Company stock. At the inaugural stockholders' meeting, Rackam was elected chairman. It was a decision that the otherwise fiscally cautious Rackam must have thanked God for in his prayers for the rest of his days.

Ford began by manufacturing high-end roadsters, but changed direction when he decided to make the Model T. He wrote in his memoirs of his vision for the new car:

> I will build a car for the great multitude. It will be large enough for the family, but small enough for the individual to run and care for. It will be constructed of the best materials, by the best men to be hired, after the simplest designs that modern engineering can devise. But it will be so low in price that no man making a good salary will be unable to own one—and enjoy with his family the blessing of hours of pleasure in God's great open spaces.

The Model T, with its innovative design, competitive price, and high-volume production, ensured the future of Ford Motor Company (and of Rackam's investment) and transformed the automobile from a plaything of the rich to an affordable convenience for the working man.

After Ford's introduction of assembly-line production methods in 1914, the company's sales and profits went stratospheric. Rackam was able to retire from his legal practice, and in 1919, at the behest of Henry Ford, he sold his stock back to the Ford family for the sum of $12.5 million. As for the horse manure crisis of 1898, it was forgotten almost overnight. The development of electric trams, motorized buses, and automobiles provided new means of transport for New Yorkers and Londoners. By 1912, there were more automobiles than horses in New York City, and the last horse-drawn streetcar in New York was withdrawn from service in 1917.

FEAR OF FLYING: MARSHALL FERDINAND FOCH

Main culprit: Ferdinand Foch

What was predicted: That aircraft would have no military use

What actually happened: The belligerent nations in World War One all had air forces and had developed fighter and bomber aircraft

Airplanes are interesting toys but of no military value.

Marshall Ferdinand Foch, Commandant, École Supérieure de Guerre, c. 1910

The long and checkered history of heavier-than-air flight begins, if you believe the Greek myth, with Icarus in ancient Crete. It takes in medieval disasters with gliders and Leonardo da Vinci's (1452–1519) ingenious but impractical "ornithopter" and "helicopter," and, in the late nineteenth century, the development of a compact, powerful, and, above all, relatively light internal combustion engine, which made flight a practical possibility. Not everyone was entirely convinced, however: The British physicist and engineer William Thomson, Lord Kelvin (1824–1907), who we have seen earlier dismissing radio, confidently asserted around the same time that, "Heavier-than-air flying machines are impossible."

In the U.S., the head of the Naval Observatory, Simon Newcomb (1835–1909) was also adamant that, "No possible combination of known substances, known forms of machinery, and known forms of force, can be united in a practical machine by which man shall fly long distances through the air." And readers might be surprised that one of the first two men to achieve the first powered flight in a heavier-than-air aircraft, Wilbur Wright (1867–1912), confessed in a speech he made in 1908 that, "In 1901 I said to my brother Orville that man would not fly for 50 years. Two years later we ourselves made flights."

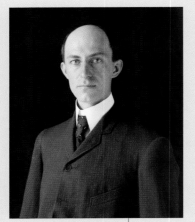

GROUNDED
Wilbur Wright himself believed that powered flight would take 50 years to achieve. Two years later he and his younger brother Orville were airborne.

Perhaps one of the oddest predictions about the future social effects of flying was penned by the English essayist and playwright Joseph Addison (1672–1719) two centuries before the Wright brothers' inaugural flight, and 70 years before two French balloonists had executed the first untethered manned flight in 1782:

> It would fill the world with innumerable immoralities and give such occasion for intrigues as people cannot meet with. You would have a couple of lovers make a midnight assignation upon the top of the monument and see the cupola of St. Paul's covered with both sexes like the outside of a pigeon house. Nothing would be more frequent than to see a beau flying in at a garret window or a gallant giving chase to his mistress like a hawk after a lark.

While the image of amorous aviators covering the dome of St Paul's Cathedral is an arresting one, the subject of this entry is not the viability of flight itself or its social consequences, but its usefulness or otherwise in war.

The idea of aerial warfare was already well established by the late nineteenth century. The ancient Chinese are thought to have used giant manned kites and hot-air balloons for communications and reconnaissance. The first recorded military use of a balloon in Europe dates to the French revolutionary wars in 1794, and in the American Civil War (1861–65) both sides used balloons for reconnaissance. But balloons and dirigibles were slow, lacked maneuverability, and were too easy to shoot down to make them effective airborne fighting machines. A truly functional military aircraft would have to wait for the development of a fixed-wing, motorized aircraft at the beginning of the twentieth century.

The Wright brothers, Orville (1871–1948) and Wilbur, are credited with the invention of the first practical heavier-than-air, fixed-wing aircraft, their first flight taking place on December 17, 1903. Their aircraft, the Wright Flier I and its successors, were made of wood, canvas, and wire, and look impossibly frail. They could just about carry the weight of their pilot, were slow, had a short range, and were difficult to maneuver. However, after many centuries of frustration and failed attempts, as soon as powered, heavier-than-air flight had been demonstrated, everyone and their grandma were taking to the skies.

THE WRIGHT STUFF

The conversion of the Wrights' prototype into a functional military aircraft was achieved in less than a decade, and its first application in wartime took place in a conflict that pitted the Kingdom of Italy and the Ottoman Empire over the control of Libya in 1911–12, when Italian planes and dirigibles bombed a Turkish military camp. In the First Balkan War (1912–13), the air forces of the Balkan League bombed Ottoman naval forces and carried out the first nighttime bombing raid. The bombs were small and probably did much more psychological than physical damage. But the action had writ the future in large letters: The next war would be fought in the skies. And in Europe, that war was just around the corner: World War One broke out in the summer of 1914, with Germany, Austria-Hungary, and the Ottoman Empire ranged against Great Britain, Russia, and France, with the U.S. entering on the Allied side in 1917.

For the French and Germans, World War One was a re-run of the Franco-Prussian War (1870–71), which had seen the humiliating defeat of France at the hands of the Kingdom of Prussia. The outcomes of the war were the fall of the Second French Empire, the creation of the German Empire, and the birth of a bitter rivalry between these European neighbors that was not to be resolved until the end of World War Two (1939–45). It is a cliché of military history that generals are always fighting the previous war. And this was something that the protagonist of this entry, the French strategist Ferdinand Foch (1851–1929), was determined to avoid.

Foch was born in Tarbes, a small town in southwestern France, near the border with Spain. In 1870, aged 19, he enlisted in the French army to fight the Prussian invasion of France. After the end of the war, he decided to remain in the army, and attended the officer-training course at the École Polytechnique, specializing in gunnery. Upon graduating, he took up his commission as a lieutenant in the 24th Artillery Regiment. His future, however, did not lie as an ordinary army officer. In 1885, he entered the elite École Supérieure de Guerre, which trained the staff officers destined to serve in the French high command. In 1895, he returned to the École as an instructor, where he taught for six years. Alternating between academic and regimental postings, he served as commandant of the École between 1907 and 1911, attaining the rank of major general. In 1913, on the eve of the Great War, he was promoted to the command of the 20th army corps of the Second Army based on the all-important eastern border between France and Germany.

AIRBORNE
A British RAF biplane in the air over France in 1918.

Foch was determined that the French army should learn the lessons of its defeat by Prussia in 1871. He studied the great military leaders of the past, including the Emperor Napoleon I (1769–1821), and published two influential books on strategy: *Des Principes de la Guerre* (*On the Principles of War*) in 1903, and *De la Conduite de la Guerre* (*On the Conduct of War*) the following year. Unfortunately for Foch and France, his theories of *l'offensive à outrance* ("extreme offensive warfare at all cost") caused the French army to lose 400,000 men, or about a third of its total of its total forces in the field, in the first year of the war, and would have lost the war had it not been for France's ally, Britain. As is well known, after initial German advances into Belgium and Northern France, the armies of both sides dug in for four years of trench warfare, during which huge offensives and counter-offensives cost millions of lives for almost no territorial gains. Foch, despite the failure of his offensive strategy, continued his rise through the ranks, finishing the war as the Supreme Commander of the Allied Armies who signed the armistice with the Germans on November 11, 1918.

World War One is known as the first modern war, in which nineteenth-century infantry and cavalry tactics made way for mechanized warfare, with an increasingly important role for aircraft and a new invention, the tank (pp. 107–10). In the area of new technology, Foch, who is generally recognized as an innovative military thinker, had a surprising blind spot. Around 1910, when he was commandant of the École Supérieure Militaire, he completely failed to grasp the military value of aircraft (see quote), dismissing them as mere toys. By the end of the war, however, the combatants on both sides had created air forces, with purpose-built fighter planes equipped with machine guns, and bombers carrying payloads of high-explosive bombs.

ON THE ROCKS:
CAPTAIN EDWARD SMITH

Main culprit: Captain Edward Smith

What was predicted: That the RMS *Titanic* could not possibly sink

What actually happened: Over 1,500 deaths and *Titanic*, the movie

I cannot imagine any condition which would cause a ship to founder. I cannot conceive of any vital disaster happening to this vessel. Modern shipbuilding has gone beyond that.

Captain Edward Smith before the maiden voyage of the RMS *Titanic* in 1912

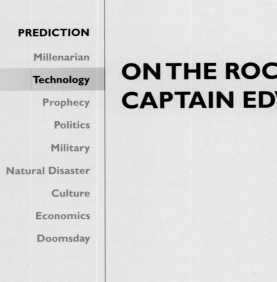

In the 1997 film *Titanic*, Cal Hockley (Billy Zane) turns to his fiancée Rose DeWitt Bukater (Kate Winslet) and, on first seeing the ocean liner that is to take them to New York, says, "It is unsinkable. God himself could not sink this ship." As neither character is based on a real-life passenger on board the RMS *Titanic*, it is unlikely that these fate-tempting words were ever uttered. However, that was probably the word on the street, or rather, on the dock when *Titanic* set sail from Southampton, England, on her maiden voyage to New York on April 10, 1912. As the largest and most technologically advanced ocean liner of its day, *Titanic* was probably considered by many—mariners, shipbuilders, and passengers alike—to be unsinkable. Those were very much the thoughts of her captain, Edward Smith (1850–1912).

The Olympic-class liner certainly lived up to her name: *Titanic* was a seagoing behemoth 882 feet 9 inches (269.1 m) long, 92 feet (28 m) wide, and 175 feet (53.3 m) high from keel to funnel top. When she set sail across the Atlantic from her last port of call in Ireland, she was carrying 2,240 passengers and crew—thankfully, as it turned out, 1,300 short of her full capacity, otherwise the loss of life would have been even greater. Much was made in the movie of the overconfidence of the designers, and such failings as insufficient lifeboat capacity, and the poor design of the hull's watertight compartments. But how much of this is Hollywood hyperbole? And to what extent was Captain Smith's confidence in his ship and in his own abilities as a mariner misplaced?

First let us deal with the issue of lifeboat capacity. According to the British government regulations of the time, ships over 10,000 tons had to carry 16 lifeboats, plus extra rafts. *Titanic* was 46,328 tons, hence 4.5 times the tonnage the lifeboat rules had been created for. The owners of the liner, the White Star Line, actually exceeded this requirement by equipping the ship with 20 lifeboats. Although lifeboat capacity was still woefully inadequate at 1,178 people, there were four more lifeboats than the law required. The company also had 16 large davits (the crane-like device that would lower lifeboats over the side) fitted on the ship, each with a capacity to handle four lifeboats; hence, on future crossings *Titanic* could have carried a total of 64 lifeboats, enough for 4,000 passengers and crew. In this, they were anticipating a change in safety regulations as passenger liners got larger and larger.

When *Titanic* set sail, Captain Smith knew that if she sank, she would not be able to save half of her passengers and crew. But he must have bet that the design, safety features, and other onboard equipment made this an extremely remote possibility. First there was the design of the ship: The hull was divided into 16 watertight compartments that could be sealed from the bridge at the first evidence of flooding. She had been designed to withstand the breeching of four compartments, and she was also fitted with the latest in pumping technology. In theory, as long as the furnaces powering the steam pumps were operational, they could have coped with a four-compartment breech. Last, but not least, the ship carried a Marconi wireless telegraph system, with two operators working in shifts around the clock.

THE MILLIONAIRE'S CAPTAIN

In *Titanic*, the movie, much is made of Captain Smith ignoring iceberg warnings, and, encouraged by his employer, the White Star Line, deciding to continue full steam ahead to New York to establish a record time for the crossing. The sinking, the film implied, was a combination of recklessness and hubris on the part of the captain and the line. If we examine Smith's career, however, and his own pronouncements before the sailing, it seems there is more to the story than this interpretation of events gives credit to.

Smith was not from a nautical family but went to sea immediately after leaving school at the age of 13. He joined the White Star Line in 1880, earning his promotion to captain seven years later. He had a distinguished career as an officer of the line, and as a commander of the Royal Naval Reserve, earning a medal when his ship the *Majestic* was requisitioned to transport troops from England to South Africa after the outbreak of the Boer War in 1899.

Smith became commodore of the White Star Line—the commercial equivalent of fleet admiral—to whom all other captains reported, and it was he who normally commanded new ships on their maiden voyages. He became known as the "millionaire's captain" because many in the English upper classes would only sail the Atlantic in a ship he commanded. In June 1911 he had concluded the maiden journey of *Titanic*'s predecessor, RMS *Olympic*, from Southampton to New York, and although the *Olympic* was involved in a collision with a British warship, which was blamed on the liner, Smith's reputation was such that he was also chosen to oversee the maiden voyage of *Titanic*. The captain had had a charmed career at sea. He confided to an interviewer:

> When anyone asks how I can best describe my experience in nearly 40 years at sea, I merely say, uneventful. Of course there have been winter gales, and storms and fog and the like, but in all my experience, I have never been in any accident of any sort worth speaking about. [...] I never saw a wreck and never have been wrecked, nor was I ever in any predicament that threatened to end in disaster of any sort. You see, I am not very good material for a story.

However, as an experienced mariner, he was also aware of the dangers from icebergs in the icy waters of the North Atlantic:

> We do not care anything for the heaviest storms in these big ships. It is fog that we fear. The big icebergs that drift into warmer water melt much more rapidly under water than on the surface, and sometimes a sharp, low reef extending two or three hundred feet beneath the sea is formed. If a vessel should run on one of these reefs half her bottom might be torn away.

Titanic with Smith at the helm sailed out of Southampton bound for New York on April 10. The ship made a brief stop at Cherbourg, France, to pick up passengers, and anchored off the port of Cobh (formerly Queenstown) in Ireland for its final stop on the European side of the Atlantic. The passenger list included British aristocrats and American socialites and financiers. Anyone who has seen the ship's portrayal in the movie will appreciate the scale and luxury of the first class accommodation.

UNSINKABLE
The Olympic-class RMS *Titanic* docked in Southampton before departing on her fateful maiden voyage to New York on April 10, 1912.

Smith received radioed iceberg warnings during the first few days of the crossing and altered his course accordingly, but he failed to get two crucial warnings on Sunday April 14 because the Marconi wireless operators were giving priority to messages from wealthy paying passengers rather than "low-priority," free traffic to the bridge. At 11:40 pm, the lookout sighted an iceberg dead ahead, but the evasive maneuver ordered by the officer of the watch failed to turn the ship in time. The iceberg buckled the side of the hull under the waterline, breaching five compartments—one more than the ship was designed to lose and remain afloat.

Titanic sent out a distress call shortly after midnight, but even then, the White Star Line did not appreciate the full gravity of the situation. Philip Franklin (1871–1939), the line's vice president, and later chairman, assured the press that, "There is no danger that *Titanic* will sink. The boat is unsinkable and nothing but inconvenience will be suffered by the passengers." What happened then is well known. The pumps managed to keep the ship afloat for two hours, but failed when they too were flooded. By then many of the lifeboats had been launched, several not filled to their full capacity. In the freezing waters of the Atlantic in April, life expectancy could be calculated in minutes. Very few who were pulled out of the waters by the two lifeboats that turned back to rescue people in the water survived the ordeal. A total of 1,517 passengers and crew, including Captain Smith, perished in the wreck.

THE ARMAGEDDON HABIT: CHARLES TAZE RUSSELL

PREDICTION

Millenarian

Technology

Prophecy

Politics

Military

Natural Disaster

Culture

Economics

Doomsday

Main culprit: Charles Taze Russell

What was predicted: The end of the world in 1914, 1915, 1918, 1920, 1925, 1941, 1975, and 1994

What actually happened: Now postponed to an unspecified date

They must see the utter wreck of Great Babylon and receive some measure of her plagues. The four years from 1910 to the end of 1914, indicated thus in the Great Pyramid, will doubtless be a time of "fiery trial" upon the Church preceding the anarchy of the world, which cannot last long.

Thy Kingdom Come (1891), Charles Taze Russell

There is something quite disturbing about a certain brand of millenarian prophet who not only predicts the end of the world in a matter of years or decades but also takes particular relish in describing the destruction of Earth and its population. The fact that these individuals necessarily believe that they will be among a select few to be saved and taken to a glorious "heaven on Earth" no doubt helps them come to terms with the impending apocalypse. Yet divine rhetoric can be inflated only so far before even the most credulous of their followers begin to re-examine their loyalties. Like a revolution eternally delayed, there are only so many disappointments a devotee can take before they turn their attentions to living in the present day.

So what will this much promised "heaven on earth" actually be like? Often it is not unlike the best parts of our own world: an unspoilt, unpolluted, and un-crowded wilderness, filled with fruit trees and flowers, docile animals and birds, and minus the "evils" of money, democratic government, and big cities—a world probably not unlike the more pristine regions of the United States during the nineteenth century. Yet, as we have seen above, the rural U.S. in the late nineteenth century was prey to a millenarian religious frenzy centered on predictions of the impending destruction of the world and humankind (see Joseph Smith, pp. 58–61, and William Miller, pp. 66–70). Without wishing to write off the sincere beliefs of many Christians, we should at least question the psychological motivations of many of the nineteenth and twentieth century's prophets of doom. Why were they so dissatisfied with their lot on Earth as to wish so fervently to see its wholesale destruction?

THE RURAL U.S. IN THE LATE NINETEENTH CENTURY WAS PREY TO A MILLENARIAN RELIGIOUS FRENZY CENTERED ON PREDICTIONS OF THE IMPENDING DESTRUCTION OF THE WORLD AND HUMANKIND.

Millenarian prophecy, however, is a powerful aid to conversion. Tell a certain kind of person that they are one of a small band of individuals chosen by God to be his elect, and who will not only survive the impending cataclysm but also run the whole Earthly show for 1,000 years, and you've got them hooked. Of course, when the promised millennium fails to occur as predicted, as happened in "The Great Disappointment" of 1844, there is bound to be a backlash. Many Millerites, for example, abandoned their beliefs altogether, but others couldn't quite kick the Armageddon habit. They contributed to the next wave of Christian millenarianism, the Adventist movement, as well as the movement that is the subject of this entry, the Watchtower Society

(WTS), later known as the Jehovah's Witnesses, who were responsible for at least seven doomsday dates between 1914 and 1975.

Charles Taze Russell (1852–1916), who was one of the founders of the WTS, was born into a family of first-generation Scots-Irish immigrants who settled in Pennsylvania. The young Charles was a precocious child who by the age of 13 was put in charge of several of his father's clothing stores. He was also precociously religious and, maybe as a result, troubled. As a teenager, he changed from the Presbyterian Church to the Congregational Church, and aged 16 had a crisis of faith, for a time rejecting Christianity altogether. He investigated Eastern religions that were becoming known in the U.S. at this time, but could not find one that satisfied him. In 1870, he attended a lecture by an Adventist minister who predicted the Second Coming for 1874.

Russell was not disillusioned when the end of the world did not materialize, and he continued his own intensive study of the Bible with Adventist friends. His co-religionists included Nelson Barbour (1824–1905), the publisher of a magazine entitled *The Herald of the Morning*, who believed that the Second Coming was to take place in 1878. So convinced was Russell by Barbour's date that he sold his clothing businesses in anticipation of the Lord's return. The two men fell out over the failed prediction and doctrinal issues, and Russell started his own magazine in 1879, *Zion's Watch Tower and Herald of Christ's Presence* (now *The Watchtower*, still the main organ of the Jehovah's Witnesses), in which he expressed views that distanced him further from mainstream Protestant Christianity and Adventism, and rejected several of their doctrines. He wrote in the first issue:

> That we are living "in the last days," "the day of the Lord"—"the end" of the Gospel age, and consequently, in the dawn of the "new" age, are facts not only discernible by the close student of the Word, led by the spirit, but the outward signs recognizable by the world bear the same testimony.

Like Miller before him, Russell turned to the Book of Daniel to calculate the date of the end of the world. In his version, however, the starting date for the countdown to Armageddon was 607 BCE. He then

THE BIBLE IN STONE

© Lebrecht Music & Arts | Corbis

PYRAMID
Russell believed that the Great Pyramid of Khufu at Giza was a "Bible in stone" that held prophecies about the fate of humanity.

interpreted Daniel 4:16 ("Let his heart be changed from man's, and let a beast's heart be given unto him; and let seven times pass over him") to mean that seven periods of 360 needed to pass, equaling 2,520 days, which converted in years (days = years principle) and added to 607 BCE gives the date October 1914. Unlike Miller, Russell also used another source for his arcane calculations: the Great Pyramid of Khufu (Cheops) on the Giza plateau just outside Cairo, Egypt. Following the earlier work of the eccentric Scottish astronomer, Charles Piazzi Smyth (1819–1900), Russell believed that the pyramid had been built by the Hebrews under divine guidance to be a "Bible in stone," which could only be understood by future generations (specifically, by Charles Russell himself).

Russell disseminated his views widely in his magazine and other writings, winning many converts in the years before 1914. In 1889, he assured his readers: "We consider it an established truth that the final end of the kingdoms of this world, and the full establishment of the Kingdom of God, will be accomplished by the end of A.D. 1914." And that same year: "In the coming 26 years, all present governments will be overthrown and dissolved." When the end did not come, he recalculated the date for 1915. He died in 1916, avoiding any further embarrassment. His successors, including the founder of the Jehovah's Witnesses, Joseph Franklin Rutherford (1869–1942), continued to produce new dates, including 1918, 1920, 1925, 1941, and 1975. After the failed 1975 prediction, however, the WTS leadership refused to endorse any dates for Armageddon.

IRON HORSES: A BRITISH STAFF OFFICER

PREDICTION

Millenarian

Technology

Prophecy

Politics

Military

Natural Disaster

Culture

Economics

Doomsday

Main culprit: A British staff officer

What was predicted: That the tank would not replace the cavalry in World War One

What actually happened: World War One was the first mechanized war and marked the end of the use of cavalry in warfare in Europe

The idea that cavalry will be replaced by these iron coaches is absurd.
It is little short of treasonous.

Comment by an aide-de-camp of Field Marshal Douglas Haig at a demonstration of the newly developed tank in 1916

The men who commanded the armies on the Western Front during World War One (1914–18) were born in the middle of the nineteenth century, and several, particularly in Britain, would have received their own military training from men who had lived in the age of heroic cavalry charges and infantry in brightly colored uniforms marching in formation onto the battlefield. The last war involving France and Germany in Europe had been the Franco-Prussian war of 1870–1, which was a German victory. The French and Germans, after 40 years of simmering animosity and border disputes, were more than ready for a rematch.

The British, however, had not taken part in a major conflict on European soil since the defeat of Napoleon (1769–1821) at Waterloo in 1815. For the most part, Britain's mid-nineteenth-century military victories were scored against the native populations of Britain's growing empire in Africa, Asia, and Oceania. The British faced peoples whose technology was no match for guns, artillery, and machine guns, but even then they were sometimes defeated, as was the case in the Anglo-Zulu War of 1879 and the Second Afghan War of 1878–80.

© Aloahwild | Creative Commons

SUNK
The new British "landships" were not invulnerable. Here a British tank captured by the Germans has been painted with the iron cross emblem.

Britain's only major war against a European power was the Crimean War (1853–56), when Britain and her ally France had fought the Russian Empire in the southern Russian region of the Crimea. That war ended in a Franco-British defeat and is best remembered for the Charge of the Light Brigade of 1854, an act of heroic but suicidal stupidity when a British cavalry unit charged a highly fortified Russian artillery position. Although over half the Light Brigade was killed, wounded, or captured, the cavalrymen were hailed as heroes embodying all the martial virtues.

While there have been innovative, farsighted military leaders, soldiering is not a profession that by its nature attracts the unconventional and original thinker. What a general wants from his officers and men is not creativity but obedience. Therefore, most senior officers and generals who have spent their whole lives in the armed forces will have a fairly conservative outlook when it comes to strategy, as well as untested military technologies. It comes as little surprise then, when in the first year of the war, a senior officer of the British Admiralty (Department of the Navy) said of a newly developed armored military vehicle: "Caterpillar landships are idiotic and useless. Those officers and men are wasting their time and are not pulling their proper weight in the war."

"Landships," or tanks, as we know them today, were not a new idea. The Renaissance painter and all-round genius Leonardo da Vinci (1452–1519) had doodled a horse-powered armored vehicle in one of his notebooks, but as with early concepts for heavier-than-air flying machines and horseless carriages, although the principle had been established centuries earlier, the world had to wait for technology to catch up before it could become a practical reality. By the early twentieth century, metallurgy was capable of producing alloys strong and light enough for armor and caterpillar tracks; the internal combustion engine provided the propulsion without the need for a furnace, stoker, and store of coal; and smokeless high explosives replaced gunpowder that would have filled the tank with choking fumes each time the gun was fired.

"THE LAND IRONCLADS"

In a short story of 1903, "The Land Ironclads," the British science-fiction writer H. G. Wells (1866–1946) showed unusual prescience in matters scientific and military by describing a future war in which a technologically advanced country defeats their brave but technically backward enemies, who are armed with rifles and riding horses, with giant armored landships. Wells' vehicles were much bigger and moved on "pedrails" (large wheels with feet) and not tracks, but otherwise they accurately anticipated the first tanks that went into service in 1916.

The British armed forces were particularly resistant to the idea of the tank because it did not fit with their conception of war. However, the first years of the conflict soon made it clear that the first side to develop an armored vehicle would gain a huge advantage—just like the antagonists in Wells' story. Much to the distaste of the British high command, technology had moved on since their victory at the Battle of Waterloo, when two armies had slugged it out on a battlefield, with the generals—Napoleon on one side, and Wellington (1769–1852) on the heights—moving their infantry and cavalry units like chess pieces.

In 1914, the Germans had tried to replicate their victory in 1871 by a rapid advance into Belgium, Luxemburg, and northeastern France, attempting to reach the French coast to cut off Paris from British help and outflank the Allied armies. After initial success, the Germans became bogged down as the French and British regrouped and then dug in along a line that became known as the Western Front. Across this imaginary line, fortified with bunkers, trenches, and miles of barbed wire, the combatants attacked each other with barrages of long-range high-explosive shells, strafed each other with machine gunfire, and poisoned each other with mustard gas. The killing fields of World War One—the area between the enemy lines—would go down in history as "No man's land." There would be no glorious charges to rout the enemy. The cavalry that the British had brought with them across the Channel remained useless in the rear, waiting for a breakthrough that would never come. The offensives that did take place were incredibly costly for little or no gain in territory. In the Battle of the Somme (July–November 1916), for example, combined German and Allied losses reached 1.5 million killed in action, a carnage that has not been equaled since in a single offensive.

Despite the misgivings of the British commander-in-chief, Field Marshall Douglas Haig (1861–1928), and his staff (see quote), the British Mark I tank went into service in September 1916 toward the end of the Battle of the Somme. The Mark I looked very different to modern-day tanks, as it had no gun turret but carried side-mounted guns. In 1917, the British Tank Corps scored its first success by breaking through the German lines at Cambrai in northern France, and in the Battle of Amiens in 1918, the first large-scale deployment of tanks overran the German lines and put an end to trench warfare once and for all. The Germans realized too late that the tank had given the Allies a decisive advantage. They produced their own tank but too late and too few in number to prevent their surrender in November 1918. It was not a mistake that Adolf Hitler (1889–1945; see pp. 140–4) would repeat 22 years later.

FAREWELL TO ARMS: PRESIDENT WOODROW WILSON

PREDICTION

Millenarian

Technology

Prophecy

Politics

Military

Natural Disaster

Culture

Economics

Doomsday

Main culprit: President Woodrow Wilson

What was predicted: That World War One would be the "war to end all wars" and would "make the world safe for democracy"

What actually happened: The Nazis and World War Two, and democracy is still being fought for in many parts of the world

What we demand in this war, therefore, is nothing peculiar to ourselves. It is that the world be made fit and safe to live in; and particularly that it be made safe for every peace-loving nation which, like our own, wishes to live its own life, determine its own institutions, be assured of justice and fair dealing by the other peoples of the world, as against force and selfish aggression.

Address to Congress by President Woodrow Wilson, January 8, 1918

It would not be an exaggeration to say that the four bloody years of World War One completely reconfigured the world's social, political, economic, military, and ideological maps. The war had been so costly in lives and money and so traumatizing for a whole generation that many, like U.S. President Woodrow Wilson (1856–1924), hoped that it would be the "war to end all wars" that would make the world "safe for democracy." In 1918, there was a huge popular groundswell against war and militarism, which gave birth to a strong movement for disarmament. Initially, there was much that was positive in the postwar settlement. The autocratic German regime that had started the war had been defeated and democratized. The multinational empires that occupied much of Central and Eastern Europe and the Balkans had been broken up into new national states, and the backward Russian empire had been overthrown by an apparently leftwing revolution.

WILSON OUTLINED THE BLUEPRINT FOR HIS NEW WORLD ORDER IN THE "FOURTEEN POINTS" SPEECH.

Wilson outlined the blueprint for his new world order in the "Fourteen Points" speech, which he delivered to Congress on January 8, 1918, ten months before the end of hostilities in Europe (see quote). His vision was of a renewed postwar world, in which international relationships would be characterized by national self-determination, free trade, democracy, and open agreements and cooperation. One of the first tangible results of the speech was the creation of the League of Nations (1919–46)—the precursor to today's United Nations (UN) and the first intergovernmental organization whose mission was to maintain world peace, resolve international disputes through negotiation, and promote the spread of democracy. The world, it seemed, was set on a new track for decades of peace and prosperity. Unfortunately, the outcome was the exact opposite: The next two decades would witness the Wall Street Crash and the Great Depression (1929–39); the failure of democracy and the rise of ultra-nationalism, militarism, and fascism in Italy, Germany, and Japan; and the failure of the League of Nations. It would culminate in the outbreak of World War Two (1939–45). What happened in those 20 short years to turn hope into despair, disarmament into armed aggression, and freedom into murderous dictatorship?

The failure of the postwar settlement, which morphed into the causes of World War Two, are complex and interweave a multitude of social and political factors. First was the staggering human cost of the war. The total number of killed, maimed, and injured is estimated at 37 million, with ten million military deaths and about seven million civilian deaths during the hostilities themselves. Of the main European combatants, Germany and France lost around four percent of their populations and Russia and Britain lost around two percent each—many of them adult men of working age. But this death toll is dwarfed by the loss of life caused by the Spanish Flu pandemic that ravaged already weakened populations between 1918 and 1920, claiming a further 50 to 100 million victims worldwide.

The economic and social dislocation caused by removing so many people from the labor force should not be underestimated. Although one of the positive effects of the war was the emancipation of women, who got the vote in many countries in the interwar period, the long-term effect was a serious downturn in economic activity. The European powers were seriously indebted to the U.S., and the problem was made much worse for Germany because the Treaty of Versailles (1919) had imposed huge war reparations. The French were particularly intransigent, wanting their revenge for the humiliation of 1871. When the Wall Street Crash of 1929 triggered the Great Depression in the U.S., it hit Germany, whose economy was already struggling, particularly hard. Unemployment rose to 33 percent, and inflation reached astronomic levels. The paper currency that the German Weimar Republic (1919–33) printed to get itself out of trouble became so worthless that it was used as wallpaper.

INTERNATIONALIST
Wilson's hope to create a new world order came to naught in part because of the Great Depression, American isolationism, and the rise of fascism.

The territorial settlement of 1919 also created problems that would only become apparent in the 1930s. At the beginning of the war, there were four empires in Europe: Czarist Russia and the Ottoman Empire to the East, and the Austro-Hungarian and German empires in central Europe. By the end of the war, the Russian Czar had been overthrown by the Bolsheviks; the already tottering Austro-Hungarian and Ottoman empires had both been broken up to be replaced by a multitude of successor states, with new national identities and aspirations; and the German Empire had been replaced by a democratic republic. Germany lost parts of her territory to France, Poland, and the Baltic States, from where German populations were either forcibly ejected or integrated into another country. The treaty also imposed the foreign occupation of the western part of Germany.

Many Germans, who had accepted the armistice of 1918 on the understanding that Germany's territorial integrity would be respected and that the peace treaty would be based on Wilson's Fourteen Points, were bitterly disappointed when the Weimar Republic meekly acquiesced to the dismembering of Germany and the loss of its colonial possessions in Africa and Asia. This was a national humiliation that would rankle for the next 20 years, and that would give the Nazi leader Adolf Hitler (1889–1945) the pretext for his so-called "liberation" of former German territories in the 1930s.

IN LEAGUE WITH THE DEVIL

Economically and politically, the postwar settlement completely failed to live up to the high ideals set out in Wilson's speech. The League of Nations in which he had placed so many hopes came into being, but without the all-important participation of the United States, which had shifted from interventionism in world affairs to isolationism, a position the country maintained to its own and the world's cost until the Japanese attack on Pearl Harbor in 1941.

The League, though it did much valuable work in the 1920s in the promotion of disarmament, was not equipped to deal with countries that were determined to flout its principles. It had no armed forces of its own, and could only call on member states to settle their disputes peacefully through negotiation. Without the economic and military muscle of the U.S. to back up its resolutions, there was little the League could do against aggressors. The first European country to turn to fascism was not Germany but Italy, which elected Benito Mussolini (1883–1945) as prime minister in 1922. Laying down a pattern that Hitler would follow a decade later, he quickly established a one-party fascist police state, giving himself the title of *Il Duce* ("the leader"). Mussolini pursued his territorial ambitions in Libya and Ethiopia with little regard to the pious reprimands of the League. The situation was replicated in East Asia, where Imperial Japan pursued a ruthless policy of military expansionism into northern China, creating its own puppet state of Manchukuo in 1932.

When Adolf Hitler came to power in Germany in 1933, the more farsighted in Europe understood that the game was up. Hitler immediately began to rearm, flouting the conditions imposed on Germany in 1919. By the mid-'30s he was ready to start his European landgrab, forcing the union of Austria and Germany, and annexing the Sudetenland, an ethnic German region of Czechoslovakia. The weak, vacillating leaders of Britain and France, still convinced that they could reach an accommodation with Hitler (see pp. 135–9), did nothing but issue strongly worded communiqués that were not backed up by any real military threat. Hitler ignored them and continued to carry out the plans that he had outlined in *Mein Kampf* (*My Struggle*, 1925–6).

Wilson's idealism was defeated by a swing in the U.S. that turned it from an interventionist into an isolationist power, but also by the realpolitik of the European countries hungry for revenge and territorial gains; by the increasing isolation of the Soviet Union, which succumbed in its turn to the totalitarian rule of Joseph Stalin (1878–1953) in 1927; and by the rise of fascism and militarism in Italy, Germany, and Japan. In 1919 Wilson was struck down by a stroke and took no further part in government for the remainder of his term, which lasted until 1921. He died three years later, spared the worst horrors of the Nazi Holocaust and World War Two.

PREDICTION

Millenarian

Technology

Prophecy

Politics

Military

Natural Disaster

Culture

Economics

Doomsday

SILENCE IS GOLDEN: HARRY M. WARNER

Main culprit: Harry M. Warner

What was predicted: That no one would want to pay to go and hear movie actors talking on film

What actually happened: Maybe he had a point...

Who the hell wants to hear actors talk?
The music—that's the big plus about this.

Harry Warner, cofounder of Warner Bros., when talkies first came out in 1927

After a few false starts, the history of commercial cinema began in Paris, France, in December 1895 with the Lumière brothers' Cinématographe — the first commercial movie projection system shown to a paying audience in a restaurant. The world's first ever picture show consisted of a program of ten shorts, running for less than 50 seconds each, which the brothers showed with a hand-cranked projector. It was a modest beginning but a foretaste of much bigger and better things to come. The Lumière brothers, however, were unconvinced about the new entertainment medium they had launched. They believed that the cinema was "an invention without any future." They soon abandoned the movie business and dedicated the rest of their careers to the development of still color photography.

One wonders how different the future of cinema would have been if its full commercial implications had been realized in France rather than in a small town ten miles east of Los Angeles by the name of Hollywood. Would all smash-hit musical tunes now be in French? And would our action heroes be called Jean-Marie, Michel, and Pierre rather than Tom, Bruce, and Sylvester? By 1915, however, Hollywood had overtaken New York as the U.S. film capital, and was on its way to achieving world domination in the new medium. World War One did the rest, strangling at birth the nascent European film industry. Even then, many wondered whether the film business had any long-term future. No less a figure than Charles "Charlie" Chaplin (1889–1977) warned in 1916: "The cinema is little more than a fad. It's canned drama. What audiences really want to see is flesh and blood on the stage." He went on to have one of the most spectacular careers in early cinema as a performer, producer, and director of silent films.

One of the greatest drawbacks of the movies from their creation until the 1920s was the absence of synchronized sound to accompany the moving pictures. Turn the sound off on your favorite TV show and put on a random CD to act as a backing track, and you can see how frustrating it can be. Although a picture can paint a thousand words, it's not always that good at giving a plot outline or revealing the emotional states and relationships of the characters. Directors tried to work around the problem by making up in body language, dramatic gestures, and facial expressions what they lacked in dialog, but that usually meant that actors weren't just hamming it up on screen, they were going for the full three-course pork dinner with all the trimmings. The alternative was to insert a few frames of commentary or dialog, but this, too, could only convey the barest bones of plot and character.

Playing movies with nothing but the click-clacking of the projector and the noise of the audience as an accompaniment was not conducive to a fun night out, so theaters quickly provided musical accompaniment to performances. In Japan and China, films had a live narrator who performed a dramatized commentary of the action.

"YOU AIN'T HEARD NOTHIN' YET."

In the early 1900s, studios began to experiment with recording the soundtrack onto old-style phonograph records that would be played with the movie. The first full-length motion picture to feature "sound-on-disc" was *The Jazz Singer* of 1927, starring the vaudeville performer Al Jolson (1886–1950). Because the soundtrack was played on a separate on-disc sound system, there were problems of synchronization, and because of the short duration of disc recording of the time, the soundtrack was only partial. The movie included several musical numbers by Jolson and others. Jolson's first synchronized dialog occured over 17 minutes into the feature, when he delivered one of his now immortal vaudeville catchphrases: "Wait a minute, wait a minute, you ain't heard nothin' yet."

The real breakthrough, however, came when the soundtrack was added to the film itself, producing full-length features with continuous synchronized dialog, sound effects, and music. With the international success of *The Jazz Singer*, it was the music that the studios were interested in. Harry M. Warner (1881–1958), the eldest of the Warner brothers, and one of the founders of the studio that bears their name, asked in all seriousness, "Who the hell wants to hear actors talk?" (see quote). He was not alone in decrying the new possibilities that sound was opening up. Chaplin complained in 1929: "Talkies are spoiling the oldest art in the world—the art of pantomime. They are ruining the great beauty of silence. They are defeating the meaning of the screen." Chaplin's reluctance to embrace the new technology is not surprising given that he was one of the performers who had made the silent medium his own.

Ironically, the man who scoffed at the future of sound, Harry M. Warner, was the very same man who put the future of his film studio on the line to finance *The Jazz Singer*. The Warner story is a rags-to-riches epic worthy of one of their Hollywood movies. Harry Warner, born Hirsch Moses Wonsal in rural Poland, came to the U.S. at the age of eight. His father had emigrated a few years before, and settled in Baltimore where he worked as a shoe repairer. After he had established his family in their new home, Wonsal senior anglicized the family name to Warner. The family moved to Youngstown, Ohio, in 1896, where the young Harry followed his father into the shoe-repair business and later opened a bicycle shop with one of his younger brothers.

For the next ten years, the Warner brothers had checkered business careers, with several failures along the way. In 1905, they went into the movie theater business, purchasing their first auditorium with the proceeds from the sale of Harry's bicycle shop. By 1912, they had gone into film production themselves, starting a new company called Warner Features. After a rocky start, they moved to Hollywood, and in 1923, established Warner Brothers Pictures Inc., to make silent movies. Their first "star" was not a sex goddess or action hero, but the Lassie of the silent era, the German shepherd Rin Tin Tin. The new studio faced stiff competition from their more established rivals and was often on the verge of going bust.

© Liang | Creative Commons

Warner Brothers had to survive by innovation. It was the first to experiment with the sound-on-disc Vitaphone system, but adding sound to movies was a costly gamble that almost did not pay off. After the company lost money on the film version of the opera *Don Juan* (1926), which had music and sound effects but no dialog, Harry forbade any more sound experiments with Vitaphone. Luckily his younger brother Sam (1887–1927) managed to persuade him to make a more popular feature with a Vitaphone soundtrack—*The Jazz Singer*. The film cost the studio almost twice its usual $250,000 budget, and Harry had to pawn his wife's jewelry and move out of his apartment to finance the project. The gamble paid off handsomely, establishing Warner Brothers as one of Hollywood's leading studios and launching

JAZZ SINGER
Despite misgivings and financial difficulties, Warner Bros made the first-ever "talkie," *The Jazz Singer*, starring Al Jolson.

sound in the movies. By 1929, nearly all films made in Hollywood were talkies, and the "Golden Age of Hollywood" had begun.

In a sense Harry Warner was right when he asked who wanted to hear actors talk. What the audience really wanted to hear was actors sing. The most successful genre of the early age of sound was the musical, starting in 1929 with MGM's *The Broadway Melody*, which itself was a prelude to the huge set-piece musical hits made by Busby Berkeley (1895–1976) during the 1930s. Rather than stifling the development of the cinema, as Chaplin feared, sound finally gave movie entertainment the dimension it had lacked for three decades. It would remain the preeminent visual medium until the invention of the small, black-and-white picture box we all know and that many love to hate: television.

WE'RE IN THE MONEY: IRVING FISHER

Main culprit: Irving Fisher

What was predicted: That the asset bubble of the 1920s would never burst

What actually happened: The worst economic depression in human history

Stock prices have reached what looks like a permanently high plateau. I do not feel there will be soon if ever a 50- or 60-point break from present levels, such as they have predicted. I expect to see the stock market a good deal higher within a few months.

**Economist Irving Fisher on October 17, 1929,
days before stock prices collapsed on the NYSE.**

The radical political economist and father of communism, Karl Marx (1818–83), was correct when he wrote that capitalism was prey to cycles of boom and bust. He thought that they were caused by the impact of the fluctuating labor costs on the economy. The ongoing economic crisis that we've been living through since the mid-2000s, however, has nothing to do with Marx' surplus labor theory, and much more with the kinds of behavior that Charles MacKay (1814–89) featured in his *Extraordinary Popular Delusions and the Madness of Crowds* (1841) — in particular, his description of economic "bubbles."

History records that the world's first speculative frenzy and subsequent crash occurred in seventeenth-century Holland over, of all things, tulips. But before we smile and write off the poor Dutch flower-fanciers as deluded dolts for their belief that the price of tulip bulbs would carry on increasing forever and therefore making them a fortune, we should look at our own conduct during the past ten years, when we bet that the prices of our stocks and real-estate assets would keep going up. The Dutch were lucky inasmuch as when the bottom fell out of the tulip market, it affected a small number of speculators in one country. The bursting of later speculative bubbles has got much bigger and more destructive. Until our own financial crisis, the one that economists muttered darkly about was the Wall Street Crash of 1929, which is given as one of the causes for the most prolonged economic recession of modern times, the Great Depression (1929–39).

"THERE MAY BE TROUBLE AHEAD...." There are some interesting parallels between the buildup to the Credit Crunch and what preceded the Wall Street Crash. The "Roaring Twenties," like the first decade of the twenty-first century, were a period of unparalleled wealth and optimism. Determined to forget the horrors of World War One, people all over the world threw themselves into an orgy of consumption and hedonism, all based on wild financial speculation. The period witnessed bubbles of all kinds: technological, real estate, and stock market, and no one—economists, politicians, or bankers—saw the storm clouds piling on the economic horizon. In 1927, the great economist John Maynard Keynes (1883–1946) affirmed, "We will not have any more crashes in our time." And in December 1928, less than a year before the crash, U.S. President Calvin Coolidge told Congress:

No Congress of the United States ever assembled, on surveying the state of the Union, has met with a more pleasing prospect than that which appears at the present time. In the domestic field there is tranquility and contentment [...] and the highest record of years of prosperity. In the foreign field there is peace, the goodwill which comes from mutual understanding.

One of the most reassuring voices of the period belonged to Irving Fisher (1867–1947). In September 1929, at the height of the speculative frenzy on the NYSE, when stock prices had reached such unsustainable levels that investors were beginning to wake up from their collective dream, Fisher assured the readers of the *New York Times*: "There may be a recession in stock prices, but not anything in the nature of a crash." He went further in October 1929 when he confidently predicted: "Stock prices have reached what looks like a permanently high plateau" (see quote). Fisher was not just another ill-informed commentator or journalist. He was a Yale alumnus and one of the most respected economic theorists of his day. Although his reputation was destroyed by his optimistic predictions for 1929, his quantity of money theory is now recognized as one of the foundations of Milton Friedman's (1912–2006) "monetarism."

OPTIMIST
Echoed in the bullish financial predictions in 2006, Fisher was sure that the Wall Street Crash of 1929 was a mere blip that would soon be forgotten.

The ink had barely had time to dry on Fisher's rosy predictions when disaster struck the NYSE. After a six-year Bull market that saw the Dow Jones Industrial Average increase in value by a staggering 500 percent, the market peaked at 381.17 on September 3, 1929. The market lost 17 percent of its value in the following month, but that was just a prelude for much worse to come. The fall had unsettled investors, and prices fluctuated wildly for the next two weeks. But like the *Titanic*, the market had struck a hidden iceberg and was taking in water at well beyond the rate that the financial system could cope with.

The Wall Street Crash started on "Black Thursday," October 24, 1929, when a record-breaking 12.9 billion shares were traded in one day. Senior Wall Street financiers and bankers met to attempt to stem the growing panic by investing heavily in the market. The strategy worked but only until Monday—"Black Monday," October 28—when the

Dow Jones lost 12.82 percent of its value, and on Tuesday—"Black Tuesday," October 29—it lost a further 11.73 percent. Fisher still assured investors that this was only a temporary blip, and that stock prices were bound to recover because stock values were not inflated. In 1930, there was a short-lived rally, which saw the Dow Jones reach a respectable 294.07, but a combination of disastrous economic reforms and a loss of investor confidence led to a further slide that continued for two years. The market hit an all time twentieth-century low of 41.22 on July 8, 1932.

Fisher was not only ruined as an economist but also as a businessman, as he himself had invested heavily in stocks. He immediately set to work to analyze where he had gone so badly wrong. He came up with debt-deflation theory to explain the effects of the 1929 crash. He focused on the bursting of the asset bubble, and how it had brought about the following nine effects: (1) the liquidation of debt and distress selling, (2) contraction of the money supply as people and businesses paid off their debts, (3) a fall in asset prices, (4) a fall in the worth of businesses, leading to business failures, (5) a fall in profits, (6) a reduction in overall economic activity, (7) pessimism and loss of confidence, (8) the hoarding of cash, and (9) a fall in interest rates but a rise in deflation-adjusted interest rates.

Stop me if this is all beginning to sound terribly familiar. Politicians, regulators, and bankers claim they have learned the lessons of 1929, and assure us that they won't repeat the same mistakes that transformed a stock market crash into a ten-year recession. However, it's a shame that they hadn't learned the lessons of 1927 and 1928 in order to avoid a repeat of 1929.

DOING THE SPLITS: ALBERT EINSTEIN

Main culprit: Albert Einstein

What was predicted: That atomic energy and weapons would never be practical propositions

What actually happened: Hiroshima, Nagasaki, Three-mile Island, and Chernobyl—maybe we should have listened

There is not the slightest indication that nuclear energy will ever be obtainable. It would mean that the atom would have to be shattered at will.

Albert Einstein, speaking in 1932

Although the ancient Greek philosopher Democritus (c. 460–c. 370 BCE) put forward the theory that matter was made up of microscopic particles, or "atoms," received wisdom for most of human history has been that humans and everything else in the cosmos were made up of the four classical elements (fire, air, water, and earth). As the centuries progressed, chemists discovered the true elements that are the building blocks of matter, such as oxygen, carbon, and hydrogen, but it took until the very end of the nineteenth century for Joseph Thomson (1856–1940) to demonstrate the existence of one of the component particles of the atom, the electron.

In 1909, the physicist Ernest Rutherford (1871–1937) proved experimentally that the atom was composed of a nucleus surrounded by one or more electrons. He gave us the planetary model of the atom that is the most familiar to laymen, with the nucleus acting like the Sun in a miniature solar system of electrons. This simplistic atomic model, however, was out of date as soon as Rutherford had published it. The new physics postulated by Albert Einstein (1879–1955) established the quantum model of the atom and its constituent particles, transforming Rutherford's model into something far more complex and uncertain. A subatomic particle could exhibit the behavior of both a discrete particle, like a marble moving in space, or of a wave, like sound or light, and in either state it was subject to the "uncertainty principle," which meant that you could measure either its charge or its position, but not both at the same time.

DUNCE
Einstein did not believe that we could commercially exploit nuclear fission or develop it as a weapon.

Despite the tremendous progress of physics in the early twentieth century, neither Rutherford nor Einstein believed that their discoveries could lead to any practical development in the fields of energy production or weapons. In 1932, when man first split the atom, Rutherford said dismissively: "The energy produced by the breaking down of the atom is a very poor kind of thing. Anyone who expects a source of power from the transformation of these atoms is talking moonshine." That same year, Einstein was even more forthright in dismissing the significance of the breakthrough, asserting, "There is not the slightest indication that nuclear energy will ever be obtainable."

Yet only 13 years later, and four decades after Einstein had published the four papers that revolutionized our understanding of the physical universe, the U.S. had successfully developed and tested a bomb that exploited the fissile nature of the atomic nucleus—the "A-bomb"—and had dropped two versions, one made of uranium, the other of plutonium, on two Japanese cities to bring the Pacific War (1941–45) to an end. It was an inauspicious and murderous beginning to the "Atomic Age." The military and civilian uses of nuclear power are so intimately linked that it would be impossible to disentangle the one from the other. Without the first experimental reactor it would have been impossible to produce the enriched uranium and plutonium to manufacture the first A-bombs; and without the impetus of World War Two, the intensive research into nuclear energy might have been long delayed.

Albert Einstein was not just a genius, he was a genius' genius. Born in Germany soon after the creation of the German Empire, Einstein is often said to have been a poor student. Generations of mothers have comforted their wayward offspring by saying, "Look at Einstein, he was a dunce at school and he got the Nobel Prize!" If the truth be told, however, Einstein was far from being a dunce. He was too bright and creative for the stifling educational methods of the day that depended on rote learning. He wrote his first scientific paper aged 16, and at the age of 17 was studying the latest discoveries in physics. He graduated in 1900 with a diploma in mathematics and physics but was unable to find a teaching post. In 1903, he settled for a job evaluating patents at the Swiss Patent Office in Bern.

$E=mc^2$

While pursuing his wholly undistinguished career in Switzerland, Einstein completed his doctorate in physics, and carried out the "thought experiments" on which he would base the four scientific articles of 1905 known as the *annus mirabilis* ("miracle year") papers. These explored the photoelectric effect, Brownian motion, special relativity, and the equivalence of matter and energy, and made all of the existing physics textbooks obsolete seemingly overnight. The paper that most concerns us here is "Does the Inertia of a Body Depend Upon Its Energy Content?", which deals with mass-energy equivalence and in which he used the world's most famous formula, $E=mc^2$. Einstein gave the following explanation of the equation:

It followed from the Special Theory of Relativity that mass and energy are both but different manifestations of the same thing—a somewhat unfamiliar conception for the average mind. Furthermore, the equation E is equal to mc², in which energy is put equal to mass, multiplied [by the] square of the velocity of light, showed that very small amounts of mass may be converted into a very large amount of energy and vice versa. The mass and energy were in fact equivalent, according to the formula mentioned before.

Einstein had established the principle that a large amount of energy could be obtained from a very small amount of matter. Humans being what they are, they imagined how large a bomb they could make, but it would take a further 40 years of research to make Einstein's principle into a functional weapon. In 1932, James Chadwick (1891–1974) discovered a hitherto unknown component of the atomic nucleus called the neutron, which became the key to atomic fission. This led experimenters in France and Italy to use neutron beams to make otherwise stable materials radioactive.

In Germany, two physicists, Otto Hahn (1879–1968) and Friedrich Strassmann (1902–80) put these discoveries together in 1938. They bombarded a uranium atom with neutrons and succeeded in confirming nuclear fission through their experiments. They realized that fission could be maintained by a chain reaction, as the splitting of atomic nuclei produced more neutrons that

DESTROYER OF WORLDS
A replica of Fat Man, the atomic bomb detonated over Nagasaki, Japan, on August 9, 1945.

continued the process until the whole of the available uranium was burned up. A controlled reaction could be used as a power source, such as a nuclear reactor, but an explosive reaction would release enormous amounts of light, heat, and kinetic energy. In other words, a small amount of the right fissile material bombarded by neutrons would give you a bomb that was many orders of magnitude more powerful than any high explosive then available.

The timing of the discovery could not have been worse. In Germany, Adolf Hitler (1889–1945) and his Axis allies were about to embark on the bloodiest war of modern times, and everyone in the world of physics had realized the potential of Hahn and Strassmann's discovery. What no one knew was whether a fission weapon was practical. British wartime premier Winston Churchill (1874–1965) said in 1939, "Atomic energy might be as good as our present-day explosives, but it is unlikely to produce anything very much more dangerous." Einstein, however, had revised his earlier opinion about nuclear power and put his name to a letter from leading physicists to President Franklin D. Roosevelt (1882–1945) warning him that Nazi Germany was conducting research into the weaponization of atomic fission and advising the U.S. to do the same.

The letter was instrumental in galvanizing the U.S. government to initiate the Manhattan Project (1942–46), in which the U.S., Britain, and Canada collaborated in the production of the first nuclear weapons. Even as the A-bomb was nearing completion, however, there were those overseeing the project who did not believe that it would work. Admiral William Leahy (1875–1959) told President Harry S. Truman (1884–1972) in 1944, "The bomb will never go off, and I speak as an expert in explosives." The 110,000 Japanese who died on the days the bombs were dropped on Hiroshima and Nagasaki bear witness to the A-bomb's awesome destructive power. The physicists who had made the bomb possible, including Einstein, were horrified at what they had created. For the rest of his life, Einstein campaigned against nuclear testing and further development of nuclear weapons. In 1949, he lamented, "I do not know how the Third World War will be fought, but I can tell you what they will use in the Fourth—rocks!"

TURNING THE RED TIDE: LEON TROTSKY

Main culprit: Leon Trotsky

What was predicted: The collapse of the Stalinist Soviet Union after a second proletarian revolution

What actually happened: The Soviet Union did collapse but not because of a second revolution

In order better to understand the character of the present Soviet Union, let us make two different hypotheses about its future. Let us assume first that the Soviet bureaucracy is overthrown by a revolutionary party having all the attributes of the old Bolshevism, enriched moreover by the world experience of the recent period. Such a party would begin with the restoration of democracy in the trade unions and the Soviets. It would be able to, and would have to, restore freedom of Soviet parties. Together with the masses, and at their head, it would carry out a ruthless purgation of the state apparatus.

The Revolution Betrayed (1936) by Leon Trotsky

From the perspective of the Cold War, and in particular American representations of the Union of Soviet Socialist Republics (USSR) during the 1950s and '60s, Russia was characterized as a monolithic totalitarian state with a disciplined population, brainwashed by the Communist Party into doing its bidding without question. The reality, of course, was quite different. There was dissent and resistance among sections of the Russian people and constant infighting within the leadership, but without a free media (and no Internet or cell phones), these went unreported, and anything that did leak out could be written off as imperialist bourgeois propaganda.

From the outset, however, the Soviet state was politically fragile, and in its early years it was almost destroyed by a combination of external invasion and internal division. Even when foreign enemies allied to the "White Russians" who wanted to restore the Czar had been defeated, there remained the great struggle for the "soul" of the Soviet Union, which was fought between two men, both Communists and both members of the ruling Politburo: Leon Trotsky (1879–1940) and Joseph Stalin (1878–1953). Stalin's victory ensured the survival of the Soviet state during World War Two but also led to its long-term decline and ultimate demise. Disgraced and exiled, Trotsky was among the first to predict the collapse of the Soviet Union. He hoped that a second proletarian revolution would sweep away the bureaucratic apparatus created by Stalin (see quote), but he also feared quite another outcome, and it was these predictions that were to prove absolutely correct.

The Bolshevik Revolution of October 1917 was the culmination of a protracted process that began at the start of the twentieth century. The autocratic regime of Czar Nicholas II (1868–1918) survived a first revolution in 1905 because of disunity among the revolutionaries, who included moderate constitutional monarchists, republicans, democrats, socialists, and Marxists led by V. I. Lenin (1870–1924), the leader of the Russian Social Democratic Labor Party (RSDLP), which itself was divided into two major factions: the radical Bolsheviks and more moderate Mensheviks. While the Mensheviks favored a gradualist approach to reform, working within the democratic process to achieve a socialist state, the Bolsheviks planned an armed uprising of the proletariat (working class).

A PLAGUE ON BOTH YOUR HOUSES

Leon Trotsky devoted his life to revolutionary politics. He came from a well-to-do farming family, and received a good education. Instead of going to college after graduating from high school, he joined the socialist Narodnik movement that sought to improve the conditions of the impoverished and oppressed Russian peasantry. Although he came across Marxism in 1897, he initially rejected it. In 1898, he was arrested by the Czar's secret police as a political dissident and was sentenced to four years' internal exile in Siberia. He spent his years in captivity studying Marxism, and he associated himself with the RSDLP that Lenin had founded in 1898. In 1902 he escaped from Siberia and sought asylum in London, where at the second RSDLP congress, the split between Mensheviks and Bolsheviks first became apparent. Trotsky initially sided with the Mensheviks against Lenin's Bolsheviks. However, he soon abandoned his partisan sympathies, preferring the role of a "non-factional social democrat" who hoped to reconcile the warring factions.

IN 1898, TROTSKY WAS ARRESTED BY THE CZAR'S SECRET POLICE AS A POLITICAL DISSIDENT AND WAS SENTENCED TO FOUR YEARS' INTERNAL EXILE IN SIBERIA.

Trotsky returned to Russia to take part in the failed revolution of 1905 as head of the first Soviet (council) of workers, founded in Petrograd (now St. Petersburg). He was arrested and sentenced to a Siberian exile for a second time, but managed to escape again, making his way back to London and then Vienna where he continued his revolutionary activities. In 1914, World War One broke out in Europe, pitting the Central powers of German and Austria-Hungary against the Entente alliance of France, England, and Russia. In the first year of the war the Central powers made rapid progress on both their eastern and western fronts. The Russian forces were no match militarily or technologically for the enemy.

The war gave the opposition in Russia the opportunity it needed to attempt a second revolution in February 1917. Trotsky played no part in the revolution as he was living in the U.S., having fled Vienna at the outbreak of war. The February revolution was led by moderate democratic parties, with whom Lenin's RSDLP had entered into an uneasy alliance. The alliance did not last, and when Trotsky managed to return to Russia in May, he sided with Lenin in the October Revolution that brought the Bolsheviks to power. From then on, until Lenin's death in 1924, Trotsky was one of the leaders of the Soviet state, holding the posts of People's Commissar for Foreign Affairs and head of the Red Army. Trotsky's reorganization of Soviet armed forces saved the young Soviet Union when it was threatened by foreign invaders and White Russian counter-revolutionaries during the civil war of 1918–20.

When Lenin died in 1924, Trotsky was his heir presumptive; however, he had a dangerous rival in Joseph Stalin, who succeeded in turning the majority of the Politburo against him. Trotsky lost his post on the Central Committee in 1927, and was exiled from the Soviet Union in 1929, seeking refuge in several countries, including Turkey and France, before finally settling in Mexico, where he spent the remaining years of his life opposing Stalin's dictatorial rule. In 1936 Stalin put prominent former Bolshevik leaders on trial in Moscow, and used the occasion to condemn Trotsky as a counter-revolutionary who had tried to assassinate him. Trotsky's response was to write *The Revolution Betrayed*, in which he made three predictions about the possible fate of the Soviet Union.

In the first, Stalin's bureaucratic state would be swept away in a second proletarian revolution that would restore Bolshevism and establish a truly communist state. In this he would be disappointed. He witnessed the consolidation of Stalin's rule, but not his ultimate triumph in World War Two, because the Russian dictator had him murdered in 1940. Trotsky's second and third predictions were the ones that actually came true. Failing a proletarian revolution, Trotsky foresaw that the bureaucracy would become entrenched as a new ruling class. He reasoned that the Communist Party elite would not be satisfied with power and honors, because "Privileges have only half their worth, if they cannot be transmitted to one's children." And that the "victory of the bureaucracy in this decisive sphere would mean its conversion into a new possessing class."

SOUR GRAPES
Disgraced and forced into exile by Joseph Stalin, Trotsky turned on the Soviet leader, and plotted his overthrow.

Trotsky was correct to suppose that this state of affairs could not last forever. By the late 1980s, the Soviet Union was on the brink of economic collapse and ripe for political reform. With what turned out to be remarkable prescience, Trotsky predicted the conversion of the Soviet Union from a Communist to a bourgeois capitalist state:

© German Federal Archive | Creative Commons

If [...] a bourgeois party were to overthrow the ruling Soviet caste, it would find no small number of ready servants among the present bureaucrats [...] The chief task of the new power would be to restore private property in the means of production. First of all, it would be necessary to create conditions for the development of strong farmers from the weak collective farms, and for converting the strong collectives into producers' cooperatives of the bourgeois type into agricultural stock companies. In the sphere of industry, denationalization would begin with the light industries and those producing food. The planning principle would be converted for the transitional period into a series of compromises between state power and individual "corporations"—potential proprietors, that is, among the Soviet captains of industry, the émigré former proprietors and foreign capitalists.

Trotsky was the only Bolshevik leader executed by Stalin who was never rehabilitated in the Soviet Union after the dictator's death. His criticism of the Soviet state were clearly too trenchant for the Communist Party elite. Although Trotsky was himself not innocent of spilling the blood of his rivals and enemies, he remained a true Bolshevik at heart—an idealist who believed in the socialist revolution he had fought for since his youth. Our next entry concerns another idealist, but from the other end of the political spectrum, who believed that peace was always preferable to war and that men of goodwill would always find a way to resolve their difficulties.

MAN OF PEACE: NEVILLE CHAMBERLAIN

Main culprit: Neville Chamberlain

What was predicted: Peace with Germany and Italy in 1938

What actually happened: World War Two broke out within a year of the Munich Pact between Germany, Italy, France, and Great Britain

This is the second time there has come back from Germany to Downing Street peace with honour. I believe it is peace for our time. We thank you from the bottom of our hearts. Now I recommend you go home, and sleep quietly in your beds.

Neville Chamberlain in a speech on his return from Munich, Germany in 1938

With a century of hindsight, the two conflicts that ripped Europe apart between 1870 and 1918—the Franco-Prussian War and World War One—have been described as the first two episodes of a single "European Civil War." The First, or "Great," War was, in part, fought as a grudge match between the Germans and the French, who had been squabbling over their common border like a pair of neighbors arguing over the position of a backyard fence. Thirty-seven million deaths later and the problem had not so much been resolved as buried under a mountain of corpses. In 1919, President Woodrow Wilson hoped that the world had finally had enough of war and would find a better way of resolving international disputes through the world's first intergovernmental organization, the League of Nations. Article X of the League's charter expressed the organization's mandate:

IN 1919, PRESIDENT WOODROW WILSON HOPED THAT THE WORLD HAD FINALLY HAD ENOUGH OF WAR.

> The Members of the League undertake to respect and preserve as against external aggression the territorial integrity and existing political independence of all Members of the League. In the case of any such aggression or in case of any threat or danger of such aggression the Council shall advise upon the means by which this obligation shall be fulfilled.

Although the U.S. did not join the League, the major players in the First War all signed up, and the organization worked with some success to promote disarmament and the peaceful resolution of conflicts throughout the 1920s and early '30s.

As we have seen above, the international settlement of 1919 came unstuck because of the vindictiveness of the European Allies who imposed punitive conditions on Germany at Versailles, and the protracted economic crisis that followed the Wall Street Crash of 1929, which the world's governments dealt with by imposing protectionist measures abroad and retrenchment at home that stifled recovery. *Revanchisme* (French for "vengeance-ism") and the faltering world economy nurtured a new form of political extremism on the right that played on nationalistic sentiment and people's yearning for strong government. The first country to succumb to fascism in the 1920s was Benito Mussolini's (1883–1945) Italy. Germany followed suit in the 1930s when it elected Adolf Hitler (1889–1945) as Reich chancellor. Yet even in 1938, with the third and final act of the European Civil

War (1870–1945) a year away, there were those in Britain and France who still believed that Germany and Italy could be bought off with concessions that would ensure "peace for our time."

The two men who decided the fate of Europe in the late 1930s could not have been more different: Hitler, who had seized power in Germany through intimidation and murder; and British prime minister Neville Chamberlain (1869–1940), an old-school Tory (Conservative) politician, who had risen through the ranks of the Westminster parliamentary system. There is probably no better example of the cliché "chalk and cheese" when one compares the styles of the two men. In the newsreels of the day we can see Hitler strutting self-importantly in his absurd paramilitary uniform, while Chamberlain wears a suit, shirt with wing-collar, and tie, which looks 50 years out of date even in 1937.

We shall concentrate on the German dictator and his long-term plans in the next entry. Here, we focus on Chamberlain and why he failed to see what Hitler was planning to do. Chamberlain was too young to have fought in any of the nineteenth century wars in Europe, and too old to be drafted to fight in the First War. Like other members of his generation, however, he had witnessed the horror of the war, which saw the slaughter of a whole generation of Europe's young men. He came from a political family; both his father and brother were Conservative members of parliament (MPs). Chamberlain began his political career in local government in his native city of Birmingham and was elected as one of the MPs for the city in 1917. He quickly rose through the ministerial ranks, becoming Chancellor of the Exchequer (minister of finance) in 1931.

Chamberlain was an able and respected parliamentarian, and under his stewardship the British economy improved, even during the difficult years of the Great Depression. Perhaps because he was so wedded to the democratic process, he put all his faith in negotiation; he could not understand the motivations of political bullies such as Hitler and Mussolini. He also had a certain amount of sympathy for Germany, which he believed had been badly treated in the postwar settlement. Instinctively, Chamberlain was a man of peace and negotiation. Given

CHALK AND CHEESE

© Getty Images

DELUSION
Chamberlain was so desperate to maintain peace that he believed everything Hitler and Mussolini told him.

this, and what was at the time the advanced age of 68 when he became premier, he was the wrong man, in the wrong job, at the wrong time.

Hitler had come to power in 1933 in a legitimate democratic election, but he quickly set about establishing a one-party police state with himself as *der Führer* ("the leader") just as Mussolini had done a decade before. To achieve his domestic aims he combined intimidation and murder with ultra-nationalism and extreme anti-Semitism, and once his position was secure, he set about rearming Germany and regaining the regions that Germany had been forced to cede to her neighbors in 1919. His plan was to create a Greater German Reich that would include all the German-speaking people of Europe and be the dominant power of the continent. Having regained the Rhineland and Saar regions in the mid-1930s, his next targets were Austria, once the heartland of the Austro-Hungarian Empire, which had been dissolved in 1919, and the Sudetenland, a German-speaking region of Czechoslovakia.

HITLER'S PLAN WAS TO CREATE A GREATER GERMAN REICH THAT WOULD INCLUDE ALL THE GERMAN-SPEAKING PEOPLE OF EUROPE AND BE THE DOMINANT POWER OF THE CONTINENT.

In March 1938, Hitler engineered the Anschluss (meaning "union") of Germany and Austria by the simple expedient of supporting a coup by Austrian Nazis against their democratically elected government. The League of Nations and the governments of Britain and France issued strongly worded communiqués but took no action to answer the Austrian government's pleas for military assistance. Hitler's next target was the Sudetenland, a German-speaking region of the former Austro-Hungarian Empire that had long agitated for independence from Czechoslovakia. Hitler, masquerading as a protector of the German people, demanded the immediate annexation of the region to Germany. Instead of taking a strong stand, Chamberlain and the French premier Edouard Daladier (1884–1970) opened negotiations with Berlin. Mussolini suggested a four-power conference, which was held in Munich in September 1938. The result was the Munich Pact (September 29–30), which effectively gave Hitler a free hand in Czechoslovakia in exchange for a promise that he would press no further territorial claims in Europe.

Chamberlain returned from Munich, famously stepping out of the aircraft waving a piece of paper. He announced to the crowd of people awaiting him at the airport:

> The settlement of the Czechoslovakian problem, which has now been achieved is, in my view, only the prelude to a larger settlement in which all Europe may find peace. This morning I had another talk with the German Chancellor, Herr Hitler, and here is the paper which bears his name upon it as well as mine.

Later, outside his official residence in Downing Street, Chamberlain produced the same piece of paper and assured his audience that he had negotiated "peace for our time." Hitler had no intention of keeping his side of the bargain he had made. In March of 1939, he invaded the rest of Czechoslovakia, and on September 1, he moved against Poland. Finally accepting that his policy of appeasement had failed, Chamberlain declared war on Germany. He resigned in May 1940, making way for Britain's wartime savior, Winston Churchill (1874–1965). He died later that year, in the darkest period of the war for the Allies. In a speech to the House of Commons three days after Chamberlain's death from cancer at the age of 71, Churchill recognized his predecessor with the following words:

> We can be sure that Neville Chamberlain acted with perfect sincerity according to his lights and strove to the utmost of his capacity and authority, which were powerful, to save the world from the awful, devastating struggle in which we are now engaged.

Chamberlain, the democrat, parliamentarian, and man of peace was no match for the demagogue, dictator, and murderer who would plunge the world into its bloodiest conflict to date, and bring the curtain down on the final tragic act of the European Civil War.

THE NAZI MILLENNIUM: ADOLF HITLER

Main culprit: Adolf Hitler

What was predicted: The establishment of a 1,000-year Reich

What actually happened: The Third Reich lasted 12 years

I intend to set up a 1,000-year Reich and anyone who supports me in this battle is a fellow-fighter for a unique spiritual—I would say divine—creation [...] Rudolf Hess, my assistant of many years standing, would tell you: If we have such a leader, God is with us.

Adolf Hitler, in an interview in 1931

Having examined the failure of appeasement in the previous entry, we shall now turn our attention to the failure of war in this and the next entry. The fascist dictator Adolf Hitler started World War Two, bringing destruction on himself and Germany. Defeated, he committed suicide in his command bunker in Berlin rather than be captured, tried, and executed by the victorious Allies, and abandoned his country to be dismembered and divided between the Western Allies and the Soviet Union. His defeat and descent into what many believe to be madness in the closing year of the war are an integral part of the Hitler myth. There could be no other moral outcome than his total humiliation and annihilation at the hands of the forces of democracy. Yet fascist dictators do not always invade the world and go insane (not necessarily in that order). A few have died in their beds of old age like Francisco Franco (1892–1975) of Spain, who managed to remain in power from 1936 until his death of natural causes 39 years later. Would it have been possible for Hitler to steer another course and create a regime that, though it probably would not have lasted his vaunted 1,000 years, might at least have outlived him?

DERANGED
As the war progressed and Hitler increasingly lost touch with reality, the German dictator began to believe his own wild claims and delusions.

The German people did not vote for Hitler on a platform of world domination. He was elected because he promised to restore German self-respect and bring the country out of the twentieth century's deepest economic recession. He may have been a megalomaniac and a murderer, but he was also an astute politician and demagogue who knew exactly what people wanted to hear. He summed up his philosophy of government in the following two quotes: "The great masses of the people [...] will more easily fall victims to a great lie than to a small one," and "What luck for rulers that men do not think."

World War Two has been portrayed as an ideological war between the forces of democracy and good on one side and of fascist totalitarianism and evil on the other. We conveniently forget that one of the U.S. and Britain's allies, Joseph Stalin, was a totalitarian dictator of the left, with as much blood on his hands as the Nazis. The conflict of ideologies between the Axis powers and the liberal democratic powers is the justification given for World War Two, but it does not really explain why Germany and its allies went to war. Although ideology played its part, the causes of the war go much further back beyond the humiliation of Germany in World War One and the struggles over land, resources, and power that states have always engaged in.

IMPERIAL PIPE DREAMS

The two countries whose actions precipitated the outbreak of World War Two in Europe—Germany and Italy—were also the continent's most recent national creations before the redrafting of national borders in the aftermath of the First War. Italy was united into an independent kingdom in 1861; the German Empire, or Reich, came into being in 1871. Until then, these two countries had been patchworks of independent kingdoms, principalities, city- and religious states, and foreign-dominated provinces of larger multinational empires. Both countries, however, could call upon glorious past traditions: Benito Mussolini's Italy looked back to the Roman Empire and consciously resurrected its symbols. We owe the word "fascist" to the Latin *fasces*, the symbol of the ancient Roman Republic. Adolf Hitler's Germany had been an empire before World War One—the Second Reich (1871–1918)—but earlier, for 1,006 years from 800–1806, the German region had been the center of the Holy Roman Empire—the First Reich—originally founded by Charlemagne (742–814).

Both dictators played on the national fears and ambitions of their peoples. Although the Italians had fought on the winning side in World War One and had made territorial gains from Austria-Hungary, they had come late to statehood and had missed out on the nineteenth-century's colonial landgrab. While Britain and France had vast overseas empires, Italy could claim only a colony in Libya. Germany, once a major colonial power in its own right, had lost its overseas possessions after the First War. Mussolini dreamed of restoring the past greatness of imperial Rome with himself as a latter-day emperor. However, the resurrection of an empire that stretched from northern England to Iraq was beyond even Mussolini's wildest dreams, but he could aim to control the Mediterranean—the *mare nostrum* ("our sea") of the Romans—so he coveted not only North Africa but also the Balkans.

Hitler's imperial ambitions were perhaps a little more realistic as they were centered on the recreation of the First German Reich, which had occupied part of France and most of Central Europe. The Third

Reich officially came into being in 1934, when Hitler became Führer. Within five years, Hitler was well on his way to achieving his aim of creating a "Greater Germany," having recovered the Rhineland (1935) and annexed Austria and most of Czechoslovakia (1938). He was allowed to act unopposed by Britain and France who still believed in appeasement, and by an isolationist U.S. that refused to intervene. Had Hitler stopped in Czechoslovakia, his regime could conceivably still be in power today. But the logic of Hitler's ideology was one of constant expansion. When he attempted to add Poland to the Reich, Britain and France declared war. The move was disastrous for France, which was forced to capitulate in 1940, and saw half of her territory occupied, and the other half governed by a puppet regime. Britain, too, faced invasion, had she not won back control of the skies in the Battle of Britain of 1940.

Again, had Hitler stopped in 1940, and negotiated from a position of strength, he might have saved his dreams of a lasting Nazi German Reich. The British briefly considered making peace with Hitler and giving him a free hand in Europe while they retained their empire. Hitler was defeated by two serious miscalculations on the part of the Axis powers: the first was his own, his invasion of the Soviet Union in 1941, and the second, over which he had no control, was the entry of the United States into the war after the Japanese attack on Pearl Harbor that same year.

© Getty Images

FALL
The 1,000-year Reich came to an end after a mere 12 years when the Red Army hoisted the Soviet flag on Berlin's Chancellery.

Hitler is an interesting psychological puzzle. Born in Austria out of wedlock at a time when being illegitimate still carried a major stigma, he was an unlikely candidate as a future ruler of Germany and would-be world conqueror. He had a distinguished military career during the First War, and entered politics soon after. He began as a socialist, opposed to the Weimar Republic (1918–34) and what he saw as its betrayal of the German people. He gradually moved to the right of the political spectrum, proving himself to be an inspirational speaker and an astute politician. After a failed coup attempt, he worked within the prewar German democratic system, being elected chancellor of

Germany after the Wall Street Crash had sent the German economy into freefall.

Although Hitler was politically ruthless, as well as a rabid anti-Semite (but there were many in Europe and the U.S. at the time who were almost as prejudiced), he was not insane—at least not at the beginning of the war. But having created an expansionist, nationalistic, racist, and militaristic state, he was trapped by its logic: Expand or face a disastrous implosion. In the end, Hitler could not control the monster he had created to win power. Caught between the world's two superpowers, the U.S. and the Soviet Union, Hitler's reign and his 1,000-year Reich lasted a mere 12 years.

HITLER'S "1,000-YEAR" REICH

German-occupied countries and allied states during World War Two. It represents the greatest extent of Hitler's "1,000-year" Reich.

- German Reich, allies, and occupied zones
- Baltic States, Belarus, Ulkraine, and Moscow and Kalrelia terr.
- Allies

ANGELS OF DEATH: CAPTAIN MOTOHARU OKAMURA

PREDICTION

Millenarian

Technology

Prophecy

Politics

Military

Natural Disaster

Culture

Economics

Doomsday

Main culprit: Captain Motoharu Okamura

What was predicted: That Japan would be saved from defeat by suicide air attacks on the Allied ships and aircraft

What actually happened: Suicide tactics proved ineffective and Japan was defeated

In our present situation I firmly believe that the only way to swing the war in our favor is to resort to crash-dive attacks with our planes. There is no other way. There will be more than enough volunteers for this chance to save our country, and I would like to command such an operation. Provide me with 300 planes and I will turn the tide of war.

Captain Motoharu Okamura in conversation with a senior naval officer in 1944

Suicide attacks have been much in the news with the wars in Iraq and Afghanistan. But it is not the first time that U.S. and British forces have been attacked by enemies who place so little value on human life that they will transform a human being into a living bomb. At the close of World War Two in the Pacific (1941–45), when U.S. and British naval forces were driving back the Japanese to the home islands, officers of the Imperial Japanese Navy and Air Force came up with a strategy that they believed would turn the tide of war in their favor. They unleashed the kamikaze ("divine wind") suicide bombers onto Allied ships and aircraft. The kamikaze was a product of Japan's centuries-old samurai tradition of Bushido (the Way of the Warrior), which placed the highest value on service to the Emperor and one's duty and honor as a warrior.

© Getty Images

Japan was another country that felt marginalized by the post-World War One settlement. Although Japan, like Italy, had fought on the winning side, and had made minor territorial gains at the expense of Germany's Asian possessions, she, too, had come to imperial-power status too late in the nineteenth century to create an empire of her own, and had to make do with near neighbors Korea and the Island of Formosa (now the Chinese Republic of Taiwan). After a brief flirtation with parliamentary democracy during the reign of the Taisho Emperor (1879–1926), the country inexorably drifted to the right under the Showa Emperor (1901–89). The weak, vacillating emperor could not resist the rise of ultra-nationalism and militarism that sought to make Japan into the dominant power in Asia.

SUICIDAL
Although the kamikaze caused havoc to Allied naval forces, they could not slow or prevent the defeat of Japan in World War Two.

Japan is extremely short of land and natural resources, two things that its giant neighbor to the west, China, has in plentiful supply. Japan's eyes were firmly fixed on the fast-disintegrating Qing Empire, which finally succumbed to a republican revolution in 1912. In the chaos that ensued, the Japanese, like the other major powers, was quick to take advantage by forcing the new Chinese government to grant her commercial privileges and territorial concessions. Asia's Second World War began much earlier than Europe's. In 1931, Japan occupied the northern Chinese province of Manchuria, and installed the former

Chinese Emperor Pu Yi (1906–67) as the ruler of the puppet state of Manchukuo. Hostilities between the two countries continued on and off until 1937, when Japan mounted a full-scale invasion of China. The League of Nations objected but was, as usual, unable to intervene in any meaningful way. The U.S., Britain, and France, preoccupied with economic problems and the rise of Hitler in Germany, woke up too late to the Japanese threat. In 1941, Japan invaded Southeast Asia and attacked Pearl Harbor to forestall American interference.

Like Hitler, the Japanese overextended themselves occupying a huge area of Southeast Asia and the Pacific, and their attack on Pearl Harbor brought the might of the U.S. into the war. After initial advances, the tide turned against Japan when its fleet was defeated at the Battle of Midway in 1942. For the next three years, the Allies drove the Japanese back toward the home islands. The war in the Pacific was a naval war, but the number or firepower of battleships and destroyers did not decide the outcome of battles, which were won or lost by carrier-based air power. The Japanese sank most of the American Pacific fleet at Pearl Harbor, but it failed to sink its all-important carriers. At the Battle of Midway, the Japanese lost most of its own carrier fleet, which crippled its offensive capability and sealed its fate.

DIVINE WINDS

The Japanese had faced the invasion of their homeland on two previous occasions, both in the Middle Ages, when the Mongol ruler of China, Kubilai Khan (1215–94), launched invasion fleets from China and Korea in 1274 and 1281. The second fleet was so large that it was only surpassed in size by the armada that ferried troops to Normandy on D-Day in 1944. The Japanese would have been defeated but for two freak typhoons that destroyed three-quarters of the enemy's ships. The storms were considered to be of supernatural origin and called "kamikaze." *Kami* is often translated as "god," but the concept is slightly different from our own, as a place, object, or human being can also be a *kami*.

When Japan faced a renewed threat of invasion for the first time in six and a half centuries, there were many who hoped for divine intervention, and some, like Captain Motoharu Okamura (1901–48), decided to give the gods a helping hand. Okamura was a typical product of the militaristic Japanese system. He was a test pilot before the war and fought in the Sino-Japanese war (1937–45) before becoming commander of an air base in the Tokyo region. Although there had been isolated suicide attacks by Japanese pilots before 1944, Okamura was the first to propose the formation of special units of suicide bombers to attack Allied shipping. Under his tutelage, thousands of young men went willingly to their deaths, like "bees who die after they have stung," Okamura said proudly.

The effectiveness of the kamikaze has never been in doubt, but the exact number of Allied ships sunk by their attacks is still a matter of debate. During the war, Japanese propaganda claimed 81 ships sunk and 195 damaged, while the U.S. Navy cited 34 ships sunk and 368 damaged. The Japanese lost over 5,000 pilots, and the Allies about 5,000 each killed and wounded in kamikaze attacks. The kamikaze, however, could not slow down the relentless advance of Allied forces on Japan. Okamura himself never flew a kamikaze mission, and he survived the Japanese defeat and surrender. According to his biography, he shot himself in 1948, out of remorse for the thousands of young men he had sent to their deaths in vain.

VIEWING THE FUTURE: DARRYL F. ZANUCK

PREDICTION

Millenarian

Technology

Prophecy

Politics

Military

Natural Disaster

Culture

Economics

Doomsday

Main culprit: Darryl F. Zanuck

What was predicted: That television would not last

What actually happened: *Big Brother, Oprah, Lost…*

Television won't be able to hold on to any market it captures after the first six months. People will soon get tired of staring at a plywood box every night.

Darryl F. Zanuck in 1946

With some relief we turn our back on the war years, and turn our attention to the intersection between culture and technology that is the world of media. Until the advent of the Internet age, media was largely synonymous with television, which, by the late 1950s, had taken over from other media as the main purveyor of home entertainment and news. Television was the technological innovation that ushered in the greatest social change in the 1960s and '70s. But in the late 1940s when it was taking off in the U.S. and Europe, it faced two fearsome competitors: radio (pp. 84–7) and the movies (pp. 116–20).

Radio has survived into the Internet age, but as a very different medium than in its heyday between the 1920s and 1950s. In addition to the news and music that it still broadcasts today, old-time radio offered children's programming, drama, comedy, celebrity news, documentaries, and quizzes—all the formats that television would make its own. Until the 1940s, the movies were the only form of mass visual entertainment. Going to a movie theater in the Golden Age of the big screen was a very different experience from a visit to one of our own shopping-mall multiplexes. For one thing there were many more movie theaters, and the grander ones were plush picture palaces. Customers could expect a lot more for their 50 cents than a few trailers, ads, and a single feature film; performances consisted of a movie serial, such as Flash Gordon or Captain Marvel, cartoons and comedy shorts, a newsreel courtesy of Pathé or Movietone News, and two full-length feature films in glorious Technicolor and stereophonic sound.

The movie theater held other attractions, especially for young couples who were still living at home and could escape parental supervision to the comparative intimacy of the back rows of the theater. The movies were big, brash, and featured the biggest stars of the day, while television was small, mono, and monochrome and populated by relative unknowns. The television broadcasts that Hollywood studio boss Darryl F. Zanuck (1902–79) saw in 1946 on a small, grainy, monochrome screen, led him to conclude that "People will soon get tired of staring at a plywood box every night." But people did not get bored. They got better and bigger TV sets, added color, invented the video recorder and the TV dinner, and it was the movie theaters that went out of business.

The invention of television was a two-stage process that began with "electromechanical" television as the precursor of our own "electronic" television. After the invention of the telegraph, the telephone, and the wireless telegraph (radio), it was a short imaginative step from the transmission of sound to the transmission of still and moving images. In 1878, a British cartoonist working for the British magazine *Punch* created the "telephonoscope"—a fictional invention that he credited to Thomas Alva Edison (1847–1931)—that would combine telephone and video technology. The cartoon predicted the new invention for 1879; however, the videophone was a bit longer in coming, with the first commercial system going into service at the Berlin Olympics of 1936.

First-generation television was known as mechanical television because simple mechanical devices captured the images that were then transmitted by radio waves. In the 1840s, the Scottish engineer Alexander Bain (1811–77) invented a kind of primitive fax machine that was capable of transmitting a still image over a wired telegraph, but it was a 23-year-old German engineering student called Paul Nipkow (1860–1940), who in 1883 invented an image-scanning disk, which improved on Bain's pendulum scanner. The Nipkow disk, which broke an image down into lines, was incorporated in the world's first operational electromechanical television system demonstrated in London in 1926 by the Scottish inventor John Logie Baird (1888–1946). After hearing of the demonstration, the radio pioneer and inventor of the vacuum tube, Lee De Forest (1873–1961), was not impressed. He said: "While theoretically and technically television may be feasible, commercially and financially it is an impossibility, a development of which we need waste little time dreaming."

The initial demonstrations of electromechanical television would not have inspired much confidence in the future of the medium. The screen was small, silent, and monochrome, and the distorted image was made up of only 30 lines. In the next decade Baird worked to improve the technology, and by 1936 the BBC was broadcasting in 240-line Baird transmissions. The Hungarian engineer Kalman Tihanyi (1897–1947)

A VIEW TO THE FUTURE

DISMISSIVE
Zanuck failed to see how the medium of television would not only take over from the movie industry but also rescue many Hollywood studios.

was working on second-generation electronic television around the same time as Baird was developing his own hybrid system. Between them, Tihanyi and Baird developed video recording (on disk and not tape), color television, and flat-panel plasma screens. The television industry spent the next 70 years catching up with their inventions.

Electronic television replaced electromechanical television by the mid-1930s, but World War Two (1939–45) interrupted the commercial development of television in the U.S. and Europe. Broadcasts resumed in 1946 with commercial stations covering most of the mainland U.S. The year 1951 saw two firsts for American television: the first coast-to-coast broadcast and later the first live national television broadcast, which featured a speech by President Harry S. Truman (1884–1972). Another U.S. president, Dwight D. Eisenhower (1890–1969), had a clearer idea of what television audiences thought of politicians making speeches on television when he said, "I can think of nothing more boring for the American people than to have to sit in their living rooms for a whole half hour looking at my face on their television screens."

SPINNING WHEEL
John Logie Baird demonstrating his version of electromechanical television at the Science Museum in London in 1926.

© SSPL via Getty Images

Just as Baird and Tihanyi were demonstrating the new medium of television, the movie industry was producing its first full-length "talkies." Darryl F. Zanuck was one of the founding fathers of Hollywood. He started in the movie business at the age of 20 writing scripts. He got a job at Warner Brothers in 1924, for whom he wrote scripts for five years before switching to production, becoming head of production in 1931. In 1933 he left Warner to found 20th Century Films. In 1935 he bought out Fox Studios to create 20th Century Fox. Zanuck's film credits include classics from the age of the silent screen such as the Rin Tin Tin movies, and blockbusters including *How Green Was My Valley* (1941), *All About Eve* (1950), and *The Longest Day* (1962).

The domination of the cinema in visual entertainment in 1946 was so complete that it is understandable why this titan of the movie business had such a low opinion of television. During the 1950s, the movies more than held their own. Although the TV shows of the period may have been great in their own way, they were small in every sense of the word: casts, budgets, locations, and they could never hope to compete with the spectacle of Cinemascope. But things changed with the introduction of color television in the late 1960s and of home video recording in the 1970s. Now it was the cinema that was losing audiences and money.

The challenge of television to moviegoing continues. The creation of outsized flat-screen digital HD and 3D televisions with surround-sound systems are now able to match the cinema experience at home. And with the advent of the Internet, and the combining of online and terrestrial broadcasting, we are firmly wedded to our not-so-small screens. Although Zanuck might applaud the improved quality of television that can at last do justice to his movies, I wonder if he would have been any more impressed by our modern-day content than he was in 1946.

ALL SHOOK UP:
VARIETY MAGAZINE

Main culprit: *Variety* magazine

What was predicted: That rock and roll would only last one summer

What actually happened: (Rock) music has never died

It will be gone by June.

Variety magazine on rock and roll in 1955

We remain in the cultural arena for this entry—a field where predictions of success (or failure) are notoriously tricky. There have been many notably poor predictions about Hollywood stars: Fred Astaire (1899–1987)—"Can't sing. Can't act. Balding. Can dance a little." And bestselling books: *Harry Potter and the Philosopher's Stone* (1997), rejected by eight publishers and published with an initial print run of 1,000 copies. But unlike technological success that depends on the usefulness of particular inventions, or economic accuracy that is based on learned theories and quantitative data, cultural success or failure is decided by the intangibles of taste, popularity, and fashion. Predictive accuracy is even more difficult when something is radically different from what has gone before, as is the case of the subject of this entry: rock and roll music, or more colloquially rock'n'roll. Even the U.S. entertainment industry's trade publication, *Variety* magazine, got it completely wrong when it predicted in 1955 that rock music would be an overnight sensation that would be forgotten in a year's time (see quote).

Rock was a product of the intersection of new sound and video technology and the huge social changes that overtook the U.S. in the postwar period. In 1948 and 1949, two new record formats replaced the old 78 rpm standard: RCA Victor's short play (single), or 45 rpm, and Columbia Records' long play (LP), or 33 rpm, initially known for the speed at which they were played on mechanical turntables. At the same time, television (see previous entry) was taking over from radio and cinema as the nation's principal entertainment medium. In the field of music production, the decade saw the development of the electric guitar and improvements in amplifier and microphone technology. The stage was set for a new type of entertainer, bearing his guitar in front of him like a knight of old carrying his shield and sword into battle, to come strutting out of the small screen to conquer both America's living rooms and the world (but more of the "King" later).

After the austerity of the immediate postwar period, the world economy revived, ushering a period of affluence not seen since the 1920s. People were more optimistic, wealthier, had more leisure time, and wanted to "let their hair down"—especially the young who were throwing off the shackles of parental control and conformity to 1940s morality. The early 1950s witnessed the beginnings of the youth counter-culture movement that would flower into the drug-fueled hippie subculture of the 1960s. Rock and roll, from the perspective of later generations, who lived through psychedelia, punk, and glam rock, and 1980s gender-bending, looks pretty tame, with its clearly defined gender roles—leather jackets, jeans, and slick-back hair for the boys and bobby socks, full skirts, and pony tails for the girls—and no substances more mind-altering than tobacco, root beer, and frothy coffee, but at the time it was seen as nothing short of a social and moral revolution.

Many younger readers, who probably think of rock and roll as being as American and wholesome as Mom's apple pie, will be surprised to learn that when it first burst onto the American scene it was slammed as an evil that would lead America's youth to perdition and ultimately to the downfall of civilization. In 1957, A. M. Meerio (n.d.), an associate professor of psychology at Columbia University in New York, warned hysterically, "If we cannot stem the tide of rock and roll with its waves of rhythmic narcosis and vicarious craze, we are preparing our own downfall in the midst of pandemic funeral dances."

The real problem was not the newness of rock music but its origins. Its antecedents included perfectly respectable middle-class "white" prewar big-band dance music, but it mixed these with the working-class and African-American styles of gospel, rhythm and blues, and country and western. In the segregated United States of the early 1950s, rock was the first musical style to be marketed to a youth audience that crossed the racial divide. In the South, it was denounced as ungodly "n***** music." Worse, rock music was associated with a dangerous, uncontrolled hedonism, as rock'n'roll was also an African-American phrase referring to the sexual act—an association that several artists exploited fully in their lyrics and stage shows. Although there cannot be said to be a direct causal relation between them, the beginnings of rock and of the nascent African-American civil rights movement coincided in the mid-1950s, and the two were associated in the minds of conservatives and racists, who saw both as signs of America's decline.

ELVIS IS IN THE BUILDING Although music historians still argue about who made the first rock and roll record, there is one artist who is, above all others, associated with rock'n'roll: the "King," Elvis Presley (1935–77). He released "It's All Right (Mama)" in 1954, which *Rolling Stone* magazine has since credited as being the first rock'n'roll record, but he was one in a generation of outstanding musicians that included the talents of Bill Haley (1925–81), Chuck Berry (b. 1926), Little Richard (b. 1932), Jerry Lee Lewis (b. 1935), and the ill-fated Buddy Holly (1936–59).

At first the establishment and the music industry did not know what to make of the rock phenomenon (hence the dismissive *Variety* review), which was fast displacing the previous generations of singers and entertainers. One of the stalwarts of the crooner generation, Frank Sinatra (1915–98), once a heartthrob and something of a fresh-faced rebel himself, said of Elvis: "His kind of music is deplorable, a rancid smelling aphrodisiac. It fosters almost totally negative and destructive reactions in young people." But in the U.S., money always talks, and the industry was forced to take notice because of the huge sales that Elvis and other rock'n'rollers were generating. The year 1956 was the breakthrough year for Elvis with his debut album *Elvis Presley* and movie *Love Me Tender*, his first chart number one, a sell-out concert tour, and his first appearances on American television.

In April and June 1956, Elvis appeared on the *Milton Berle Show* to acclaim from his youthful fans but to negative reviews from cultural commentators who accused him of the "lowest depths in the 'grunt and groin' antics" and earned him the nickname "Elvis the pelvis." Ed Sullivan (1901–74), who hosted what was then America's most popular variety show, vowed that he would never have Elvis on his show because he was "unfit for family viewing." There were several comical attempts to control the King's gyrating hips: A judge in Jacksonville, Florida, threatened to send him to jail if he moved his body suggestively during a live stage show in the town. In response Elvis stood stock still during the performance but wiggled his finger to ridicule the ban. Television producers attempted to censor the singer by showing him from the waist up, but to little avail as the studio audience's response to Elvis' stage show made sure that the folks at home could imagine what was going on. One story goes that Sullivan was so shocked by footage of Elvis that he was sure he had a coke bottle stuffed down his trousers.

ILLEGAL
Repeated efforts were made to control the King's gyrating pelvis, ranging from a court injunction to filming him from the waist up on TV.

When Elvis' appearance on the rival *Steve Allen Show* dethroned the *Ed Sullivan Show* from the top ratings spot for the first time, Sullivan relented and booked Elvis for three appearances. Sixty million viewers—a record-breaking 83 percent of the national television audience—watched Elvis' first appearance on the show on September 9, 1956. From then on, Elvis was a national and soon an international phenomenon, and rock'n'roll was established as the leading popular music genre of the 1950s and early 1960s until The Beatles led the "British invasion" of the U.S. music market with their own brand of rock 'n' roll-influenced music.

Music historians will argue, probably forever, whether the bands of the 1960s and beyond can be classed as rock music, as their sound was so different from that of the original rockers. But the term "rock" has endured, in the names of a plethora of musical styles, including folk rock, soft rock, glam rock, hard rock, progressive rock, indie rock, punk rock, and progressive rock. In addition to the rock label, the "live fast, die young, and make as much noise as possible" ethos of rock'n'roll lives on in today's sophisticated, commercialized music scene. Despite *Variety*'s prediction and Don McLean's (b. 1945) hit song "American Pie," the music never did die, and rock'n'roll is very much alive and kickin', although in the present day it may be in Lady Gaga's Perspex high heels.

ATOMIC DREAMS: ALEXANDER LEWYT

PREDICTION

Millenarian

Technology

Prophecy

Politics

Military

Natural Disaster

Culture

Economics

Doomsday

Main culprit: Alexander Lewyt

What was predicted: Nuclear vacuum cleaners, cars, home boilers, aircraft . . .

What actually happened: While mobile nuclear reactors were designed and tested by the U.S. and U.S.S.R. during the 1950s and '60s, these were only for military use

Nuclear-powered vacuum cleaners will probably be a reality in ten years.

Alexander Lewyt, president of Lewyt Corp., in an interview with the *New York Times* in 1955

The "Atomic Age" began a long time before the bombing of Hiroshima and Nagasaki in 1945, and it began badly. In 1898, two years after the French scientist Antoine Becquerel (1852–1908) had discovered radioactivity, Marie Curie (1867–1934) isolated a new radioactive element that she christened "radium." One of the properties of radium is that it phosphoresces—glows in the dark. Unaware of the danger that she was exposing herself to, Curie kept lumps of radium in her desk because she liked its glow. She died of cancer, most probably caused by her exposure to radiation during her scientific work. Even now her papers are kept in lead-lined cases because they retain traces of radioactivity over 70 years after her death. Today, we associate radioactivity with mortal danger, but in the 1910s and 1920s, radium was seen as a miracle substance that was added to toothpastes and patent medicines to give one that "inner glow."

Radium's phosphorescence gave rise to the element's most bizarre and ultimately most tragic use. Between 1917 and 1926, thousands of factory workers, most of them young women, were employed by the U.S. Radium Corporation to paint watch dials with "Undark," a phosphorescent paint containing radium. The girls were never warned of the lethal dangers of exposure to Undark, and in addition to their contact with it at work, they would take the paint home, and use it as nail varnish, makeup or in several cases to paint their teeth for evenings out. As a result hundreds died slow and painful deaths from bone degeneration and cancer.

FATAL
The early pioneers of atomic science, Becquerel (pictured here) and Marie Curie, were unaware of the deadly danger from exposure to radiation.

Another high-profile fatality associated with radium poisoning was that of American socialite and industrialist Eben Byers (1880–1932), who imbibed vast quantities of "Radithor," a patent medicine containing radium. After consuming 1,400 bottles of the nostrum, Byers suffered from massive bone necrosis. After his death from radium poisoning, the *Wall Steet Journal* ran with the headline: "The Radium Water Worked Fine Until His Jaw Came Off."

These two cases led to far-reaching reforms of the laws governing safety at work and food additives in the U.S., but humans unfortunately have very short memories. The second phase of the Atomic Age took place during World War Two when the U.S., Britain, and Canada collaborated to develop the atomic bomb before Nazi Germany. The Manhattan Project created uranium and plutonium fission bombs, which were dropped on Japan to end the Pacific War (1941–45). The bombings caused immediate revulsion all over the world. Robert Oppenheimer (1904–67), the American physicist who headed the Manhattan program, quoted the Hindu scripture, *Bhagavad Gita*: "Now I am become Death, the destroyer of worlds."

The Atomic Age's third phase lasted from the dropping of the A-bomb in 1945 to the Cuban Missile Crisis in 1962. It was characterized by marked contradictions about attitudes to all things nuclear. On the one hand, it was the decade that witnessed the beginnings of the Cold War (1947–91) and of the nuclear arms race after the first successful Soviet nuclear test of 1949. As the decade progressed, there was a growing realization on both sides of the ideological divide that the next world war would be fought with nuclear weapons and would result in the wiping out of the human race. At the same time, there was unbridled optimism about the potential benefits of nuclear power that would produce clean, safe, and environmentally friendly electricity that would be "too cheap to meter," and would power everything from our cars to our vacuum cleaners (see quote).

Just as the nuclear arms race between Russia and America was hotting up, with both sides working in secret on long-range nuclear bombers and intercontinental ballistic missiles (ICBMs), President Dwight D. Eisenhower (1890–1969) announced his "Atoms for Peace" campaign in a speech to the U.N. General Assembly in 1953. He said:

> The United States pledges before you—and therefore before the world—its determination to help solve the fearful atomic dilemma—to devote its entire heart and mind to find the way by which the miraculous inventiveness of man shall not be dedicated to his death, but consecrated to his life.

On cue, the first nuclear power stations went on line in the Soviet Union and the U.S. in 1954, followed a year later by Britain's first commercial reactor. Compared to the low-tech, dirty coal power stations that provided most of the world's power in the 1950s, nuclear plants must have looked like the shape of things to come, with their sleek concrete towers producing nothing more harmful than white water vapor.

NUCLEAR FAMILIES

The world was completely schizophrenic about nuclear technology: fearing an impending atomic Armageddon while at the same time contemplating nuclear home appliances, cars, and aircraft. Alex Lewyt (1908–88), president of the Lewyt Corporation, who had made his mark with a clip-on bow tie specially designed for use by undertakers, invented and marketed an innovative vacuum cleaner that did not require a bag—a bestseller in postwar America—that earned him an award from the American Society of Industrial Engineers for "leadership in the vacuum-cleaner field." Thankfully his vision of the atomic vacuum cleaner never got anywhere near the drawing board, but it was symptomatic of the wild optimism surrounding all things nuclear.

Another nuclear prophet from 1955, Robert Ferry (n.d.), who worked for the U.S. Institute of Boiler and Radiator Manufacturers, enthused:

> The basic questions of design, material and shielding, in combining a nuclear reactor with a home boiler and cooling unit, no longer are problems [...] The system would heat and cool a home, provide unlimited household hot water, and melt the snow from sidewalks and driveways. All that could be done for six years on a single charge of fissionable material costing about $300.

This idea, too, was never developed. But one product that did get as far as the design stage was the "Nucleon," a nuclear-powered concept car developed by Ford Motors in 1957–58. The sleek futuristic lines of the Nucleon, typical of the gas-guzzlers of the 1950s, complete with chrome detailing and tail fins, looks a bit like a cross between a spaceship and a pickup truck. The reactor and its shielding are carried on a long rear section, well back from the passenger compartment to give the driver extra protection. Ford's engineers predicted that a Nucleon could run 5,000 miles (8,000 km) on one atomic pile, which was designed for easy removal and replacement in a future chain of nuclear service stations. The technology in the Nucleon's reactor was not unlike that used in nuclear submarines, but on a much-reduced scale. The reactor would superheat steam that turbines would convert into kinetic and electrical energy. As added bonuses, the car would produce little noise and no harmful emissions. What stopped Ford was not any concern about radioactivity or what might happen in an accident, but simply that the reactors of the day were too big to fit into the rear of a family sedan.

Unlike the atomic automobile, the nuclear aircraft actually did get off the ground. The difference was that the interest in nuclear-powered aircraft was military and did not have to be commercially viable. In the late 1950s, both the U.S. and the Soviet Union fitted planes with small nuclear reactors. The projects in both countries got as far as test flights, powered not by the reactor itself but by conventional engines, in order to test the shielding of the reactors. The programs were abandoned when the development of long-range ICBMs made bombers redundant. At present the size and weight of a nuclear reactor makes it suitable only for very large applications, such as the engines of submarines or ships. The U.S., Russia, China, Britain, and France all operate fleets of nuclear subs, and there are also a limited number of civilian and military nuclear-powered surface vessels, including U.S. Navy aircraft carriers and Russian icebreakers.

After the Cuban missile crisis had brought the world to the brink of World War Three, and with a growing number of civilian and military nuclear accidents unsettling Western electorates and their representatives, nuclear power generation was almost abandoned in the developed world. The predictions of peak oil (see next entry) and the failure of renewables to meet the energy shortfall in the short term, have given a new lease of life to nuclear power, both fission, and the new hope for tomorrow, fusion. In a way, Lewyt was not entirely wrong when he said that the nuclear-powered vacuum would be with us within the decade, because by 1965 nuclear power plants were providing a growing share of the developed world's electricity, and hence powering its iceboxes, washing machines, boilers, and vacuum cleaners.

NAVAL POWER
Nuclear power has transformed the submarine as a military weapon, extending its range and capabilities.

PREDICTION

Millenarian

Technology

Prophecy

Politics

Military

Natural Disaster

Culture

Economics

Doomsday

HIGH AND DRY:
M. KING HUBBERT

Main culprit: M. King Hubbert

What was predicted: That crude oil production would peak in the mid-1990s and enter into an irreversible decline with serious consequences for the future of industrial civilization

What actually happened: There is disagreement as to whether peak oil has taken place, will take place sometime in the future, or will not take place at all

If the world should continue to be dependent upon the fossil fuels as its principal source of industrial energy, then we could expect a culmination in the production of coal within about 200 years. On the basis of the present estimates of the ultimate reserves of petroleum and natural gas, it appears that the culmination of world production of these products should occur within about half a century, while the culmination for petroleum and natural gas in both the United Sates and the state of Texas should occur within the next few decades.

M. King Hubbert in "Nuclear Energy and the Fossil Fuels" in 1956

The industrial revolution of the eighteenth and nineteenth centuries was built on the coal that powered its steam engines, drove its trains, and worked its factories and mills. The consumer revolution of the twentieth century depended on plentiful supplies of the cheap oil that drove its cars and was the base material for its plastic consumer goods. The affluent lifestyles that we enjoy in the twenty-first century are dependent on a mix of energy sources, including nuclear and renewables, but are still heavily reliant on fossil fuels: coal, oil, and natural gas. By their very nature, these resources are finite, as the geologist and petroleum specialist M. King Hubbert (1903–89) explained in a paper he presented at a meeting of the American Petroleum Institute in 1956:

> The fossil fuels, which include coal and lignite, oil shales, tar and asphalt, as well as petroleum and natural gas, have all had their origin from plants and animals existing upon the Earth during the last 500 million years [...] When we consider that it has taken 500 million years of geological history to accumulate the present supplies of fossil fuels, it should be clear that, although the same geological processes are still operative, the amount of new fossil fuels that is likely to be produced during the next few thousand years will be inconsequential. Therefore [...] we can assume with complete assurance that the industrial exploitation of the fossil fuels will consist in the progressive exhaustion of an initially fixed supply to which there will be no significant addition during the period of our interest.

At the time, the idea that we might one day run out of fossil fuels was a shocking theory that went against the established orthodox view that supply would always outstrip demand. In the 1950s, Hubbert's ideas were rejected, but when U.S. production peaked around 1970 as he had predicted, people began to sit up and take notice. At the same time, oil was becoming politically much more problematic. Once, most of the producing countries had been colonies or subservient allies of the major Western powers that consumed most of their production. But from the 1970s onward, producers realized that their huge reserves of oil and gas gave them the upper hand in negotiations and organized themselves into the OPEC (Organization of Petroleum Exporting Countries) cartel. As a result, the 1970s was the decade of the "oil shocks" and "oil crises."

HUBBERT'S PEAKS AND TROUGHS

Texas-born M. King Hubbert was no rabid environmentalist with a green ax to grind (Greens didn't exist back in 1956). He was an oilman through and through, who worked for Shell Oil for two decades. After retiring from the oil industry, he divided his time between academic posts at the universities of Stanford and Berkeley and geophysical work for the U.S. Geological Survey (USGS). His contribution to the science of energy is the Hubbert peak theory, with which he used to predict the lifetime of worldwide fossil-fuel reserves. The theory is based on a complex mathematical formula but is illustrated rather simply and starkly by the "Hubbert curve."

The curve is a roughly symmetrical bell-shaped distribution with a single peak. In the case of oil, it is made up of three components: (1) production to the time Hubbert made the original calculation, from the 1850s to the mid-1950s; (2) proven reserves of oil, which he thought would take us to around 1970–80; and (3) an estimate of future discoveries, which peak around 2000 (he specified 1995), and trail off to zero around 2200. Hubbert based his theory on the assumption that once oil is discovered in a specific country or region, production increases quickly, as more and more efficient extraction facilities come on stream. After the peak is reached, the rate of decline in production to exhaustion matches the earlier increase.

Environmental campaigners have enthusiastically endorsed peak oil theory in order to argue for the rapid development of renewable energy resources. Not only is our dependence on fossil fuels damaging the environment because they are the major source of greenhouse gases and therefore the main cause of global warming, but they are also fast running out. And when the supply and demand go seriously out of kilter, they predict, we will experience an economic shock so profound that it will make us look back at the current financial crisis with dewy-eyed nostalgia.

Hubbert peak theory, however, has a good number of critics, though admittedly many of them come from within the oil industry and the fossil fuel energy sector. Let us first look at the arguments relating to the total reserves of oil that exist on the planet and that can be physically exploited. While Hubbert's calculations might hold true for conventional oil supplies, Leonardo Maugeri (b. 1964), vice president of the Italian energy company ENI, argues that the next century will not be one of energy shortages and power cuts in the developed world, but that it will "overflow with petroleum." In "The Crude Truth About Oil Reserves" (*Wall Street Journal*, November 4, 2009), he gives three reasons why Hubbert was wrong.

First, although he agrees with Hubbert that the world's oil resources are finite, he questions the USGS' estimates of how much is left and what we should include in the reserves. Stocks of conventional oil are estimated at seven to eight trillion barrels (we consume about 30 billion barrels annually), and two trillion of these are deemed to be recoverable with current technology. However, Maugeri goes on to point out that there is at least the same amount of "unconventional oils"—ultra-heavy oils, tar sands, and shale oils—much of which are in the politically stable Canada and, even better, in the Midwest. Second, Maugeri reminds us that technology does not stand still, and our ability to recover oil from mature existing fields is improving:

> Today, we recover on average less than 35% of the oil contained in known fields, up from 20% in 1980. Even the most mature oil country, the United States, still holds huge volumes of unexploited oil underground. Although the country's proven oil reserves are now only 29 billion barrels, the National Petroleum Council (NPC) estimates that 1.124 trillion barrels are still left underground, of which 374 billion would be recoverable with current technologies.

Naturally, he admits, new, more efficient recovery technologies and the extraction of oil from unconventional sources do not come cheap. But with the steady increase in the price of oil, he claims that these deposits might soon become commercially attractive—not to mention the fact that much of it is in the U.S.' backyard.

Third, Maugeri explains that much of the world's surface remains unexplored: "Oil exploration has been mainly a North American phenomenon, with the U.S. and Canada accounting for around 90 percent of all oil-exploration wells ever drilled on the planet." In contrast, the world's largest producer, Saudi Arabia, accounts for

CURVE BALL
Environmentalists point to Hubbert's correct prediction of peak production in the U.S. as an indication that world production has also peaked.

only 300 exploration wells, and the figure drops even lower for other major producers such as Iraq, Iran, and Russia. Additionally there are sizeable undersea resources that are largely unexplored and untapped. Maugeri is undoubtedly an oil optimist, but he is not alone. Other researchers, including the Cambridge Energy Research Associates and the Association for the Study of Peak Oil and Gas, delay peak oil to some point in the future as technology and exploration make up for the shortfall in supply. Mention undersea resources and Canadian tar sands and the environmentalist lobby will immediately scream ecological vandalism. Look at the Deepwater Horizon oil spill, they say. And extracting oil from unconventional sources produces far more CO_2 and damage to the environment than current oil production techniques.

Hubbert himself foresaw another solution to the oil depletion predicted by his theory. Taking the very long view of 10,000 years, 5,000 years back to the earliest civilizations to 5,000 in the future, he claimed that, "The discovery, exploitation, and exhaustion of the fossil fuels will be seen to be but an ephemeral event in the span of recorded history." Speaking at the most optimistic period of the Atomic Age (see previous entry), he predicted a ten percent annual increase in nuclear energy in the U.S. that would seamlessly replace the country's dependence on fossil fuels. He concluded rather optimistically: "Provided mankind [...] does not destroy itself with nuclear weapons, and provided the world population can somehow be brought under control, then we may at last have found an energy supply adequate for our needs for at least the next few centuries of the 'foreseeable future.'"

FLY ME TO THE MOON: LEE DE FOREST

Main culprit: Lee De Forest

What was predicted: That man would never land on the Moon

What actually happened: The U.S. put a man on the Moon in 1969

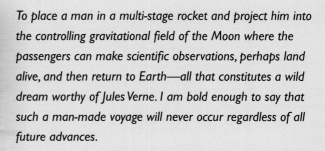

To place a man in a multi-stage rocket and project him into the controlling gravitational field of the Moon where the passengers can make scientific observations, perhaps land alive, and then return to Earth—all that constitutes a wild dream worthy of Jules Verne. I am bold enough to say that such a man-made voyage will never occur regardless of all future advances.

Lee de Forest in a *New York Times* interview, 1957

While many modern technologies have earlier antecedents, powered, heavier-than-air flight is historically relatively recent. The first manned ascent in a hot-air balloon in Europe dates back to the late eighteenth century (the Chinese, as usual, probably got there a lot earlier), and we had to wait more than 100 years until the turn of the twentieth for the Wright brothers to get airborne in a heavier-than-air flying machine. Even then, the altitudes they reached in their early flights could be measured in feet rather than miles, so the idea that man could ever reach space, let alone our closest celestial body, the Moon, which is 238,857 miles away (384,403 km), must have seemed an absurd pipe dream to scientists well into the twentieth century. In 1926 Professor Alexander Bickerton (1842–1929) of Canterbury College, Christchurch, New Zealand, expressed the accepted scientific wisdom of the day when he explained:

> This foolish idea of shooting at the Moon is an example of the absurd length to which vicious specialization will carry scientists working in thought-tight compartments. Let us critically examine the proposal. For a projectile entirely to escape the gravitation of Earth, it needs a velocity of seven miles a second. The thermal energy of a gram at this speed is 15,180 calories [...] The energy of our most violent explosive—nitroglycerine—is less than 1,500 calories per gram. Consequently, even had the explosive nothing to carry, it has only one-tenth of the energy necessary to escape the Earth.

The absence of a workable flight technology and a total ignorance of what might await them beyond the Earth's atmosphere, however, have not been a bar to history's inspired space pioneers. The first would-be astronaut, and probably the wackiest in the history of space exploration, was a Ming Dynasty (1368–1644) Chinese scholar official called Wan Hoo (d. c. 1500), who devised a scheme to travel to the Moon by strapping gunpowder rockets to a wicker chair. The consequences of the rocket-chair's "launch" were predictably dramatic, but suffice it to say that Wan Hoo was "blown away" by the experience.

The Chinese, inventors of gunpowder, gave the world the first functioning rockets, which they used as weapons of war, as well as more peacefully

BLAST OFF
Apollo 11, carrying Buzz Aldrin and Neil Armstrong, blasts off from Cape Canaveral, to take the first men to the surface of the Moon.

for fireworks displays. The Mongols, who had conquered China and were planning to add Western Europe to their empire, brought gunpowder technology westward. The Arabs were the first to adopt it and they in turn passed it on to the Europeans. The Mongols failed and left, leaving the rockets behind. Gunpowder rockets developed more slowly than artillery and firearms, but by the early nineteenth century they were part of the arsenal of the major powers. In the Battle of Baltimore (1814) during the War of 1812 (1812–15) between Britain and the U.S., the British use of rockets inspired the phrase "the rockets' red glare" in the "Star-Spangled Banner."

The theory and technology of modern rocketry had all been worked out by the early twentieth century but were only fully realized with the liquid-fueled V2 rockets built by Adolf Hitler's Third Reich in an attempt to avoid defeat at the hands of the Allies in World War Two. Hitler was defeated despite his rockets, and it was the Russians and Americans who benefited from Nazi research to develop their long-range ballistic missiles and first space shots. The V2 is the first manmade object to reach space. A USAF V2 left the atmosphere on a parabolic trajectory but did not orbit Earth. That prize was won by the Soviet Union with the Sputnik 1 satellite in 1957—an achievement followed four years later by the first manned orbit of Earth by Soviet cosmonaut Yuri Gagarin (1934–68) in Vostok 1. With the Soviet Union doing all the running in the space race, the U.S. administration was determined that it would get the next major prize first. In a speech to Congress in May 1961, President John F. Kennedy (1917–63) announced:

> I believe that this nation should commit itself to achieving the goal, before this decade is out, of landing a man on the Moon and returning him safely to the Earth. No single space project in this period will be more impressive to mankind, or more important in the long-range exploration of space; and none will be so difficult or expensive to accomplish.

There were probably many, like inventor and radio pioneer Lee De Forest (1873–1961), who found the whole idea of getting a man to the Moon and back a complete absurdity worthy of the novels of French sci-fi writer Jules Verne (1828–1905) (see quote). As with robots (pp. 188–93), writers and filmmakers had got to the Moon much earlier

"A WILD DREAM WORTHY OF JULES VERNE"

than the NASA astronauts. Verne's *De la Terre à la Lune* (*From the Earth to the Moon*), written in 1865, 104 years before the first Apollo Moon landing, is uncannily prescient in its description of the lunar space shot. The spacecraft is manned by three astronauts, leaves Earth from Florida, is catapulted around the Moon by its gravity, and then returns to make a splash landing in the ocean where it is picked up by a U.S. warship — the only major difference being that Verne's spacecraft is launched, not on a multi-stage rocket, but fired from a giant cannon, and like Apollo 8, in December 1968, it orbits the Moon without making a landing.

It was left to another visionary science-fiction writer, H. G. Wells (1866–1946), to imagine the first Moon landing in his novel *First Men in the Moon* (1901). Wells' Moon has an atmosphere, a flora and fauna, and the "Selenite" civilization of intelligent insects. The Moon that Neil Armstrong (b. 1930) and his Apollo 11 crew member Buzz Aldrin (b. 1930) stepped onto was to prove quite different — a barren lump of inert rock without an atmosphere.

We have met Lee De Forest in an earlier entry ridiculing the commercial viability of television in 1926. But in that prediction, he was understandably protecting his own position as a pioneer of radio broadcasting. De Forest was not a stupid man, nor was he shortsighted in scientific matters; his discovery of the vacuum tube revolutionized electronics. But he was a man of the nineteenth-century scientific revolution who failed to grasp the full implications of the technologies of the twentieth, and how they would turn Jules Verne's fantasy into the first manned expedition to the Moon.

GREAT LEAP BACKWARD: MAO ZEDONG

Main culprit: Mao Zedong

What was predicted: That China would equal Britain's steel output by 1965

What actually happened: After initial gains, the Chinese economy stalled and agricultural production slumped, causing a famine that killed between 20 and 40 million people

With eleven million tons of steel next year, and seventeen million the year after, the world will be shaken. If we can reach forty million tons in five years, we may possibly catch up with Great Britain in seven years.

Mao Zedong in a speech to the Communist Party congress in 1958

© Time & Life Pictures | Getty Images

In two previous entries we looked at predictions about the world's first communist state, the U.S.S.R., and its ideology, Marxism-Leninism. In this entry, we shall turn to the next major power to join the communist fold in the post-World War Two period, China, and the predictions made about its future by its leader for almost three decades, Mao Zedong (1893–1976). For millennia, Chinese civilization led the world in technological and cultural attainments, but by the early twentieth century, the empire was bankrupted intellectually, economically, and politically, and under siege by the Western powers and Japan. In 1912, five years before the Russian Czar was to face the same fate, the last Qing emperor was forced to abdicate, and China became a republic.

China's democratic experiment was a short-lived and unmitigated failure. The country's second president, Yuan Shikai (1859–1916), abolished China's fledgling democratic assemblies and followed the route taken by many strong leaders and would-be reformers throughout Chinese history by declaring himself emperor in 1915. But the Chinese had had enough of emperors and dynasties; Yuan was quickly deposed and died in 1916. Leaderless, China sank into anarchy, becoming what we would now call a "failed state," with an ineffectual central government, which left large areas of the country under the rule of independent warlords or occupied by foreign powers.

Two political movements, the Chinese Communist Party (CCP) that looked to the newly founded Soviet Union for inspiration and support, and the rightwing Kuomintang (Nationalist Party, or KMT), slugged it out for dominance. The KMT came out on top during the period running up to the Japanese invasion of China in 1937. During the war against Japan, which lasted until 1945, the CCP and KMT agreed an uneasy truce to fight the invader. However, the civil war resumed in 1945 and was ultimately won by the CCP, led by Mao Zedong, in 1949.

THE COMMUNIST EMPEROR

The vast country that Mao now ruled was predominantly agricultural, with a few industrial urban areas that had latterly been under foreign control. Historically, Chinese society had resembled a gigantic pyramid, with the emperor and court at its apex above a class of landowning officials, which were both supported by the peasantry that accounted for 90 percent of the population. The emperor and court had been removed in 1912, but now Mao was going to replace it with the Central Committee of the CCP and its bureaucracy, with himself at its head. For ideological reasons, Mao never aspired to the imperial throne, but he had the powers and attributes of a Chinese sovereign in all but name. In life and later in death, he was revered as much as any divine Son of Heaven.

It is unlikely that many among China's huge rural population were communists at this stage. But after a century of social disintegration, civil war, and foreign invasion, they were happy to support any government that promised them stability, security, and most important of all, land reform. The majority of China's peasants were tenants of the old feudal ruling class, who were the backbone of the imperial and republican civil service. China had an urban proletariat, but one that was even smaller than Russia's in 1917. According to Marx's original theory of communism, Russia and China would need to be transformed socially and economically before they would be ready for true socialism. However, neither Russia nor China had the time to engage in gradual change.

Immediately after the revolution of 1917, the Soviet Union had been attacked by foreign powers supporting the forces of counter-revolution. The Soviet Union survived, but after Lenin's death the struggle for power within the Soviet hierarchy had one clear winner, Joseph Stalin (1878–1953), who assumed full power in 1927, and immediately set about liquidating his enemies and rivals. Stalin was not unlike Mao: He was a man of humble origins who distrusted intellectuals. In order to survive and compete with the major European powers, Stalin realized that the Soviet Union had to modernize its industry and agriculture. Between 1927 and 1939, he applied his own interpretation of socialist principles to achieve this aim. He established a command economy with five-year plans that controlled every aspect of industrial production and distribution. The power no longer rested in the proletariat and the Soviets but in the state and its bureaucrats.

Stalin succeeded in modernizing Russian industry, and his success enabled the Soviet Union to survive and repel the German invasion during World War Two. Where he failed spectacularly was in his

© Zhang Zhenshi | Creative Commons

IDEOLOGUE
Mao put ideology before scientific knowledge and common sense and so triggered a massive crisis in the Chinese economy.

reform of agriculture. He forced through a policy of collectivization of all agricultural land, which, coupled with the pseudo-scientific theories of the geneticist Trofim Lysenko (1898–1976), led to a famine that killed between six and eight million people between 1932 and 1933. Stalin's propaganda machine kept the disaster a secret so well that its full extent was not revealed until the liberalization of the 1980s. By the late 1940s, Russia had not only defeated Germany and occupied half of Europe, but she also seemed about to topple the U.S. from its position as the world's leading superpower.

Stalin extended every assistance to his eastern neighbor, providing funds, engineers, and technology transfers to China. While Stalin was alive, Mao was firmly wedded to Stalin's version of communism and wanted to emulate his apparently shining example in modernizing China's industry and agriculture. In the process, he unwittingly repeated Stalin's mistakes, but on a much bigger scale. Starting in 1949, Mao inaugurated the first five-year plan, but his task was far greater than Stalin's. European Russia in the 1910s and '20s was more developed than any region of China in the late 1940s, and after the defeat of Hitler, Stalin had been able to strip Eastern Europe of everything that could be loaded onto trucks and taken back to Russia to aid its reconstruction and development. China, on the other hand, had its huge population and natural resources but little else. What little industrial, scientific, and commercial expertise there was had been in the hands of foreigners or of the discredited ruling class.

LEAP INTO THE DARK Dissatisfied with the progress the Chinese economy was making, and gradually drifting away from his alliance with the post-Stalinist Soviet Union, Mao decided on a far-reaching reform policy, which he called the "Great Leap Forward." The five-year plan that would run from 1958 to 1963 would see China's industrial production catch up with the world's developed economies. He focused on two areas: increasing the yields of Chinese agriculture and China's steel production, which he saw as the key to the country's industrial development. His boast to the CCP congress in 1958 was that China would equal Britain's steel production by 1965. Although British steel production is now dwarfed by that of China, in 1958 the UK still ranked among the leading industrial economies in the world. Mao's pledge was little more than a dream, but one that would soon turn into a nightmare for the Chinese people.

Mao imitated Stalin in his modernization of agriculture. He embarked on a program of collectivization, taking land away from the peasants who had so recently acquired it and creating vast collective farms consisting of thousands of households. He also introduced new planting techniques inspired by Lysenko's bogus theories that had caused so much damage in the Soviet Union. Lacking the industrial infrastructure to achieve his massive increase in steel production, he promoted the building of thousands of backyard furnaces all over the country that would turn scrap metal into steel. For a brief moment it seemed that the plan was working. Favorable weather in 1958 produced a bumper harvest and the peasants dutifully melted pots and pans and any other scrap they could find to increase China's steel production. Unfortunately, what they produced was low-grade and largely useless pig iron, and the lack of transport infrastructure meant that whatever was produced could not be taken to the cities.

Collectivization and new agricultural techniques, combined with poor weather, floods, and drought in 1959 and 1960, and the lack of manpower that had been diverted to other projects, meant that agricultural production slumped. Despite growing food shortages that were fast turning to famine, Mao pursued his genocidal policies, exporting grain to the cities while the peasants starved. Just like in Stalinist Russia during the 1930s, the scale of the catastrophe was kept secret until after Mao's death in 1976. Estimates of the death toll from starvation for the years 1959 to 1961, when the Great Leap Forward was consigned to the trashcan of history, range from 20 to 40 million souls.

PREDICTION

Millenarian

Technology

Prophecy

Politics

Military

Natural Disaster

Culture

Economics

Doomsday

NOWHERE MAN: DICK ROWE

Main culprit: Dick Rowe

What was predicted: That groups and guitar music were on their way out, and that The Beatles would go nowhere

What actually happened: The Beatles are arguably the biggest band of all time and Decca no longer exists

We don't like their sound, and guitar music is on the way out.

Decca Records' Dick Rowe's comment to The Beatles' manager, when he rejected them after their audition

We return to the arenas of culture and popular music for this entry on the musical style that dethroned rock'n'roll, and the band that above all others embodies the pop music of the 1960s, The Beatles. Every reader will have his or her memories of The Beatles. Those over 50 will remember The Beatles as a band—their early hits, movies, and sell-out tours. Younger readers might remember their solo careers and the murder of John Lennon (1940–80) in New York.

In the modern era, a musical generation, it seems, lasts about ten years. A decade after Elvis (1935–77) had taken the U.S. by storm, it was the turn of The Beatles. Although they used the same combo of drums, and electric and acoustic guitars, they sounded very different from the rock'n'rollers, and they also looked very different. Where the rockers favored slick-back hair, jeans, T-shirts, and leather jackets, The Beatles wore their hair in their trademark "mop tops"—not quite the long hair they would sport in the late 1960s, but long enough to shock the conservative American press and public. They wore suits, white shirts, and pencil ties, but somehow their smart clothes and grooming made them look even more subversive than the self-consciously rebellious rockers.

The Beatles did not spring into existence fully formed but had a long gestation that began when a 17-year-old John Lennon founded a skiffle-cum-rock'n'roll band call The Quarrymen in his native Liverpool in 1957. The 14-year-old Paul McCartney (b. 1942) joined the band later that year, and George Harrison (1943–2001) in 1958. After high school Lennon went to college to study art, where he met another guitarist Stuart Sutcliffe (1940–62), who joined the trio in 1960. It is Sutcliffe who is credited with coming up with the name "The Beatles," as a tribute to Buddy Holly's (1936–59) band, The Crickets. The band then finally acquired a permanent drummer, Pete Best (b. 1941).

The Beatles' first break came when they were booked to become the resident band at a music club in Hamburg (then in West Germany). Although they were well received by their American and German audiences, their first stint went badly for legal reasons. Harrison, who was underage, was deported, soon to be followed by Best and McCartney for arson, after they had set fire to a condom in their hotel room. However, the band was back in Hamburg the following year, while also developing a following in their hometown of Liverpool, where they performed in the now famous Cavern Club. It was in the Cavern that they met their future manager, music shop proprietor and music writer Brian Epstein (1934–67), who, realizing the potential of the band, began to remake their image in preparation for launching their recording careers.

THE AUDITION There now occurs one of the strangest episodes in pop music history, and surely one that had Decca executives waking up in the middle of the night in a cold sweat for decades. In 1961 Epstein had been visiting the A&R departments of several of the major record companies in London with little success when he hit lucky with Decca, who agreed to give The Beatles an audition in their north London recording studio on New Year's Day, 1962. By that time, Sutcliffe had decided to leave the band to resume his art studies in Germany in 1961, so the line up was Lennon, McCartney, Harrison, and Best.

Decca was no fly-by-night operation. Founded in the UK in 1929, it had set up a successful U.S. subsidiary (sold off in 1939), and for a time was the second largest record company in the UK. In the late 1950s, it marketed and released Elvis' hits in the UK. The producer for the audition, Tony Meehan (1943–2005), was himself a successful musician who had played the drums for the British band The Shadows. The Beatles drove down from Liverpool on New Year's Eve, but their driver lost his way and the band arrived in London late at night, exhausted after a ten-hour drive. They were probably not in the best physical and mental shape when they showed up for the audition at Decca's north London studio the following day.

Epstein chose the 15 tracks that The Beatles performed and recorded, which featured only three Lennon and McCartney originals: "Like Dreamers Do," "Hello Little Girl," and "Love of the Loved," and a dozen covers, including Chuck Berry's (b. 1926) "Memphis, Tennessee," Phil Spector's (b. 1939) "To Know Her Is to Love Her," and Buddy Holly's (1936–59) "Crying, Waiting, Hoping." It might not have been the best playlist to showcase the band's original sound. Meehan completed the demo and sent it to his boss Dick Rowe (1921–86). At a meeting with Epstein, Rowe said the now infamous line: "We don't like their sound, and guitar music is on the way out, Mr. Epstein."

The comment about guitar music is a strange one, as Rowe immediately decided to sign another pop guitar band, The Tremeloes, instead of The Beatles. In fairness to Decca, it is possible that the audition did not show the band in the best light. They were tired, and the material that Epstein chose might not have been the best to showcase their talents. We must also remember that the band was not yet the slick, disciplined, and well-groomed performers that they became under Epstein's tutelage. The manager was not disheartened by Decca's rejection and he continued his search for a record deal. He next approached the UK's leading label EMI, but they, too, initially rejected the band. It was only after George Martin (b. 1926), a producer with the EMI subsidiary Parlaphone, heard The Beatles' Decca demos, that the band got its first recording contract. The Decca audition, it turned out, had not been a complete failure.

Martin produced The Beatles' first recording session in June 1962. It was he who suggested that the band drop Best and replace him with a session drummer (one was used on one track), but for the other tracks Best was replaced by Ringo Starr (b. 1940), who completed The Beatles' final lineup. The band released their first album, *Please Please Me*, which featured their chart-topping hit "Love Me Do," and was recorded under Martin's supervision at the now legendary Abbey Road Studios in St John's Wood, London, in three live sessions on a

MOP TOPS
The Beatles, with their trademark suits and mop top haircuts, arrive to take America by storm, creating as much of a stir as Elvis did at the start of his career.

single day. The album topped the charts for 30 weeks, before being replaced by the band's second album, *With the Beatles*, released in 1963. In the same year, they issued one of their most iconic early tracks, "She Loves You," which was the first single to sell over one million copies, and held the record for bestselling single until overtaken by a later McCartney hit in 1978. Having triumphed in the British and European markets, the Beatles were ready to take on America. Until then traffic had been one way from the U.S. to the UK, spearheaded by the likes of Presley and other rock and rollers. Capitol Records released "I Want to Hold Your Hand" in late 1963, and the song's strong performance in the U.S. charts boded well for the band's U.S. tour, scheduled to begin in

New York in February 1964. Despite press criticism of their music and iconic "mop top" haircuts, the band received a rapturous, sometimes riotous, welcome from American fans wherever they performed. They appeared twice on *The Ed Sullivan Show*, garnering an unprecedented audience of 74 million viewers. From then on until The Beatles split in 1970, their releases consistently topped the album and singles charts on both sides of the Atlantic.

The Beatles' conquest of America not only heralded the "British invasion" of the American music market during the 1960s, it also confirmed The Beatles as one of the most successful rock bands of all time. Dick Rowe and Decca certainly had a lot of time to reflect on what must surely be the biggest goof in musical history. They managed to redeem themselves, however, when, in 1963, they signed an up-and-coming band called The Rolling Stones. Rowe went on to have a highly successful career in the music industry, signing, in addition to the Stones, Van Morrison, Tom Jones, The Animals, and The Moody Blues.

MAD: NIKITA KHRUSHCHEV AND JOHN F. KENNEDY

PREDICTION

Millenarian

Technology

Prophecy

Politics

Military

Natural Disaster

Culture

Economics

Doomsday

Main culprits: Nikita Khrushchev and John F. Kennedy

What was predicted: The destruction of the planet in a nuclear conflict

What actually happened: World War Three was almost declared during the Cuban Missile Crisis of October 1962, but the U.S. and Soviet Union reached a secret deal to defuse the crisis

Mr. President, we are rapidly approaching a moment of truth both for ourselves as human beings and for the life of our nation. Now, truth is not always a pleasant thing. But it is necessary now to make a choice, to choose between two admittedly regrettable, but nevertheless "distinguishable," postwar environments: one where you got twenty million people killed, and the other where you got a hundred and fifty million people killed.

General Buck Turgidson in the black comedy
***Dr. Strangelove* (1964)**

We have seen two predictions concerning the Atomic Age: the first about the splitting of the atom and the second about the possible, if rather improbable, practical applications of nuclear power. We now come to our third and final Atomic Age prediction: about nuclear Armageddon, World War Three. With the dissolution of the Soviet Union and end of the Cold War in Europe in 1991, and the liberalization of the Chinese economy in the post-Mao (1893–1976) period, the risk of nuclear war between the superpowers has thankfully receded.

We now fear more localized nuclear conflicts in the Middle East or the Indian subcontinent, or the acquisition by terrorists of nuclear material to make a "dirty bomb." The results of localized nuclear war or terrorism, while catastrophic, would not match the extinction of all life on Earth that faced humanity from the 1950s through to the late 1980s. Those four decades were the era of MAD (mutually assured destruction), when Armageddon was only the flick of a switch away. According to most historians, the moment the U.S. came closest to all-out nuclear war with the Soviet Union was in October 1962 during the Cuban Missile Crisis.

POKER FACE
President Kennedy bluffs Soviet foreign minister Gromyko by not admitting that he knew of the Russian missile buildup in Cuba.

The quote at the head of the entry is entirely fictional, as it is part of the dialog between General Buck Turgidson (George C. Scott; 1927–99) and President Merkin Muffley (Peter Sellers; 1925–80) in Stanley Kubrick's (1928–99) chilling black comedy *Dr. Strangelove or: How I Learned to Stop Worrying and Love the Bomb*, which was due to be released in November 1963, a year after the Cuban Missile Crisis, but was delayed by three months by the assassination of John F. Kennedy (1917–63). Made at the height of the Cold War, the film deals with the repercussions of a nuclear bomber attack on the Soviet Union launched by an insane U.S. Air Force general.

While President Muffley and General Turgidson go through various scenarios if nuclear war were started accidentally, the Russian premier reveals the existence of a "Doomsday Machine" that will wipe out all life on Earth if a nuclear attack is launched by either side. At the end of the movie, the president succeeds in recalling the bombers, except for one, which drops its payload on its Soviet target, triggering the Doomsday device. While the plot of *Dr. Strangelove*, one hopes, was wholly fictional, the tenor of the discussions between the president and his senior military adviser must have reflected real conversations during the MAD era between U.S. presidents and Soviet premiers and their military advisers—the lunatic calculations of what might constitute "acceptable losses" on both sides or the chances of a "preemptive strike" disabling the enemy's ability to respond in kind. What scientists and tacticians soon realized, however, was that the detonation of enough nuclear weapons would destroy the whole planet through poisonous nuclear fallout and/or the triggering of a nuclear winter from the debris thrown up into the atmosphere. Nuclear war was always going to be a lose-lose scenario, whichever side started it.

DOWN HAVANA WAY

The Cold War, simmering since 1947, broke out in June 1948 with the year-long Soviet Blockade of Berlin. Although the U.S. and the Soviet Union had been allies during World War Two, their ideological differences were so great that many believed that they were bound to go to war sooner rather than later. What prevented them was the development of nuclear weapons—at first, because only the Americans had the bomb, and later because they both had the bomb and a conflict would have been fatal to both sides. The Americans developed the A-bomb in 1945, and the Russians, through a combination of homegrown talent, spying, and German World War Two research, successfully detonated their own bomb in 1949. The French and British joined the nuclear party a few years later.

However, until the late 1950s, what both sides lacked—Moscow and Leningrad being a long way from Washington and New York—were long-range delivery systems that could take the bombs to their desired targets. Both sides had short- and medium-range ballistic missiles capable of delivering nuclear warheads, thanks to German research with V2 rockets, and medium-range bombers, but long-range intercontinental ballistic missiles (ICBMs) were only just coming on stream. The U.S. Air Force came up with a solution in 1961, by deploying intermediate range ballistic missiles (IRBMs) in southern Italy and Turkey. The Russians were naturally displeased at having U.S. nukes on their metaphorical doorstep, and in 1962 the then Soviet premier Nikita

Khrushchev (1894–1971) cooked up a scheme with his new best friend Fidel Castro (b. 1926) to get his own back on Uncle Sam.

After the Bay of Pigs fiasco of April 1961, when a force of Cuban exiles backed by the U.S. military had tried and failed to invade Cuba and overthrow Castro, the Cuban leadership, fearing another imminent U.S. invasion, was only too pleased to cooperate with the Soviet plan. Khrushchev dispatched military specialists to Cuba in the guise of agricultural specialists. By the summer, the Russians were building nine missile sites, six for medium-range R-12 missiles, with a range of 1,200 miles (2,000 km), and three for R-14 IRBMs with a range of 2,800 miles (4,500 km), putting most of continental U.S. within range of the Soviet missiles. Also included in the deal was a squadron of Ilyushin Il-28 bombers, which would have completed the Soviet's Cuban nuclear arsenal. Despite the highest levels of secrecy in Russia and Cuba, and constant public denials by Khrushchev that he had any plans to arm his Cuban allies, the Americans finally discovered the scheme in August, but it was only in October that a U2 spy plane got photographic confirmation of the construction of IRBM launch sites. The first consignments of R-12 missiles arrived on the island in September.

Khrushchev believed that Kennedy was too young, inexperienced, and too hesitant after the Bay of Pigs to intervene strongly, and that he would be forced to accept the missile deployment as a *fait accompli*. Kennedy was not about to stand down, however. The military strongly advised an invasion of Cuba, but Kennedy bided his time, preferring a blockade of Cuba backed by the U.S.' Latin-American allies. When, on October 26, Khrushchev complained that this was an act of aggression, tantamount to a declaration of war, U.S. forces went to DEFCOM 2, putting the U.S.' bomber and missile forces on full alert. With the Russians refusing to back down, an invasion appeared increasingly likely, along with a nuclear strike on the Soviet Union in case she decided on retaliatory military action in Europe.

Just as the U.S. and Soviet military were planning a nuclear endgame, secret negotiations were taking place between Kennedy and Khrushchev through various intermediaries, including the president's younger brother Robert Kennedy (1925–68) and U.N. Secretary General U.

Thant (1909–74). On October 28 a deal was brokered in which the Soviets agreed to dismantle their missile bases in Cuba in exchange for the removal of the IRBMs in Italy and Turkey, and a promise that the U.S. would not invade Cuba. The world was saved, but it was a very close thing. For 14 days, the very survival of the human race had been put into question.

MAD brought a new perspective to human history. Although, as we have seen, supernatural doomsdays have been predicted since civilization began, for the first time it became a very real possibility—and not at the hands of a spiteful god but of something infinitely worse—a human being. Until the Atomic Age, humans were always at the mercy of forces greater than themselves but, after Hiroshima, they had become, like the gods, "the destroyer of worlds."

HESITANT
Soviet premier Khrushchev believed that Kennedy's youth and inexperience would lead to him backing down and accepting the Soviet missile deployment.

PREDICTION

Millenarian

Technology

Prophecy

Politics

Military

Natural Disaster

Culture

Economics

Doomsday

METAL MICKEY: MEREDITH THRING

Main culprit: Meredith Thring

What was predicted: Domestic robots by 1984

What actually happened: The household robot still seems to be many years away

We could have a robot that will completely eliminate all routine operations around the house and remove the drudgery for humans.

**Meredith Thring in "A Robot in the House"
in N. Calder's The World in 1984 (1964)**

We return to technology for an entry on the household robot, an invention that, unlike the telephone, radio, and the automobile, has yet to become a reality despite more than half a century of predictions to the contrary. The idea of mechanical servants made in the image of humans or animals begins with ancient Greek mythology. The god Hephaestus (Vulcan to the Romans) had metal handmaidens who helped him with his work. Ancient myths are full of statues that come to life, not necessarily as domestic helpers but often as monsters that attack the hero. Robot-like creatures, designed to be the servants of humans, exist in many cultures. In the Jewish tradition, for example, there is a story of artificial humanoids, the golems, which, while not machines in the conventional sense of a mechanism made of metal with moving parts, broadly conform to our idea of robots.

A common theme that runs through these narratives, however, is that far from being the servants of humanity, they are often made by the gods or men to be its implacable foes. This is an idea that has been picked up in science fiction with a number of common plot variations: The robot that becomes self-aware and decides that the world would be better run by machines, like the artificial intelligences in the *Matrix* and *Terminator* movies; the robot that takes over to save humans from themselves, like the superbrain in *I, Robot* (2004); and the robot that blows a fuse and starts killing people, like the on-board computer HAL in *2001, A Space Odyssey* (1968). Our ambiguous relationship with humanoid robots, or "androids," was first dramatized in Karel Capek's (1890–1938) play *R.U.R.* (*Rossum's Universal Robots*). Capek is also credited as the inventor of the word "robot," and is perhaps best described in Isaac Asimov's (1920–99) short-story collection, *I, Robot* (1950), and Philip K. Dick's (1928–82) novel *Do Androids Dream of Electric Sheep* (1968), better known to moviegoers as *Blade Runner* (1982).

I, ROBOT
Asimov's short-story collection dramatizes the ethical issues that are likely to arise as we develop ever more human-like robots.

What these authors, and many scientists, including Meredith Thring (1915–2006), professor of mechanical engineering at Queen Mary College, University of London (see quote), took completely for granted was that humanoid robots (but not necessarily exact artificial copies like Dick's "replicants") would be a reality within a few years or decades at most. Artificial Intelligence (AI) pioneer, Professor Marvin Minsky (b. 1927) of the Massachusetts Institute of Technology, who in 1967 predicted that all the problems connected with AI would be solved within a few years making robots a reality, has since revised his opinion. Analyzing the predictions about robots, he noticed an inverse ratio between the date of the prediction and its supposed realization: "In the fifties, it was predicted that in five years robots would be everywhere. In the sixties, it was predicted that in ten years robots would be everywhere. In the seventies, it was predicted that in 20 years robots would be everywhere. In the eighties, it was predicted that in 40 years robots would be everywhere."

FROM AUTOMATA TO ACTROIDS

Undaunted by the difficulty of the task, inventors and scientists have been trying to build robots since Antiquity. The Greek inventor Hero of Alexandria (c. 10–70 CE) is credited with the creation of the first automata—comparatively simple mechanisms powered by water, several of which were in the shape of human beings. Doll-like automata from the Arab world and Japan could carry out simple tasks such as writing, pouring cups of tea, and playing musical instruments. Although these devices performed autonomous actions by following simple programming, they were not robots in the true sense of the word because they were not able to interact with their environment or with humans.

Until the twentieth century, technology lagged far behind the imagination of writers such as Frank Baum (1856–1919), who invented Tik Tok, the mechanical man in the Oz books, and filmmakers such as Fritz Lang (1890–1976), who portrayed an evil android robot in his silent science-fiction classic *Metropolis* (1927). But in 1937, a team from Westinghouse finally managed to approximate the robots of science fiction with their seven-foot (2 m), 265-pound (120 kg) metal robot nicknamed Elektro. Readers with Internet access can see a video of Elektro performing at the 1939 New York World's Fair on YouTube.

In the video, Elektro towers rather ominously over the human presenter who introduces it to the public. It walks and moves its metal body, rather slowly and clumsily, by using mechanical gears and electric motors encased in its aluminum skin. It could "see" the colors red and green using its photoelectric "eyes" and was equipped with primitive sound-recognition technology that allowed it to respond to voice commands transmitted by telephone. It even had a vocabulary of 700 words recorded on 78-rpm disks and played back on a built-in gramophone. Its "brain," Elektro explains on the video, was like an old-style telephone switchboard, with wires and 48 relays.

Looking at Elektro, you begin to understand the range of problems that aspiring robot designers will have to solve to create a functional domestic robot. The first is the question of scale. Although Elektro's abilities were very limited, it was still outsized. Not only was there the issue of the psychological unease caused by a seven-foot robot not unlike the B-movie death-dealing machine in *The Day the Earth Stood Still* (1951), but there was also the practicality of it functioning within an ordinary human-scaled domestic interior. With miniaturization and new materials, size and weight are now no longer an issue.

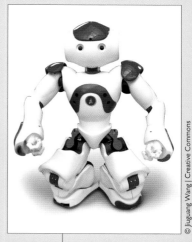

The Honda Corporation's ASIMO robot, first released in 2002, is an unthreatening 4 ft 3 in (1.3 m) tall, and weighs a manageable 120 lb (54kg). Looking like a child-sized astronaut, ASIMO is remarkably agile with articulated arms, legs, and hands that can mimic many human movements. It can walk at a top speed of 1.6 mph (2.7 km/h) and run at a respectable 3.75 mph (6 km/h). However, a series of YouTube videos showing ASIMO falling off a staircase at a public demonstration in Japan reveal why full bipedal locomotion, which we take completely for granted, remains one of the greatest robotic challenges. Walking doesn't just involve the leg muscles but dozens of postural muscles in the rest of the body, as well as a complex feedback system that constantly monitors our balance, the evenness of the ground, and a dozen other factors, including the footwear we're wearing, what we may be carrying, and any obstacles in our way. Walking, running, and going up and down stairs are incredibly complex tasks that our bodies carry out completely automatically. For a robot they require an enormous amount of processing power, and hundreds of moving parts. A robot has to think about walking all the time, otherwise it will just fall over.

If walking is a difficult task for a robot, imagine how much more difficult it would be for a machine to cook an egg sunny side up, for example.

LIVING DOLL
Miniaturization has enabled the construction of much smaller, more functional robots in the past decade that are capable of walking and carrying out simple manual tasks.

© Jiuguang Wang | Creative Commons

What we find a relatively simple procedure consists of hundreds of complex muscle actions controlled by our brains. Picking up something as fragile as an egg without crushing it requires considerable dexterity, as does cracking it and separating the contents from the shell, before pouring and cooking it in a pan. At the moment, ASIMO is able to carry a tray from one side of a room to another.

Most daily activities that take place in and around the home — cleaning, washing up, cooking, doing the laundry, and gardening — take huge amounts of processing power, which brings us to the human data processor, storage, and retrieval unit, the brain that fits neatly into our skull. Until comparatively recently, computers (pp. 204–8) were room-sized and weighed tons. It is only in the past decade that processors and data storage systems have become small enough to fit into a mobile unit the size of ASIMO. But the current robot brain is still many times slower and less powerful than our own. In addition, the human body is equipped with the most sophisticated array of sensors to monitor the outside worlds, including the eyes, nose, tongue, ears, and skin receptors (to name just the basic five). ASIMO can hear and see, and can recognize faces and objects so as not to bump into things, but that's a long way short of what it would need in order to do the full range of tasks needed to run a household.

ASIMO CAN HEAR AND SEE, AND CAN RECOGNIZE FACES AND OBJECTS.

In a parallel development, the Japanese electronics company Kokoro Company in collaboration with Osaka University has been manufacturing "actroids" — android robots that are designed to look as human as possible. The company has produced several models, all based on (surprise, surprise) attractive young Japanese women. The robot, which is reminiscent of a theme-park animatronic figure, has lifelike movements of the face and upper body, and speech recognition and production software. However, the actroid still has limited lower-body mobility. Although actroids look like our idea of humanoid robots, they are functionally much more limited than ASIMO.

One final problem with the current humanoid robot technology is power: ASIMO's systems are powered by a 13 lb (6 kg) lithium-ion battery, with a running time of 40 to 60 minutes (if they're anything like my laptop battery, you can halve that). The robot needs three hours to recharge from a special docking port, so there is no danger that these babies are going to rebel and conquer the Earth any time soon, unless they can do it in under 40 minutes.

Although the domestic humanoid robot that will "eliminate all routine operations around the house" is still many years away, Thring was not entirely wrong when he predicted that robots would be abolishing human drudgery. By 1984, many tasks on the world's assembly lines had already been entrusted to robots. Robots play an ever-increasing role in scientific research and in industrial production. They have made their way onto the battlefield and into other hazardous environments where the risk to human life is considered too great. Even in the home, a new generation of "smart" domestic appliances is gradually introducing automation to the domestic setting. It may not have a head, arms, or legs, but one day soon you might find yourself having a conversation with your icebox or your washing machine.

IRON MAIDEN:
MARGARET THATCHER

Main culprit: Margaret Thatcher

What was predicted: That a woman would not become prime minister of Great Britain in her lifetime

What actually happened: Margaret Thatcher was elected prime minister in 1979 and was elected for three successive terms

I don't think there will be a woman Prime Minister in my lifetime. And I don't think it depends so much on whether it's a man Prime Minister or a woman Prime Minister as whether that person is the right person for the job at that time. And it's very difficult to foresee what may happen many, many years ahead.

Margaret Thatcher in a BBC interview in 1973

There will never be a black president; there will never be openly gay and lesbian politicians; there will never be a woman prime minister. These statements tell us just as much about the state of the society in which they are made as about the beliefs and values of the people making them. It might not be a case of prejudice and discrimination on the part of bigots and racists, but just as much about the speaker not believing that their gender, ethnic origin, or sexual orientation disbars them from high political office. In each case, the assertion has been proved completely wrong, and often much earlier than many commentators would have anticipated.

To give the most recent example, in the 2008 presidential campaign the American electorate was suddenly faced by an embarrassment of firsts: a choice between the first African American and the first woman presidential candidate in the Democratic primaries, and the first Republican woman vice-presidential candidate. In the end, Democrats picked Barack Obama (b. 1961) over Hilary Clinton (b. 1947), and Sarah Palin (b. 1964), the darling of the Tea Party movement, is waiting in the wings as a potential presidential candidate. What once seemed an impossible barrier to overcome is suddenly the new normality. Whatever Obama does in office, whether his economic policies fail or succeed, he will have achieved the greatest transformation in American politics since the birth of the civil rights movement by simply holding the country's highest office.

Turn the clock back three decades, to the United Kingdom, when Margaret Thatcher (b. 1925), then a cabinet minister in the Conservative government of Edward Heath (1916–2005), declared in a television interview in 1973 that there would not be a female prime minister in her lifetime. Why was she so adamant that a British woman would not achieve the land's highest political office when the UK's head of state since 1953 has been a woman, Elizabeth II (b. 1926)? Did she perceive some particular impediment in British society or its political system that made it an unbreakable glass ceiling? Did she believe that women weren't up to the job? Or was it her own upbringing that made her so reticent to endorse a female political leader?

The UK has a long tradition of women's rights, beginning with Mary Wollstonecraft's (1759–97) *A Vindication of the Rights of Woman* (1792), which argued that men and women were equal and that any disparity between them was due to education. The women's suffrage movement born in the nineteenth century took off in the early twentieth, when the redoubtable Emmeline Pankhurst (1858–1928) took the lead. Thanks to her efforts, women over 30 obtained the vote in 1918, and full female suffrage at the age of 21 was won in 1928.

Women served in political office from the very first elections held with women's suffrage. The first woman member of the House of Commons to take her seat was the American-born Nancy Astor (1879–1964), who represented the seat of Plymouth Sutton for the Conservatives from 1919 to 1945. The first woman minister was appointed in the Labour government of 1924. In 1970, the UK passed the Equal Pay Act, followed five years later by the Sex Discrimination Act. By 1973, the UK was a mature democracy, with a tradition of women's rights going back to the eighteenth century and advanced equality legislation in operation or about to be passed. So why did the prospect of a female prime minister seem so far-fetched?

Outside of the UK, there were two very famous examples of women heads of government in the 1960s and 1970s: Indira Gandhi (1917–84), prime minister of India from 1966 to 1977, and Golda Meir (1917–56), who served as Israeli premier from 1969 to 1974. Yet in Britain, the political hierarchy, both Conservative and Labour, seemed steeped in a patriarchal culture quite out of keeping with the social changes that had overtaken British society since the 1960s.

THE GROCER'S DAUGHTER

Margaret Thatcher, née Roberts, was nicknamed the "grocer's daughter," often in a derogatory way by those who felt either that she had betrayed her class origins, or that she was not of the right social class to lead the Conservative party. Her father was, in fact, not a humble grocer, but a businessman who owned grocery shops. She became active in the Conservative party while attending Oxford University, where she studied chemistry. After graduating, she trained as a barrister. She stood unsuccessfully for Parliament in the 1950 and 1951 general elections, but was passed over in the 1955 election. She was finally elected in 1959 for the north London constituency of Finchley, which she represented until her retirement from the House of Commons in 1992.

She held her first junior government post in 1961, and climbed steadily through the ranks until she was appointed Secretary of State for Education and Science in the Heath cabinet in 1970. Her tenure is remembered for her abolition of free school milk for 7- to 11-year-olds, which earned her the epithet: "Margaret Thatcher, Milk Snatcher." It was in 1973, during her tenure at the Department of Education and Science, that, when interviewed by the BBC, she made the fateful comment about a woman prime minister in the UK. She didn't reject the idea of a woman leader out of hand, citing the examples of Indira Gandhi and Golda Meir, but put the possibility into an indeterminate future "many, many years ahead," and certainly not in her lifetime (see quote). When asked why, she admitted it was partly because of prejudice, but also because:

> I don't think we have enough women with the same range of experience in politics as men have had. And it is important, whoever becomes Prime Minister, that they've had quite a wide range of experience in top political jobs. And we haven't yet worked up sufficient women.

Asked whether she had ambitions of becoming prime minister herself, she fell back on the same answer.

> My goodness me, it's a pretty penetrating question, isn't it? I would not wish to be Prime Minister, dear. I have not enough experience for that job. The only full ministerial position I've held is Minister of Education and Science. Before you could even think of being Prime Minister, you'd need to have done a good deal more jobs than that.

This might strike some as strange, as by that time Thatcher had been active in politics for a quarter of a century, and had held junior ministerial portfolios in power or opposition for 14 years. She was probably considerably more experienced than Tony Blair (b. 1953) when he came to power in 1997.

A year later, Edward Heath lost the election to the Labour party. Her declaration of 1973 forgotten, Thatcher challenged him for the leadership of the Conservative Party in 1975, becoming the party's first woman leader, the first woman Leader of Her Majesty's Opposition, and the first woman prime minister in waiting. The Labour government was

© Margaret Thatcher Foundation | Creative Commons

"I'M A LADY"
Despite years of experience in government, the Conservative Thatcher could not quite bring herself to believe that women were as able as men.

soon mired in deep economic troubles that led to a period of industrial unrest known as the "Winter of Discontent" (1978–79). Promising smaller government, lower taxes, and more freedom for business and the individual, Thatcher led the Conservatives to victory in the 1979 election and embarked on a far-reaching program of reforms that transformed British society during the next decade. After the British victory in the Falklands War against Argentina in 1982, she won a second term with a huge majority in 1983.

She won her third and final term in 1987, leaving office three years later not because she had lost the support of the electorate but that of her own party. In all she had served as prime minister for 11 years—the longest-serving British premier of the twentieth century and without doubt one of its most influential. Thatcher is fairly unique in the annals of poor predictions for proving herself so spectacularly wrong.

CHILL OUT: *NEWSWEEK* AND *TIME* MAGAZINES

PREDICTION

Millenarian

Technology

Prophecy

Politics

Military

Natural Disaster

Culture

Economics

Doomsday

Main culprit: *Newsweek* and *Time* magazines

What was predicted: A steady period of global cooling leading to a collapse in agricultural production and possibly leading to a new ice age

What actually happened: Global warming

The central fact is that after three quarters of a century of extraordinarily mild conditions, the Earth's climate seems to be cooling down. Meteorologists disagree about the cause and extent of the cooling trend, as well as over its specific impact on local weather conditions. But they are almost unanimous in the view that the trend will reduce agricultural productivity for the rest of the century.

"The Cooling World," *Newsweek,* **April 28, 1975**

In the TEOTWAWKI (the end of the world as we know it) stakes, the frontrunner this decade has undoubtedly been climate change. Climate is after all a vital, if not *the* vital, factor in deciding the long-term survival of the human race. A change of a few degrees either way could spell disaster for the species, turning agriculturally productive areas of the planet into arid desert or frozen tundra. The major worry today is, of course, global warming, and the big culprit in the frame is carbon dioxide (CO_2). From my rather distant memory of high-school chemistry, CO_2 used to be a fairly innocuous gaseous component of our atmosphere, a byproduct of photosynthesis, breathing, and other natural processes. Now it's seen as the chemical equivalent of the Antichrist, worse than radioactive fallout, heroin, and nicotine put together.

COLD FRONT
Newsweek, the first edition of which is shown here, featured the global cooling story as the main threat to the survival of human civilization.

Global warming, however, has not always been what makes climatologists wake up in the middle of the night in a cold sweat. In the 1970s, it was the complete opposite: the prospect of global cooling, and the possible onset of the next ice age that might have been triggered by natural factors or humanity's wanton behavior. In the mid-1970s both *Time* and *Newsweek* (see quote) ran articles warning about the coming collapse of civilization because the climate was getting steadily colder.

The Earth is no stranger to extreme climatic oscillations. In its 4.5-billion-year history, the planet is thought to have experienced five periods of extensive cooling known as "ice ages," because of the presence of ice sheets covering a large part of the Earth's surface. The most extreme of these events, known as the "Cryogenian," saw the whole Earth cocooned in ice for 220 million years. The current ice age—the Quaternary-Pleistocene glaciation— began about 2.6 million years ago.

Hold on, I hear you say, you said earlier that scientists in the 1970s feared a new ice age, and now I'm telling you that we're already living through one. I'm afraid that's what comes from sloppy use of terminology. Ice ages are themselves divided into colder periods, called "glacials," when the ice sheets advance from the poles, and warmer "interglacials," when the ice retreats but not completely. Periods when there are no polar ice know for sure why the Earth is so prone to regular periods of warming and cooling, but you can be sure that they've come up with a lot of theories to explain it.

The most obvious potential cause of climatic variation is the distance between the Earth and the source of the world's heat, the Sun. The Earth's elliptical orbit and its axial tilt cause the annual round of the seasons, but there are much longer cycles—the Milankovitch cycles— measured in tens of thousands of years that change the shape of the Earth's orbit around the Sun, the Earth's tilt through its axis, and its axial precession (the change of the Earth's direction in relation to the fixed stars). A more recent discovery is the change in the Earth's orbital inclination relative to other planets in the solar system that takes 100,000 years, which is, as we shall see below, a rather significant number. Another extraterrestrial factor put forward as a possible cause of Earth's cooling is variation in the Sun's energy output.

In addition to these factors, we have to consider changes that have taken place on the Earth's surface in the past hundred million years. First, the surface of the planet is not fixed but is divided into continent-sized moving tectonic plates. As the configuration of the continents changed over millions of years, it affected the circulation of the ocean currents, allowing or preventing the flow of warmer waters into the Polar regions. Second, the rise and fall of landmasses also changed patterns of air circulation. Third, the Earth has been prone to periods of intense volcanic activity. Supervolcanic eruptions added billions of tons of greenhouse gases to the atmosphere, and could have precipitated global warming and ended past ice ages. Last but not least, we humans have been implicated in climate change, not just since the industrial revolution 250 years ago when we started to pump CO_2 and pollutants into the atmosphere, but from the very beginnings of human civilization when we began our transformation of the Earth's surface through deforestation, agriculture, and animal husbandry.

The succession of glacial and interglacial periods occurred initially in cycles of 41,000 years but then changed to 100,000-year cycles. Interglacials, however, tend to be a lot shorter than glacials and were once believed to last approximately 10,000 years. The current warm period, the Holocene, began 12,000 years ago, and corresponds to the

SUPERVOLCANIC ERUPTIONS ADDED BILLIONS OF TONS OF GREENHOUSE GASES TO THE ATMOSPHERE, AND COULD HAVE PRECIPITATED GLOBAL WARMING AND ENDED PAST ICE AGES.

period during which humans developed agriculture and settled patterns of life. In fact, our whole civilization is a product of what are unusually benign climatic conditions. Humans managed to survive glacial periods, but in small bands of hunter-gatherers, which lived on the very brink of extinction. A minor cooling in the climate would spell disaster for food production, and we would soon be faced with famine on a worldwide scale. A 12.5°F (7°C) drop in global temperatures would send us into a new glacial phase, and that would spell doom for a large proportion of the Earth's population.

BLOWING HOT AND COLD

The fact that the Holocene interglacial is now 12,000 years old led several climatologists in the 1970s to conclude that our time would very soon be up, and that we all better learn how to build igloos and how to hunt seals. *Time* featured the story in June 1974, and *Newsweek* followed suit in April 1975. They both quoted experts and provided the scientific facts and figures, but the theories and evidence they put forward to explain global cooling did not always agree.

In *Newsweek*, for example, "Rainy Britain, on the other hand, has suffered from uncharacteristic dry spells the past few springs." While in *Time*'s article, "In England, farmers have seen their growing season decline by about two weeks since 1950, with a resultant overall loss in grain production estimated at up to 100,000 tons annually"; or *Time*'s, "Since the 1940s the mean global temperature has dropped about 2.7°F." To *Newsweek*'s, "A survey completed last year […] reveals a drop of half a degree in average ground temperatures in the Northern Hemisphere between 1945 and 1968."

The two magazines go for slightly different explanations as to the cause of the phenomenon. *Newsweek* goes for "large numbers of pressure centers in the upper atmosphere" that by breaking up air flow and creating stagnant air produce, "extremes of local weather such as droughts, floods, extended dry spells, long freezes, delayed monsoons and even local temperature increases." *Time* has another take on the science with an "expansion of the great belt of dry, high-altitude polar winds—the so-called circumpolar vortex," which blocks moisture-bearing winds and causes drought in the subtropical belt, as well as causing tornadoes in the Midwest. Both publications, however, agree that this means one thing: the global climate is cooling, and the results that this means one thing: the global climate is cooling, and the results for human civilization are bound to be disastrous. *Newsweek* is the only one to suggest a solution: "Melting the Arctic ice cap by covering it with black soot," which it concedes is a fairly unrealistic prospect.

A more recent take on global cooling was dramatized in the 2004 movie *The Day After Tomorrow*. The film is based on the premise that global warming could trigger an ice age by melting the polar ice cap and dumping huge amounts of cold water into the north Atlantic, disrupting the Gulf Stream that keeps much of the northern hemisphere temperate. In the film, brave, outspoken paleo-climatologist Jack Hall (Denis Quaid) faces down the skeptics as the climate cools in a matter of days, and Europe and North America are entombed under a sheet of snow and ice. He then sets out to rescue his son Sam (Jake Gyllenhaal), who is trapped in the Public Library of a frozen New York. One climate scientist has dismissed the movie as "The *Towering Inferno* of climate science movies," while another said that although he was heartened that Hollywood had finally made a movie addressing climate change, he deplored its science, giving it "a D minus or an F."

Although I have no wish to side with the climate-change deniers, it is interesting to note that quite a lot of the evidence cited in *Time* and *Newsweek* in the 1970s to make the case for global cooling—droughts, floods, and other freak weather events—has reemerged in support of global warming. Of course, now we know a lot more about how the climate works (don't we?), and it's not just a handful of scientists with limited evidence but the vast majority of the world's climate scientists with three decades of studies behind them. But who knows, our relentless exploitation of the planet's fossil fuel reserves may be the one thing keeping the next ice age at bay.

PREDICTION

Millenarian

Technology

Prophecy

Politics

Military

Natural Disaster

Culture

Economics

Doomsday

DOES NOT COMPUTE: KENNETH OLSEN

Main culprit: Kenneth Olsen

What was predicted: That the PC would never catch on

What actually happened: PC sales in 2010 were estimated to be 366.1 million units

There is no reason anyone would want a computer in their home.

**Kenneth Olsen, president
of Digital Equipment
Corporation
in 1977**

While many crystal gazers and scientists expected that one day (soon) there would be a robot in every home to do the chores for them, what almost no one foresaw is that instead, by 2010, most households would have one or more artificial brain to do their thinking for them. The personal computer (PC) is an intriguing invention. Compared to other inventions that we have examined in this book—the telephone, the lightbulb, and the airplane—which had an immediate and easily grasped function that improved our daily lives, in the 1960s and '70s, it was far from obvious why a computer in the home would be useful let alone indispensible.

PCs have become so small and ubiquitous that they surround us in the home, in shops, in the car, and at the office. The standard desktop is now an unwieldy dinosaur when compared to the ever-shrinking varieties of PC: the laptop or notebook—as heavy as a brick! The tablet (e.g., iPad)—still too big! The ultra-mobile and the pocket PC—now you're talking. How small will PCs get? The only limitation to size, it seems, is the ability of our big, clumsy fingers to use an input device such as a pen or keyboard, and the ability of our eyes to read the small print on the screen.

The history of all-purpose, electronic, digital computing begins in wartime, when the UK, U.S., and Germany each developed computers to aid in their war efforts during World War Two. The British built Colossus, which they used to crack German military Enigma codes, and the Americans had ENIAC (Electronic Numerical Integrator And Computer). But we're not talking portable here, even if you had a forklift truck—not so much desktops as "roomtops." Early computers were monsters. ENIAC was 8.5 ft x 3 ft x 80 ft (2.6 m x 0.9 m x 24 m), consumed 150 kW of juice, contained around 18,000 vacuum tubes, and weighed around 30 tons. It took weeks to program, and its dependence on fragile vacuum tubes meant that it was not particularly reliable.

FROM "ROOMTOP" TO DESKTOP

ENIAC was a very fast and sophisticated adding machine capable of thousands of complex calculations per second—fine for the military, a government department, big business, or a research lab, but of very little use to the general user. Looking to the future in 1949, the magazine *Popular Mechanics* predicted: "Where a calculator on the ENIAC is equipped with 18,000 vacuum tubes and weighs 30 tons, computers in the future may have only 1,000 vacuum tubes and weigh only 1.5 tons." In 1943, president of IBM Thomas J. Watson, Sr. (1874–1976) hit the nail on the head when he said, "I think there is a world market for maybe five computers." ENIAC-like machines operated until the mid-1950s, gradually improving in speed and storage capacity, but they were experimental one-offs, built for a specific purpose, and costing millions of dollars each.

The next stage of the computing revolution began with the commercial application of the transistor in the mid-1950s. One of the bestselling "second-generation" computers was the IBM 1401, first marketed in 1959. The company's literature proudly boasted:

> The all-transistorized IBM 1401 Data Processing System places the features found in electronic data processing systems at the disposal of smaller businesses, previously limited to the use of conventional punched card equipment. These features include: high-speed card punching and reading, magnetic tape input and output, high-speed printing, stored program, and arithmetic and logical ability.

The 1401 was a lot smaller than ENIAC, but not very small. You still needed a large, air-conditioned room to house its punch reader, processor, and printer, each the size of a photocopier. Neither was the 1401 particularly user-friendly: There was no screen or keyboard, and data entry was through punch cards and later magnetic tape. Again, the target customer was business, but even here, many expressed doubts as to its long-term future. The business book editor at publishers Prentice Hall commented in 1957: "I have traveled the length and breadth of this country and talked with the best people, and I can assure you that data processing is a fad that won't last out the year." Not only were computers large and expensive, but they also needed specialist operators versed in the arcane computer languages to program the machine and manage its input and output.

We were still a very long way from the age of the home PC. The current third generation of computers came about after Robert Noyce (1927–90) and Jack St. Clair Kilby (1923–2005) came up with the integrated circuit in 1958, and Ted Hoff, Jr. (b. 1937) of Intel produced the first commercial microprocessor and RAM chip in 1971. The elements of the PC were now in place. We already had the keyboard (from the electric typewriter) and the cathode-ray tube (from TV); storage was always going to be a problem because of the limited memory of the day's RAM chips, but early machines solved this with cassette and disk drives that loaded the applications and stored and saved the data. While the earliest PCs were sold in kit form to computer hobbyists, in 1977, three fully assembled models hit the market at the same time: the Commodore PET, the Tandy TRS-80, and last but not least, Steve Wozniak's (b. 1950) Apple II.

Even teenagers who have never seen or even heard of floppy disks would be able to recognize the Apple II as a PC. It could do sums, but also word process, and with sound and color, was also an early games platform. It was not very portable, having no independent power source, and it came in three parts (four if you added a printer). But the era of home computing had finally arrived. At this moment, Ken Olsen (b. 1926) made his oft-quoted comment (see quote). Olsen was no Luddite; he was a techie through and through. While studying at MIT, he built an experimental transistorized computer, and in 1957, he founded the Digital Equipment Corporation (DEC). In the 1960s and '70s DEC's innovative designs challenged IBM in the business market, but the company missed the PC boat in the 1980s and was finally bought out by Compaq in 1998.

The computing revolution of the past two decades has caught out many IT analysts and hardware manufacturers. The market is so complex and fast-moving that last year's success story can be this year's flop. The home PC market was initially driven by innovation—miniaturization, which made machines smaller and cheaper, the availability of faster chips, and larger memory storage, which made a growing range of applications available to the domestic user. But alongside these PC-specific developments have come the appearance of the Internet and the cell phone, two inventions that really came into their own in the 1990s. Both impacted the home PC market in ways that were almost impossible to predict.

OLSEN WAS NO LUDDITE; HE WAS A TECHIE THROUGH AND THROUGH. WHILE STUDYING AT MIT, HE BUILT AN EXPERIMENTAL TRANSISTORIZED COMPUTER.

The Internet requires a specific type of PC, with a fast chip, plentiful memory to load pages, and high-end graphics and video capability to display their content. But even in the 1990s, only the most farsighted analysts understood how much people would want to use the Internet at home and the kinds of activities they would be conducting online: email, video conferencing, Internet telephony, watching TV, listening to radio, and downloading movies. Convergent machine evolution has transformed the cell phone into a miniature PC, especially since the arrival of Apple's iPhone and the new generation of Android phones all equipped with Internet access and apps. Today few of us could imagine not being connected to the Internet 24/7, not just at home, but on our cell phones as well.

I am indebted to the debunking website snopes.com for their clarification of the Olsen quote. Rather than questioning why anyone would want a computer at home, the website explains, Olsen was referring to the computerized home, with everything controlled by a CPU à la HAL in *2001, A Space Odyssey* (1968). I have no reason to doubt that this is true, but the fact remains that DEC, once a leading industry player, remained in the business computer market, while IBM was wisely investing in the home PC market. They produced their IBM PC in 1981, establishing the dominance of DOS and later Windows machines that has lasted to the present day. Even the huge success of Apple Macintosh in recent decades has not managed to make up for the enormous lead established by the IBM PC and the hundred of clones that it has spawned. As for the computerized house, with your Wi-Fi devices chatting to one another, and soon to your intelligent air-con, icebox, washer, boiler, and dishwasher, it's only a matter of time.

STORMY WEATHER: MICHAEL FISH

PREDICTION

Millenarian

Technology

Prophecy

Politics

Military

Natural Disaster

Culture

Economics

Doomsday

Main culprit: Michael Fish

What was predicted: Strong winds for October 15–16, 1987

What actually happened: The hurricane-force Great Storm of 1987, which killed 22 people in the UK and France, destroyed buildings, overturned ships, wrecked cars, felled 15 million trees, and cost over £7 billion ($10.5 billion)

Earlier on today, apparently, a woman rang the BBC and said she heard there was a hurricane on the way; well, if you're watching, don't worry, there isn't, but having said that, actually, the weather will become very windy, but most of the strong winds, incidentally, will be down over Spain and across into France.

BBC weatherman Michael Fish (b. 1944) on October 15, 1987

Picture the scene: the peaceful, idyllic southeast of England with its pastures and fields enclosed in neatly trimmed hedgerows, its quiet villages with their thatched cottages and old country churches, its ancient deciduous woodlands, its city suburbs with tree-lined streets and manicured parks and gardens. It is a mature, well-cared-for landscape, verdant from plentiful but gentle rain and occasional sunshine.

The weather in southeast England, although the locals seem to find it so fascinating that they talk of little else, is unusually gentle and temperate, with no extremes of temperature, wind, or precipitation — 85°F (30°C) is a "heat wave" and 20°F (-5°C) with a few inches of snow is an "Arctic winter." Compared to their American cousins who live through tornadoes, hurricanes, blizzards, and droughts, the English are unusually blessed with one of the world's most boringly predictable climates: "Sunny with showery intervals" and "showers with sunny intervals" are probably the phrases you'll hear most on the lips of the British weatherman or woman.

The weather on October 15, 1987, on land at least, was not particularly bad. That evening, those viewers who tuned into the BBC news saw weatherman Michael Fish (b. 1944) forecast strong winds for the following day, but nothing particularly out of the ordinary for mid-October. He even jokingly referred to a phone call that the BBC had received earlier that day about the possibility of a "hurricane" (see quote), reassuring viewers that there was no danger of a storm and that the strongest winds would remain over Spain and France. People went to their beds, only to be woken up by the worst weather to hit London and the southeast in several centuries. The event would go down in the annals of British meteorology as the Great Storm of 1987, and haunts Michael Fish to this day. He commented in a recent interview, "I wish I had a penny for each time that clip had been broadcast, I'd be a millionaire!"

"NO PEN COULD DESCRIBE IT"

The storm was the worst in living memory, but not the worst in the history of British climatology. On November 26–27, 1703, the south of England was struck by a hurricane-force storm that was witnessed by the author of *Robinson Crusoe*, Daniel Defoe (c. 1660–1731). In 1704, he published a book of eyewitness accounts of the event entitled *The Storm*. The destruction was so great that Defoe wrote: "No pen could describe it, nor tongue express it, nor thought conceive it unless by one in the extremity of it." At the peak of the storm, winds reached 120 mph (190 km/h), causing massive destruction on both land and sea.

A British fleet returning from the continent was wrecked with the loss of 1,500 sailors; on the river Thames, the winds broke the moorings of some 700 sailing ships and barges, which Defoe described as being "crushed together" in the Pool of London a little way downstream of London Bridge. Thousands of buildings in London and the surrounding counties, being of much frailer construction than in the twentieth century, were destroyed or damaged. Even major buildings were not proof against the violent winds: London's Westminster Abbey lost part of its leaded roof, and the Royal Family had to hide in a cellar when chimneys and part of the roof of St James's Palace collapsed. In all, an estimated 8,000 to 15,000 people, many of them sailors, perished in the disaster.

In 1703, there were no weather forecasts, and citizens and mariners had to content themselves with the tried and tested method of looking out of the window. Professional weather forecasting began 150 years later when the British government established the world's first national weather agency, the United Kingdom Meteorological Office (now the Met Office) in 1854, gathering information by telegraph, and relaying it to ports when storms were expected. A daily weather forecast issued by the Met Office was published in *The Times* from 1860.

© David Wright | Creative Commons

CRUSHED
Fallen trees and crushed cars litter the streets of London and southeast England after the Great Storm.

Great storms, which are yearly occurrences in some parts of the world, are tri-centennial events in merry old England, and few but the best informed of historians would have known of the events of November 1703, 284 years later. In the fall and winter, depressions forming over the Atlantic sweep across the British Isles, bringing cold winds and rain, but nothing of the severity of the hurricanes that habitually blow up in the Gulf of Mexico and batter the U.S. coastline. On October 15, an area of low pressure was moving northward from the Bay of Biscay (between Spain and France) toward the English Channel. Just before midnight, the Met Office issued warnings to shipping of

Force 10 winds (55–63mph; 88–101 km/h). A few days before, the Met Office's computer models had suggested that the storm would stay in the Channel and affect only the southernmost coastal counties, but contrary to expectation the storm kept traveling northeastward, crossing southeast England during the night and reaching the Humber Estuary on the east coast at 5.30am, leaving a trail of death and destruction in its path.

REAL THING
A tropical hurricane crosses the U.S. coast. The Great Storm, though it had hurricane force winds, was not the "real McCoy."

The strongest winds recorded were 120 mph (190 km/h), well above Force 12 (73 mph/117 km/h), which is the hurricane threshold. The storm brought with it huge fluctuations in temperature and barometric pressure. As the storm front passed through Hampshire, southwest of London, the temperature rose from 47° F (8.5°C) to 63.5° F (17.5°C) in 20 minutes, and pressure dropped more than 20mb in three hours. According to the BBC weather website, however, the Great Storm of 1987 was not a hurricane, as this terms refers specifically to weather events that take place in the tropics.

Hurricane or not, the destruction was considerable, in a countryside that was completely unprepared for such a violent onslaught. The greatest damage was reported in London and the southeast. The botanical gardens at Kew in west London, Hyde Park in the center, and Hampstead Heath in north London lost thousands of mature trees. Fallen trees blocked roads and railway lines, damaged cars and buildings, and knocked down electricity cables, causing widespread blackouts. On the coast, in the port of Dover a large ship capsized, temporarily blocking the harbor, and a passenger ferry was driven ashore at the nearby port of Folkestone. The Shanklin Pier on the Isle of Wight was broken into three sections by huge waves. Damage was also severe in western France, in the coastal regions of Brittany and Normandy, where forests were flattened and utilities were cut to millions of homes. In all 22 people died—a death toll probably mercifully small because the storm had struck during the middle of the night.

The man who has earned so much opprobrium and ridicule for his forecast on the night of October 15, Michael Fish, was no pinup weatherboy hired for his looks and flashing smile. He was one of the

BBC's most experienced meteorologists, employed at the corporation for three decades, from 1974 to 2004. In his defense, Fish later claimed his remarks about a hurricane referred not to possible weather conditions in the UK, but to a storm that was then affecting Florida. The woman caller, he explained, was the mother of a BBC employee who was traveling to the Caribbean. He added that he had concluded his forecast that evening with a warning of high winds, and advised viewers to "batten down the hatches." Despite his denials, the forecast has given rise to the "Michael Fish Effect," in which British weathermen prefer to cry wolf than be caught out like their now infamous predecessor.

Could the Great Storm forecast fiasco happen again? The British Isles and northern Europe only had to wait three years for a weather event of a similar magnitude that struck with little or no warning. On January 25, 1990, on Burns' Day, when the Scots celebrate the birthday of their national poet, a hurricane-strength storm hit the UK, causing flooding, knocking down millions of trees, and causing major damage to buildings. Because the storm struck during the day, the death toll was also much greater, with the loss of 47 lives in the UK alone, and more on the Continent. Despite an ever-growing array of weather satellites and the application of the latest supercomputer technology to weather modeling, it seems the Earth's weather remains as unpredictable as ever.

CARRIED AWAY: HAL LINDSEY, EDGAR C. WHISENANT, AND MANY OTHERS

Main culprits: Hal Lindsey, Edgar C. Whisenant, and many others

What was predicted: That the rapture would take place in September 1988

What actually happened: The dates for the rapture have been revised over and over again

When the Jewish people, after nearly 2,000 years of exile, under relentless persecution, became a nation again on 14 May 1948 the "fig tree" put forth its first leaves. Jesus said that this would indicate that He was "at the door," ready to return. Then He said, "Truly I say to you, this generation will not pass away until all these things take place."

Hal Lindsey in *The Late, Great Planet Earth* (1988)

We return to the area of religious prophecy for the last time in this book (but, I predict, not the last time in the future history of predictions), with a topic that seems to have captured the imagination of evangelical Christians worldwide in the past few decades: the imminent occurrence of the "rapture," when the "true believers" will be "extracted" from the Earth by a crack team of angelic commandos. This much-anticipated event takes us back to the second entry in this book about the predictions for the Second Coming of Christ and its accompanying events: the times of tribulation, the millennium, and the last judgment. We saw in our discussion of millennialism (see pp. 25–8) that this comes in three basic flavors—pre-, a-, and postmillennialism—depending on the exact sequence of events. Therefore, there is a great deal of disagreement within evangelical circles as to when, how, or even if the rapture will take place.

The evidence that rapture prophets have used includes pyramidology and a study of recent world events, but mainly rests on their own divinely inspired interpretation of verses from the Bible. The biblical passage that is most often quoted consists of three verses from The First Epistle of Paul to the Thessalonians (1. Thessalonians):

> $_{15}$ For this we say unto you by the word of the Lord, that we which are alive and remain unto the coming of the Lord shall not prevent them which are asleep.

> $_{16}$ For the Lord himself shall descend from heaven with a shout, with the voice of the archangel, and with the trump of God: and the dead in Christ shall rise first.

> $_{17}$ Then we which are alive and remain shall be caught up together with them in the clouds, to meet the Lord in the air: and so shall we ever be with the Lord.

Paul of Tarsus (c. 5 – c. 67 CE), who is also known as the "apostle of the gentiles," wrote the epistle (letter) from the Greek city of Corinth, to the fledgling church of Thessalonica in Macedonia, northern Greece, in around 52 CE. He had spent some time preaching in the city, and made converts to the new faith of Christianity. During the early history of the Church, Christianity was often seen as a breakaway Jewish sect rather than a religion in its own right. The confusion was compounded by the fact that many early Christians were themselves Jews, that Christianity was often preached in synagogues, and that Christians performed Jewish customs and ceremonies. This led to tensions between the established Jewish communities in the Roman world and the Church, which they saw as a heretical offshoot of orthodox Judaism.

Paul was concerned about the wellbeing of the Thessalonica converts, and sent his disciple Timothy (d. c. 80 CE) to check up on them. Timothy reported that the Thessalonians had misunderstood what Paul had preached about salvation. In particular they believed that those converts who had died before the Second Coming would not be resurrected or saved. Paul wrote the First Epistle to explain that Christ would resurrect Christians who had died before his coming ("And the dead in Christ shall rise first"), while those who were still alive at the time would be, in Paul's words rendered from the original Greek into Latin and later into English, "caught up" by Jesus, "to meet the Lord in the air." A second oft-quoted New Testament passage is Matthew 24:36–41, in which Christ compares his Second Coming to the Great Flood, when only Noah and his family had been warned by God of the approaching disaster. Upon Jesus' return, some will be "left" and others will be "taken"—interpreted by evangelical prophets to mean that the chosen few will be carried away by Christ before the destruction of the world.

PROMISED LAND
The return of the Jews to the Holy Land is an important part of rapture theology, as it prefigures the coming of the Antichrist and the end times.

The original Greek for "caught up"—*harpazo*— occurs 17 times in the New Testament, sometimes with the negative connotations of "seize or carry off by force," like a wolf seizing a lamb, or slightly more positively as "to seize on, claim for oneself eagerly" or "to snatch out or away." In both cases, however, the action is sudden or even violent, which is why some later versions of the Bible qualify the verb "caught up" with the adverb "suddenly." The verses from Matthew quoted above also indicate the suddenness of the rapture, and suggest that those who would be left behind would not realize what had happened, as if the raptee had been invisibly "beamed up" in *Star Trek* fashion. This has led some prophets to claim that the rapture has actually taken place, with the mysterious disappearance from the Earth of the elect.

© Getty Images

To non-believers or non-Christians, who have their own eschatological traditions, the scriptural foundations for the rapture might appear a bit thin. But as we have seen earlier in this book, this has not stopped Christian prophets who have spun out the flimsiest of evidence into cast-iron theories and predictions. The great advantage that modern doomsday prophets have in disseminating their ideas over their nineteenth-century predecessors, such as Joseph Smith and William Miller, is that in addition to the printed word, they have at their disposal all of the twentieth century's media tools: radio, television, and film, and the twenty-first's, which is perhaps the most powerful of all, the Internet. Hence an Internet search on the word "rapture" will turn up hundreds of sites devoted to the subject, and often to the denunciation of rival sites as being "false prophets."

There are so many evangelical rapture prophets that it is difficult to know where to start (or stop). I've picked two not entirely at random, Hal Lindsey (b. 1929), the author of *The Late, Great Planet Earth* (1970), and Edgar C. Whisenant (1932–2001), who wrote *88 Reasons Why the Rapture Will Be in 1988* (1988). What draws them together, apart from the date 1988, is that they both chose that particular year because it was 40 years after the creation of the state of Israel in 1948—40 years being interpreted as one biblical generation, which harks back to the prophecy that once the temple of Jerusalem was rebuilt, Jesus would return within one generation (Matthew 24:34).

Texas-born Hal Lindsey began his training for the ministry at the age of 29 after a stint as a tugboat captain on the Mississippi. He worked in several evangelical missions and taught Sunday school, but what shot him to stardom in conservative evangelical circles was his first book, *The Late, Great Planet Earth*, which the publisher claims has been translated into 54 languages and sold 35 million copies worldwide. The book, which is still in print, was made into a movie narrated by Orson Welles (1915–85) in 1979. Lindsey is a "Christian Zionist" but not because he has any great love for Judaism, the Jewish people, or the state of Israel. In some respects, you could argue the exact opposite. He strongly supports the Jewish state because he believes that its restoration and survival is an important part of the realization of the biblical prophecies that predict the end times, rapture, and Second Coming.

"THE LAST DECADE OF HISTORY"

In *The Late, Great Planet Earth*, Lindsey drew parallels between world affairs: the wars between Israel and her Arab neighbors, the Cold War between the U.S. and the Soviet Union, and the evolution of the EEC (European Economic Community, now the EU [European Union]), and specific biblical prophecies in the Old Testament books of Daniel and Ezekiel, and New Testament passages from Matthew and Revelation. The key event in the book is the foundation of the state of Israel, which he equates with the rebuilding of the Temple of Jerusalem. The events that he predicted for the 1980s were a Soviet attack on Israel, the transformation of the EEC into a revived Roman Empire ruled by the Antichrist, and the usual sundry famines, wars, and natural disasters that are precursors to the whole seas boiling, skies pouring with fire end of the world that God has planned. In a later book, *The 1980s: Countdown to Armageddon* (1980), he predicted, "the decade of the 1980s could very well be the last decade of history as we know it."

The 1980s have come and gone. Israel remains intact, and the Soviet Union has ceased to exist. As for the revived Roman Empire under the rule of the Antichrist, perhaps we should check whether the 11th president of the EU, Jose Manuel Barroso (b. 1956), has been sacrificing virgins and conducting black masses at EU headquarters in Brussels. The failure of the world to end and the rapture to take place in 1988 or 1990 has not disheartened Mr. Lindsey or his followers, and does not seem to have hurt his book sales. His latest offering, *The Everlasting Hatred: The Roots of Jihad* (2002) claims that the current war on terror is part of "A struggle driven by a hatred that goes back over 4,000 years." An interesting claim, since Islam was founded in 610 CE, exactly 1,400 years ago.

"ONLY IF THE BIBLE IS IN ERROR AM I WRONG."

Our second rapture prophet, Edgar C. Whisenant, had an unusual pedigree for an evangelical Christian, as his first career was as an engineer working for the U.S. space program. A student of the Bible, he came to prominence at the age of 56 with the publication of *88 Reasons Why the Rapture Will Be in 1988*, in which he claimed the rapture would occur during Rosh Hashanah (Jewish New Year), September 11–13, 1988. He, too, interpreted the 40 years after the foundation of Israel as the length of time predicted between the restoration of the Temple and the Second Coming.

He was so confident in his prediction that he claimed, "Only if the Bible is in error am I wrong." He distributed 300,000 free copies of the book to ministers in the U.S., and a further 4.5 million copies were sold. On those fateful September days in 1988, the influential evangelical Trinity Broadcast Network (TBN) interrupted its programming to broadcast shows dealing with the rapture, with instructions for non-believers about what to do in case family members and friends were suddenly "caught up" and the Earth entered its time of tribulation (presumably, convert in a hurry).

When Rosh Hashanah 1988 passed without the promised rapture, Whisenant revised the date for September 15, specifying the time 10:55am. When a second revised date of October 3 passed without incident, he insisted that the rapture would take place within a few weeks. Having been proved wrong again, he wrote in *The Final Shout — Rapture Report 1989* that he had made an error in his calculations, and that the rapture would now take place during Rosh Hashanah 1989. The passing of this and subsequent Rosh Hashanahs prompted Whisenant to publish further predictions, including *The Final Shout — Rapture Report 1990, 1991, 1992, 1993, 1994*, covering himself for the next five years.

Needless to say, Mr. Whisenant's later predictions did not attract very much attention, but he continues as a presence in odd corners of the Internet's evangelical fringe as either an inspired or a false prophet. Whisenant died in 2001, leaving the field open to Lindsey and many other rapture prophets who continue to set dates, and continue to attract the support of their followers, despite the repeated failure of their predictions to come true.

The growth of the rapture business is now, like everything else, on the Internet. The reader can enter "rapture" as a term in a search engine and get around eight million hits, though not all of them deal with Christian evangelical eschatology. I shall only cover one of these websites, not to give it undue prominence or publicity, but because "Rapture Ready" (raptureready.com), founded in 1995, is typical in tone and content of rapture theology available online.

INTERRUPTION
The Christian Trinity Broadcast Network interrupted its regular broadcasts with special programs on the days the rapture was predicted to occur.

Starting with a modest seven articles in 1997, grouped together in a "Rapture Index," Rapture Ready has grown exponentially to feature thousands of articles on every conceivable subject from prophecy to peak oil, via gay marriage and creationism, with sections in Spanish, French, German, and Japanese. The stated aim of the website is to inform rapture believers about what they need to do to prepare for the great event, and also to give advice and warnings to non-believers about the perils that they run if they miss the heavenly airlift. A handy FAQs section gives readers access to all the information they need, including the answers to the burning questions: "What is the 'rapture' and when will it happen?", "What if all of my family and friends do not accept Jesus before the rapture?", "Will the rapture happen this year?", and the intriguing "How do you plan to maintain this site after the rapture?", which suggests that the webmaster is pretty sure that he's going to be "caught up" with the other elect.

To my mind, the most striking aspect of the whole modern rapture phenomenon is how a huge eschatological superstructure has been built on the most flimsy of foundations. Millions of words have been written, broadcast, and published on the Internet, principally on the basis of a 33-word verse in the New Testament, originally written in Greek, translated into Latin and later into English. The rapture is also an American phenomenon, a revisitation of the Smith-Miller-Russell tradition of Doomsday prophecy. What is it in the psyche of the citizens of God's own country, the United States of America, we have to ask again, that makes them particularly susceptible to these kinds of apocalyptic fantasies?

HISTORY MAN: FRANCIS FUKUYAMA

PREDICTION

Millenarian

Technology

Prophecy

Politics

Military

Natural Disaster

Culture

Economics

Doomsday

Main culprit: Francis Fukuyama

What was predicted: The triumph of Western liberal democracy as the dominant form of government on the planet

What actually happened: The emergence of militant Islam and the economic domination of a capitalist-communist China

What we may be witnessing is not just the end of the Cold War, or the passing of a particular period of post-war history, but the end of history as such: that is, the end point of mankind's ideological evolution and the universalization of Western liberal democracy as the final form of human government.

Francis Fukuyama in *The End of History and the Last Man* (1992)

For many of us, history consists of lists of presidents, kings, and queens, military defeats and victories, and peace treaties, and the discovery of hitherto unexplored bits of the planet—in other words, a school student's history of dates and people, and their roles in major world events. But this is not the kind of history discussed in Francis Fukuyama's (b. 1952) *The End of History and the Last Man*, published to much acclaim and criticism in 1992. The book features a much more philosophical view of history, which sees it as an evolutionary process leading to a definable end point. This is a view that Fukuyama shares with the eighteenth-century philosopher Georg Hegel (1770–1831), and also with the father of Communism and one-time Hegelian, Karl Marx—although in each case, the historical destination of humanity's historical express is different.

Before we examine Fukuyama's book and predictions, let us remind ourselves of the state of the world in 1992. The big news of the decade was the end of the Cold War (1947–91) between the U.S. and the Soviet Union. The Berlin Wall that had divided the former and current German capital since 1961 fell in 1989, and the following years saw the dissolution of the Eastern Bloc and the collapse of the Soviet Union. In the Middle East, the U.S. and its allies, led by U.S. President George Bush, senior (b. 1924) defeated Iraqi dictator Saddam

NEW ORDER
U.S. president Ronald Reagan and Soviet general secretary Mikhail Gorbachev in discussion at a 1985 summit in Geneva, Switzerland. Both men played a central part in the thawing of Cold War relations between the two countries.

Hussein (1937–2006), who had invaded the neighboring oil-rich state of Kuwait. During the First Gulf War of 1991, the Iraqi dictator was expelled from Kuwait, but left in power. Bush, however, was not the one to benefit from the "peace dividend," as he was defeated in the 1992 presidential election by Bill Clinton (b. 1946).

In just a few short years, the geo-political and ideological maps of the world had been completely redrawn, wiping out 70 years of history, and giving cartographers a field day as new countries came into existence almost daily. The liberal-democratic, capitalist West had defeated the communist, totalitarian East without the spending of a single soldier's life. The last generation of Cold War warriors, Margaret Thatcher (b. 1925) and Ronald Reagan (1911–2004), had retired to make way for younger, more liberal-minded politicians. The 1990s were a decade of unbridled optimism, accompanied by a steadily improving economy in the U.S. and the countries of the newly formed European Union (1992). To quote Tony Blair's (b. 1953) campaign song, who was to come to power in the UK in 1997, "Things Can Only Get Better."

Fukuyama first outlined the thesis contained in *The End of History* in an article of the same name (with an added "?" in the title), published in 1989 while he was an adviser in the State Department working for then Secretary of State James Baker (b. 1930), a stalwart of the Reagan-Bush years. His work for Baker and for the U.S. government's leading think tank, the RAND Corporation, will give the reader an idea of Fukuyama's political sympathies, which have always been to the right of the political spectrum, shading into full-blown neoconservatism. But Fukuyama is no backstreet rabble-rouser or demagogue: He is a Cornell graduate in Classics (Latin and Greek studies) with a PhD in political science from Harvard, his specialist subject being the foreign policy of the Soviet Union. And don't let the Japanese-sounding name fool you into thinking that he is a recent import from the land of the rising microchip. Fukuyama, senior, was a second-generation Japanese-American and a minister in the Congregational Church who later lectured in theology.

THINGS CAN ONLY GET BETTER

The big idea in *The End of History* is not the triumph of capitalism over communism: It is definitely not a book about the Cold War and how we won it. Taking the long historical view—going back to cavemen—Fukuyama examines the development of humanity's political institutions and analyzes how various systems came into being and succeeded one another. In the flow of seemingly random, disconnected events we call "history," he discerns a pattern. Just as Karl Marx believed that history was an evolutionary process leading to a socialist utopia, so Fukuyama believes that the end point of political history is liberal-democracy. In other words, we are it. Our system of government is the best humanity can hope or strive for (God help us!). Hence the "end" of history does not mean the end of presidents, kings, queens, dates, or even wars—it is not the end of the history of events, but rather that the fall of Soviet communism was the effective end of the age-old conflict between democratic and non-democratic forms of government.

Like Marx, Fukuyama points to science and technology and their impact on the development of a state's economy as one of the main factors influencing its political evolution. Marx saw industrialization in a very negative light, as a relentless process of exploitation of labor by capital, leading to the ultimate overthrow of the bourgeoisie in a proletarian revolution. Fukuyama posits a much more positive view of capitalism. In an interview with Brian Lamb in 1992, he explained:

> The underlying cause of many of the recent transitions to democracy [...] has to do with the fact that as economic development occurs, as a country industrializes, as it becomes more urban, it becomes, therefore, more educated. You create a certain kind of middle class that is raised and trained to be literate, to take an understanding of their own affairs. And ultimately, I think, people like that, a middle class society like that begins to demand a certain degree of democratic participation.

But according to Fukuyama, that can only be half of the story. He disagrees with Marx that only economics matter, and goes back to Marx's predecessor, Hegel, to a concept that he himself calls "thymos." The Greek word *thymos* comes from the work of the ancient Athenian philosopher Plato (c. 428–c. 348 BCE), who divided the soul into three parts: the desiring part, the rational part, and the thymos, the part that wants the recognition of others, which to quote Fukuyama is the part that says, "Yes, I am a human being. I have a certain dignity of worth and I am proud of that worth."

This fundamental human drive, Fukuyama believes, has shaped civilization throughout the ages. It created the first master and the first slave, as early humanity sorted out its original political systems. Of course, Fukuyama admits, this has often led to tyranny—the likes of Stalin (1878–1953) and Saddam Hussein, who impose their thymos on their own people. But it is also positive in that it drives the desire for democracy—the only political system in which, theoretically, we all have an equal opportunity to get the recognition we yearn for. He suggests the intriguing possibility that if Adolf Hitler (1889–1945) had been born in the U.S. and not Germany and had applied his talents to business and not politics, he might have become another Henry Ford (1863–1947) rather than an insane military dictator.

Apart from the collapse of Soviet communism, Fukuyama points to many other hopeful signs that heralded the triumph of democracy: the democratization of Spain and Portugal in the 1970s, the fall of the Chilean junta and other Latin American dictatorships in the 1980s, the economic liberalization of China post-Mao (1893–1976), and finally the example of a "democratic" country that will strike us as laughably inaccurate in the light of events since 1992. He claims, "Khomeini's Iran or the post-Khomeini Iran I think can claim the title to being a more or less democratic country. They have elections of sorts. They're not the fairest elections, but there are elections."

It is much too early to say whether Fukuyama is wrong or right about his long-term prediction that liberal democracy will become the only form of government on the planet, supplanting all other political systems. However, in the short term, his claim that we have reached the "end of history" is a tad premature. In 1992, everything in the garden was rosy: The economy was on the up, and the world was almost at peace. But then it all went wrong: It started with 9/11, which led to the invasions of Afghanistan and Iraq, and then the world economy went into meltdown in 2007. A new ideology of militant jihadist Islam has arisen to take the place of militant communism, and the War on Terror has replaced the Cold War.

Although there are more liberal democratic states in the world today, with the democratization of the countries of Eastern Europe and of several of the former Soviet republics, China has struck out with a new political model that manages to combine phenomenal economic growth with a one-party socialist political structure. As for Fukuyama himself, he has since revised many of his opinions, and his support for neoconservatism and the Bush policy in Iraq has turned from enthusiastic support to fierce opposition. History has been around for a very long time, and as Professor Fukuyama has discovered, the old girl has got a few tricks left up her sleeves.

JIHAD
The 9/11 attacks on New York and Washington signaled the new challenge to liberal democracy from fundamentalist Islam.

SUICIDE CULTS: MARSHALL APPLEWHITE, BONNIE NETTLES, AND OTHERS

Main culprits: Marshall Applewhite and Bonnie Nettles; Luc Jouret and Joseph Di Mambro

What was predicted: The promise of life on another planet or dimension after death by suicide

What actually happened: Mass suicide-murders of cult members

The idea of the passage from one world to another might worry some of you. I assure you that you are going towards a marvelous world which could not be, in any case, any worse than the one you are leaving. Know from now on that after the passage, you will have a body of glory but you will still be recognizable.

Excerpt from documents from the Order of the Solar Temple found in Switzerland in 1993

The popular image of the adherents of that hotchpotch of beliefs known as the "New Age" is that of a bunch of brown rice-eating crystal wavers who live in eco-teepees and practice aromatherapy and foot massage while listening to whale songs on their iPods—weird but mostly harmless. However, wading into the murky waters of belief is always a dangerous enterprise; extremism, literalism, and fundamentalism are rarely far from the surface. This entry deals with two New Age cults that led to the tragic deaths by murder and suicide of their leaders and believers. The first, the Order of the Solar Temple (OST), looked back to the traditions of the medieval order of the Knights Templar, while the second, Heaven's Gate, anticipated the arrival of an alien spaceship that would rescue cult members from a dying Earth.

In both cases, the cult leaders died with their followers, promising that their souls would be reborn on another planet or dimension. Neither group was millenarian, although they both believed that the Earth would be destroyed, and neither believed in the coming of a better world. Their fate was to leave to find a new life away from our earthly reality. As such they were very different from the millenarianism of nineteenth-century doomsday prophets. While after the Great Disappointment, when Jesus did not return, many Millerites abandoned their faith, the followers of the OST and Heaven's Gate, by contrast, would only be disappointed when they didn't wake up on Planet X—a rather terminal problem with their theology.

L' Ordre du Temple Solaire (the Order of the Solar Temple) was one of the many European secret societies that traced their imaginary roots back to the Poor Fellow-Soldiers of Christ and of the Temple of Solomon, better known as the Knights Templar. A number of books have examined the forged Dossiers Secrets d' Henri Lobineau, on which were based the "factual" *The Holy Blood, the Holy Grail* (1982), and the fictional *Da Vinci Code* (2003). In *Holy Blood*, the Knights Templar were said to have protected the secret of the Grail—Jesus' bloodline—and paid for it with their lives. In 1307, the king of France ordered the arrest of the Templars, who were then tortured into confessing to being heretics, sodomists, and devil worshippers. It was not, however, to find out the whereabouts of the Grail, but more mundanely to extort from them their money and estates.

The sordid truth of what really happened to the Knights Templar, however, never disturbed OST members who performed strange rituals dressed as medieval crusaders in order to reach a higher spiritual plane and usher in the New Age. The two founders of the order were Joseph Di Mambro (1924–94) and Luc Jouret (1947–94). Di Mambro was born in Pont-Saint-Esprit, a small town in southwestern France, whose only claim to fame was a mass poisoning in 1951, which was rumored to be a covert CIA LSD trial. He was a member of at least one secret society in the 1960s before he set up a pseudo-Templar order called the Golden Way in Geneva, Switzerland. In 1984 he met Luc Jouret, in whom he found a kindred spirit. Jouret was born in the Belgian Congo, and had a colorful career as a Marxist radical and then a paratrooper before training as a homeopathic doctor in the late 1970s. It was during one of his lecture tours that Jouret met Di Mambro, and the pair set up the OST, with the charismatic Jouret as the front man and Di Mambro as the behind-the-scenes organizer.

The aims of the order were to promote the spiritual development of members and bring about the New Age. While Jouret and Di Mambro exercised considerable authority over their followers, there is no reason to think that they did not themselves believe what they were preaching. The OST was not a moneymaking con. The organization attracted a growing following in the French-speaking world, with temples in France, Switzerland, and the Canadian

SUPPER
Luc Jouret, one of the leaders of the Order of the Solar Temple. He and several of his followers killed themselves after eating a "last supper" in a local restaurant.

province of Quebec. But as they grew, their activities began to attract the attention of the authorities. Di Mambro was arrested in Quebec for trying to buy handguns. In 1993, as the above quote shows, the two cult leaders had decided that they and their followers should quit planet Earth, as their plans for the New Age were not working out. They promised their followers that after they took their own lives, they would "transit" to a planet orbiting the star Sirius.

All didn't turn out well, however. On September 30, 1994, a Swiss-British couple—Tony and Nicky Dutoit—along with their three-month-old son, were murdered in Quebec on Di Mambro's orders because he believed the child to be the Antichrist and blamed him for the failure of his mission on Earth. On the night of October 4, he, Jouret, and a dozen of their followers went for a "last supper" in a restaurant near their Swiss headquarters. That night the inner circle, including Di Mambro and Jouret, took poison, while another 40 or so cult members were drugged and shot or smothered in two locations. The houses had been rigged with remote-controlled arson devices that set them alight. The suicides did not stop with the deaths of the OST leaders. Surviving members killed themselves on the solstices and equinoxes in 1995, 1996, and 1997, in the belief that they would join their brethren who had already transited to Sirius.

Our second group, Heaven's Gate, was a homegrown American phenomenon, founded by Marshall Applewhite (1931–97) and Bonnie Nettles (1928–85). Texas-born Applewhite had a difficult private life. He was estranged from his wife and family, and is thought to have been a closeted homosexual who could not come to terms with his sexuality. He lost his job as a music teacher in 1970 because of "emotional problems," and admitted himself several times to psychiatric hospitals for depression, and, it has been suggested, because he was seeking to be "cured" of his homosexuality. It was during one of his stays in hospital in Houston in 1972 that he met Bonnie Nettles who, despite her beliefs about herself and her patient, was then working as a nurse. It was she who convinced Applewhite that they were both 2,000-year-old aliens who were living in human bodies on Earth, and that the planet was about to be "recycled" and "renewed"; in other words, destroyed.

Applewhite later persuaded himself and his followers that the alien he was now incarnating had previously been Jesus Christ, combining Christianity with Ufology. Despite this bizarre set of beliefs, the pair managed to attract followers in the U.S. and Canada. The group moved peripatetically across the Western states before settling in a mansion, the Rancho Santa Fe, in San Diego County, California. Nettles died of cancer in 1985, leaving Applewhite as sole leader of the cult. The members led ascetic lives, and autopsies revealed that eight male members of Heaven's Gate, including Applewhite, had had themselves castrated to preclude all sexual activity.

In March 1997, Applewhite, fearing persecution and torture by the authorities, decided that the time had come for the group to leave Earth before it was recycled. He persuaded his followers, whom he claimed were all reincarnated members of his original alien crew, that a spaceship hidden in the tail of the comet Hale-Bopp would take their souls to a higher plane of existence—a "level above human." Wearing costumes reminiscent of science-fiction shows such as *Star Trek*, Applewhite and 39 followers took overdoses of the sedative phenobarbital mixed with applesauce and vodka. They also tied plastic bags over their heads in case the drug cocktail did not kill them. Two surviving cult members killed themselves in 1997 and 1998.

HEAVEN CAN'T WAIT

What draws Di Mambro, Jouret, Nettles, and Applewhite together is not their bizarre beliefs, but the powerful charismatic and very disturbed personalities that were strong enough to persuade others to take their own lives. What it says about our culture tragically confirms what the author G. K. Chesterton (1874–1936) said in the last century: "When people stop believing in God, they don't believe in nothing—they believe in anything."

ELECTRONIC ARMAGEDDON: GARY NORTH

Main culprit: Gary North

What was predicted: The disastrous crash of the world's computer systems and embedded microchips on January 1, 2000, triggering an electronic Armageddon

What actually happened: Nothing

At 12 Midnight on January 1, 2000 (a Saturday morning), most of the world's mainframe computers will either shut down or begin spewing out bad data. Most of the world's desktop computers will also start spewing out bad data.

**Gary North in "The Year 2000 Problem:
The Year the Earth Stands Still," c. 1998**

The year 1999 now seems an age away: So much has happened in the intervening years to make us forget the hope and foreboding that greeted the Common Era's second millennium. There was no shortage of Christian apocalyptic fervor, and, of course, we were treated to the revived astrological predictions of Nostradamus. On New Year's Eve 1999, I can't remember much panic on the streets or people running for the hills. Those people who were going to run to the hills had retired there long before, and the rest of humanity was making whoopee at the world's biggest party.

According to several sources, however, not everyone was having a good time. Computer programmers and IT managers worldwide stayed up all night, sitting by their mainframes, networks, and desktops, to see whether, when the clocks turned from 11:59 on December 31, 1999, to 00:00, January 1, 2000, their systems would crash, go haywire,

or even explode. This was the prediction made with undisguised glee by the likes of Christian reconstructionist economist and publisher Gary North (b. 1942). North disseminated his electronic doomsday predictions on the Internet—the very medium he predicted would be annihilated during the year 2000—"the year the Earth stands still" (see quote).

The problem that concerned governments, businesses, the more hysterical sections of the media, and Mr. North was the millennium, or Y2K, "bug." Although the use of the word "bug" suggests some kind of virus, it was in fact more of a programming glitch that many believed would lead to an irretrievable breakdown of computerized systems running our banking, power, transit, communications, and defense. Given our dependence on computers and the Internet by the end of the twentieth century, how justified was that fear? And how much was doomsday hype?

The problem with computers is that, for all their awesome calculating ability, their speed, and their storage capacity, they do not think. They are dumb. So when a computer comes up against an impossible command or a conflict in its programming, it just crashes or returns

AGE CONCERN
Although modern machines were not thought to be immune, the most serious problems were predicted in the "heritage" systems created in the '70s and '80s when the 1999 problem was still far in the future.

a nonsensical answer. Computer programs are written in computer languages—to the layman seemingly random assemblages of letters, numbers, and symbols from the ASCII character set. In the old days, when people still had to program with punch cards and computer memories were limited, it was more economical to use two instead of four digits to denote a year. Hence, 1964, would be 64, and 1976, 76. In 1976, the millennium was 34 years away—an eternity in computer programming terms, when programs only had a shelf life of a few years. And in 1976, there were far fewer computers in the world—no PCs, no laptops, and no Internet.

As early as 1958, a farsighted IBM programmer called Robert Bemer (1920–2004) realized that there would be a problem when we reached the end of the century, which was also coincidentally the end of the millennium. As the date rolled over at midnight on January 1, the date could not go up to 100 in a two-digit system, giving the program a serious case of indigestion. It could go to 00, in which case it would revert to the year 1900, or 99 years into the past. Bemer attempted several times to warn the IT community of the looming Y2K problem but was largely ignored. From the 1980s onward, new applications to handle large databases were created with much longer lifespans than earlier programs. However, even then, many of these stuck to earlier two-digit year convention.

Gary North, who made some of the most apocalyptic Y2K predictions, is not a computer scientist, or even a scientist of any kind. He is, in fact, a man of letters and a man of faith. He holds a PhD in history from UC, Riverside, with a special interest in economic history. He is an adherent of Christian reconstructionism, a school of Protestant thought that combines support for small government and laissez-faire economics with a belief that the U.S. should be run according to Old and New Testament law. In *Political Polytheism: The Myth of Pluralism* (1989) he expressed his political credo in the following terms:

NORTHERN EXPOSURE

> The long-term goal of Christians in politics should be to gain exclusive control over the franchise. Those who refuse to submit publicly to the eternal sanctions of God by submitting to His Church's public marks of the covenant—baptism and holy communion—must be denied citizenship, just as they were in

ancient Israel. The way to achieve this political goal is through successful mass evangelism followed by constitutional revision.

This Handmaid's Tale vision of America might come about if there were to be a major collapse of the banking system and stock market. And this is exactly what North was predicting when he wrote:

> Months before January 1, 2000, the world's stock markets will have crashed. Who is going to leave his money in his bank if he thinks his bank's computer is not reliable? A worldwide run on the banks will create havoc in the investment markets [...] How reliable will stocks and mutual funds be if the banking system has closed down? How will you even get paid? How will your employer get paid? How will governments get paid?

Back in the real world, several governments, especially the U.S. and UK, who were perhaps more computer-dependent than most, were particularly concerned and mounted major campaigns to inform the public and business as to the potential dangers of Y2K. Other governments, such as Italy, Russia, and China, did not take the problem as seriously, and did comparatively little preparatory work. The estimated global cost of Y2K remediation was $300 billion for the checking, patching, and upgrading of older IT systems. Supporters of remediation claim that it was money well spent. They point to the fact that there were very few problems caused by the Y2K bug, and that this was due to the work done in the run-up to the rollover date.

THE ESTIMATED GLOBAL COST OF Y2K REMEDIATION WAS $300 BILLION FOR THE CHECKING, PATCHING, AND UPGRADING OF OLDER IT SYSTEMS.

There were, however, a few glitches: In the UK, card-swipe machines issued by the HSBC bank stopped working for four days from December 28, 1999, to January 1, 2000; stores reverted to using paper slips to process credit-card payments. On New Year's Day itself, 150 slot machines stopped working in the state of Delaware; bus ticket validation machines failed in two Australian states; Japan's NTT cell-phone network had problems relaying SMS messages, and there were two minor equipment failures at nuclear power plants that caused no risk to the public. Finally, websites in several countries displayed the date as "01/01/19100."

Critics of Y2K remediation, including *The Wall Street Journal*, claimed that Y2K was all hype—"the hoax of the century"—and that the whole exercise had been a complete waste of time and money. They pointed out that countries such as Italy that had not made major preparations had not been affected in any significant way. In the U.S. three-quarters of the public school system and approximately 1.5 million small businesses did not undertake any Y2K remediation, yet again, there were no major problems reported in January 2000. Finally, skeptics pointed out that if problems were going to occur, they would have made themselves known in the course of 1999, as the financial year 2000 for many institutions and corporations would have started well before the New Year.

When I heard of the Y2K bug in the late 1990s, I decided to try a simple experiment. Having backed up my hard drive (just in case, you understand, because I was sure nothing bad would happen), I opened the "date and time" panel on my PC and entered the fateful date January 31, 1999, and the time of 11:59 and waited a minute to see if my computer would start "spewing out bad data," as predicted by Gary North, or possibly blow a fuse and stop working. In the event, nothing at all happened as the manufacturer had already patched the machine's operating system to ensure that 60 seconds later, the date read 01/01/2000.

OVER THE RAINBOW: GORDON BROWN

Main culprit: Gordon Brown

What was predicted: The end of cycles of boom and bust

What actually happened: The financial crisis and credit crunch

We will not return to the old boom and bust.

Gordon Brown in his budget speech to the House of Commons in 2007

© Cloki | Dreamstime

A reinvigorated Labour Party, renamed "New Labour" by its leader Tony Blair (b. 1953), swept into power in May 1997, ending 18 years of Conservative rule, 11 of which had been under Margaret Thatcher (b. 1925). The party's election coincided with a resurgent economy after years of recession and stagnation, the peace dividend from the end of the Cold War, and three years before the second millennium, which most people welcomed with optimism rather than pessimism. Blair (44) and his deputy Gordon Brown (b. 1953) were young, brimming with new ideas, and untainted by the accusations of political "sleaze" that bedeviled the final years of Conservative rule. In contrast with Blair and co., the outgoing Conservatives, led by the less-than-charismatic John Major (b. 1943) looked old, tired, corrupt, and politically bankrupt.

As New Labour and its supporters celebrated their victory on election night, it was to the strains of the party's campaign song "Things Can Only Get Better" (1994) by D:Ream, which carried with it echoes of an earlier British prime minister's remark after his general election victory in 1959, "You've never had it so good." That statement characterized Britain's economic, social, and cultural resurgence during the 1960s, just as D:Ream's optimistic anthem foreshadowed the boom times of New Labour's "Cool Britannia" during the early 2000s. But what were the boom times built on—sound economic bases or the shifting sands of stock-market speculation and inflated house prices? Gordon Brown, who became Chancellor of the Exchequer (Minister of Finance) in the Blair government and remained in post for ten years, repeatedly claimed that his "prudent" economic policies had brought an end to the cycles of "boom and bust" that have always characterized capitalist economies. It was a bold claim, and one that was to be proved spectacularly wrong.

I do not wish to be unnecessarily unkind or hurtful when I say that physically Gordon Brown is not the most prepossessing of individuals. In general appearance and demeanor he looks like a strict high-school history teacher telling you you've come bottom of the class in your term paper, or a minister of religion who's caught you doing something bad in Sunday school class. The impression is not helped by the fact that he is visually impaired in one eye, due to an unfortunate accident while he was playing rugby at high school that almost cost him his sight. In the media age, when presentation counts for just as much as policy, Brown was always going to be at a serious disadvantage when compared to the charismatic Blair, or his Conservative successor as prime minister, the youthful, eloquent David Cameron (b. 1966).

The most tragic miscalculation of Brown's premiership and 2010 reelection campaign were not policy gaffes but his attempts at smiling. No doubt advised by a well-meaning image consultant that he should try to be more of a "people person," Brown appeared on YouTube and television interviews occasionally breaking from his usual serious frown when he remembered that he had to smile. However, instead of creating the impression of a warm, friendly person, Brown contorted his features into a ghastly rictus worthy of Bela Lugosi (1882–1956) as Count Dracula.

Although personal charm is an important asset for a political leader — look at Bill Clinton (b. 1946), for example — it is not so critical for a second in command — look at Al Gore (b. 1948). In the Blair-Brown double-act, Blair had the looks and charm, but, it was generally agreed, Brown had the brains, common sense, and staying power. Brown seemed physically and temperamentally well suited to the job as Chancellor of the Exchequer. He looked like a man you could trust with your money — not the kind of smooth operator who was going make a sudden flit to Rio after he'd blown all the cash on fast living and fast women. But was the British public's trust misplaced between 1997 and 2007? Who is Gordon Brown, and what were his qualifications for the job? Did he get things right or spectacularly wrong? Should we praise him as the savior of the world's banking system or slam him as one of the main instigators of the world's worst financial crisis?

SON OF THE MANSE

Born in the small town of Kirkcaldy on Scotland's east coast, Brown is the son of a minister of the Church of Scotland, which gave him one of his own favorite epithets, "son of the manse" (manse being the current or former home of a minister). Unusually for a future British chancellor and premier, he did not go to Oxbridge (the abbreviation for Britain's elite "Ivy League" universities of Oxford and Cambridge), but attended the University of Edinburgh, where he graduated in history and where he completed his doctorate on the Scottish Labour Party in the early twentieth century. Between 1976 and 1983, Brown had a career as a university lecturer in politics and as a television current affairs journalist. Considering his future ten-year tenure as chancellor, Brown had no background in economics, and no first-hand work experience of the financial sector. Politically, he was on the center-left of the Labour Party and a lifelong Christian socialist, and therefore not naturally sympathetic with New Labour's newfound affection for free enterprise and big business.

Brown was elected to Parliament in the 1983 election, the second to be won by Margaret Thatcher. It was during his first term as an MP that he met his long-time political ally and colleague, Tony Blair. The two men climbed the party ranks quickly, both becoming members of the Shadow Cabinet. The crucial event during Brown's time in opposition was the unexpected death of Labour Party leader John Smith (1938–94), which left the party leaderless, and its two heirs apparent, Blair and Brown, with a problem: Who would be the next leader? According to New Labour legend, the two made a deal in a north London restaurant one evening in 1994, agreeing that Blair would be premier, and Brown chancellor, and that at some point in the future Blair would step down and Brown would take over. Blair became prime minister and Brown chancellor. In New Labour's first administration it seemed to be an ideal arrangement, and the government and country prospered.

However, in the light of recent events, we have to ask whether that prosperity was built on Brown's fiscal prudence and his farsighted economic policies, or was the result of fortunate economic circumstances? When analyzing the causes of the current financial crisis, which is now agreed to be the worst in recent history, rivaling the Great Depression, economists look back to the late 1990s and early 2000s, and the decisions taken by men such as Brown in the UK and Chairman of the Fed Allan Greenspan (b. 1926) in the U.S. In particular, they focus on three areas: deregulation of the financial sector, lack of control of the housing market, and fiscal policy in response to the bursting of the dotcom bubble of 2000.

IMAGE
In the television and Internet age, the serious (verging on dour) Gordon Brown suffered a major image problem during his premiership.

Financial deregulation began with the Big Bang in 1986, but continued apace through the era of Reaganomics, and accelerated under the Democratic and New Labour administrations in the U.S. and UK. As a result, financial institutions developed ever more arcane and riskier products—mortgage back securities (MBS), collateralized debt obligations (CDO), and credit default swaps (CDS); at the same time, interest rates were being kept artificially low in response to the bursting of the dotcom bubble. In other words, the world economy was awash with cheap cash, and, my god, did we spend it! We shopped ourselves stupid using our credit cards, and when we'd filled our homes full of clothes, white goods, and electronics, we thought it'd be a grand idea to buy a bigger home. The deregulated finance sector dreamed up sub-prime mortgages to pay for ever higher house prices. Banks realized that there was more money to be made from repackaging mortgage debt and selling it on, so it was spread evenly throughout the whole of the economy.

When the housing bubble burst in 2006, the whole complex financial edifice it had supported collapsed with it, threatening to take the world's leading banks with it. It became apparent that the prosperity of the previous six years had not been built on prudent fiscal measures and economic policies but on the equivalent of going to Vegas and putting everything on red in roulette. Gordon Brown had neither foreseen what was happening, nor had he taken any measures to control the worst excesses of the financial sector and housing market. Thinking he had put an end to boom and bust, he himself contributed to the biggest bust since 1929. After Tony Blair stood down in June 2007, just before the financial storm hit, Brown succeeded him in office as premier. He limped on for another three years, his credibility crumbling as fast as the British economy. Defeated in the general election of 2010, he resigned before the Conservative and Liberal Democrat parties had even agreed to form a coalition, leaving the country and his own party leaderless.

BRING OUT YOUR DEAD: DR MARGARET CHAN

Main culprit: Dr. Margaret Chan

What was predicted: The death of millions from pandemic flu

What actually happened: Fewer people died in the HIN1/09 pandemic than from seasonal flu

All countries should immediately now activate their pandemic preparedness plans. Countries should remain on high alert for unusual outbreaks of influenza-like illness and severe pneumonia.

Statement by Dr Margaret Chan (b. 1946), Director-General of the World Health Organization, April 29, 2009

We are right to fear pandemic diseases. As the human population has grown, and become more concentrated in villages, towns, and cities, so the risk of epidemics and pandemics has increased. A "pandemic" is an epidemic disease outbreak that not only affects a large number of people but is also distributed over a large geographical area. During the Middle Ages and Age of Exploration, several pandemics were caused when a disease was introduced from one part of the world into regions where the native population had no experience of it and therefore no immunity.

One of the most deadly of the great historical pandemics was the fourteenth-century "Black Death," a European outbreak of bubonic plague. The disease's original home was central Asia, where its animal host was the flea of the black rat. The plague traveled westward with the invading Mongol armies, and the Black Death is thought to have begun in the Crimea in southern Russia in 1346. Merchant ships returning from the Crimea to European ports brought with them infected black rats, which passed the disease on to humans and European rats.

CRY WOLF
WHO director Margaret Chan has been accused of exaggerating the threat from H1N1, costing governments millions in unused antiviral drugs.

The plague's first European port of call was the capital of the Byzantine Empire, Constantinople (now Istanbul, Turkey), and quickly spread throughout the whole of the Mediterranean world and northern Europe with disastrous consequences. It abated in 1350, having killed between one and two-thirds of Europe's population. The equivalent death toll in today's U.S. would be between 100 and 200 million, and between 20 and 40 million deaths in the UK. The second pandemic of this type occurred in the Americas after the Europeans arrived in the fifteenth century. The native populations had no immunity to Old World diseases such as smallpox, typhus, and cholera, and it is estimated that during the next two centuries epidemics wiped out between 90 and 95 percent of the pre-Columbian population.

The most recent pandemic of this type has been the spread of the Human Immunodeficiency Virus (HIV), the cause of Acquired Immune Deficiency Syndrome (AIDS), which was first identified in the U.S. and Europe in 1981. Epidemiologists believe that it was originally a West African simian virus that passed into the human population at some time during the twentieth century or possibly earlier. Once the virus had left its animal host and become a human disease, it spread quickly through unprotected populations, making particular inroads in sub-Saharan Africa and Southeast Asia in the past three decades. Although HIV is fatal without treatment and has killed over 25 million people between 1981 and 2006, it is relatively difficult to catch, being principally passed on through blood-to-blood transmission during sex and intravenous drug use, and thus fairly simple to avoid with measures such as the sterilization of needles and the use of condoms.

Today, given the amount of travel both between and within countries and continents, there are very few places in the world left that are so remote that they haven't been exposed to the full Pandora's Box of human infectious diseases. The danger is now not so much from a completely unknown disease but from viruses that are genetically unstable and can mutate or combine with other viruses to create new, deadlier strains. The most dangerous of these unstable viruses is perhaps also the most common: the influenza or flu virus. We are all used to the seasonal flu that comes back without fail every fall and winter, like an annoying relative who we just can't seem to shake off at Thanksgiving or Christmas time. Seasonal flu is a serious disease. It affects between five and 15 percent of the world population (340 million to 1 billion), and kills between a quarter and a half million people annually, principally among high-risk groups: people with underlying health conditions, the under-fives, and the over-60s. Healthy young adults do contract seasonal flu, but they are much less likely to develop fatal complications than those in high-risk groups.

However, there are also potentially far more dangerous types of viral flu that originate in animals and can be transferred to humans by close contact. Historically, these new strains have not been as picky as seasonal flu when it comes to selecting their victims. The World Health Organization website carries the following advice about animal-to-human flu pandemics:

> The severity of disease and the number of deaths caused by a pandemic virus vary greatly, and cannot be known prior to the emergence of the virus. During past pandemics, attack rates reached 25-35 percent of the total population. Under the

best circumstances, assuming that the new virus causes mild disease, the world could still experience an estimated 2 million to 7.4 million deaths. Projections for a more virulent virus are much higher.

In order to monitor new flu outbreaks, the WHO has devised a six-level scale for the severity of pandemics. At the lowest threat levels 1–2, the virus is only active in animals and there are no or very few cases of animal-to-human transmission. At levels 3–4 human-to-human transmission takes place at increasing rates and the disease begins to spread through the population of one of the WHO world regions (roughly the continents). At levels 5–6, the outbreak is declared a full-blown pandemic with efficient and sustained human-to-human transmission of the virus in at least two of the WHO's regions.

The H5N1 influenza strain, known as "avian" or "bird flu," has been causing concern since the early 2000s. H5N1, which is found in wild and domesticated birds, can jump the species barrier and infect mammals, including humans. At present, cases have been reported in people who live and work with infected birds, and human-to-human transmission is extremely rare. As of August 2010, human cases of avian flu had been confirmed in 15 countries, mostly in Asia, with the highest death toll reported in Indonesia (139). The total number of deaths from H5N1 worldwide is 300, out of 505 cases, making it lethal in about 60 percent of cases. The most westerly fatal human cases have been reported in Turkey, with four fatalities. The virus has yet to appear in humans in the Americas and Western Europe. The fear is that the virus will mutate or "reassort" (acquire genetic material from another flu strain), and become much more infectious and much deadlier. The WHO threat level from H5N1 at the time of writing is level 3.

In 2009, the world's health authorities were busy planning for a possible pandemic outbreak of a mutated form of H1N1, when out of the blue, in March, there was an outbreak of another strain of flu, A/H1N1, soon christened "swine flu" because it is originally a pig influenza strain, reported in Mexico. By June 2009, Dr Margaret Chan, WHO Director-General, announced that the outbreak had become a level 6 global pandemic, confirming people's worst fears about a possible new and potentially deadly flu strain.

H1N1 is not a new virus. Along with A/H3N2, a subtype of human H1N1 is responsible for seasonal flu infections that affect around 0.1 percent of the world's population every year. H1N1's most deadly manifestation in the twentieth century was the Spanish Flu pandemic of 1918–20, which broke out immediately after World War One. The outbreak began in Spain, hence its name, but thanks to improved transport links spread quickly to the whole world. European populations already weakened by four years of war were particularly vulnerable. A third of the world's population (around 500 million) contracted the virus, and between 20 and 100 million died, a death toll that even managed to dwarf the carnage of World War One. The particular tragedy of the Spanish Flu outbreak was that it affected young, healthy adults who would not have been so prone to die of seasonal flu.

The latest outbreak of H1N1 was first identified in Mexico City in March 2009, but had probably started much earlier, possibly as early as the fall of 2008. The pathogen was identified as a new subtype of the H1N1 virus, which combined an existing human, avian, and pig viral reassortment with a different type of H1N1 pig flu virus. One of the most worrying aspects of the illness was that, like Spanish Flu, it affected healthy young adults as much as high-risk groups. The symptoms of mild swine flu were the same as those of seasonal flu: fever, sore throat, chills, tiredness, aching joints, coughs, and runny nose, but a small number of patients had much more severe symptoms, which sometimes led to viral pneumonia and death caused by acute respiratory failure.

In the early stages of the epidemic there was no vaccine available, but like other flu strains H1N1 could be treated with antiviral drugs. The most effective of these (though by how much is still a matter of debate) is oseltamivir, better known under the brand name Tamiflu. However, in summer 2009, worldwide stocks of the drug could not have met demand in the event of a worldwide pandemic.

The Mexican authorities moved quickly after the first cases were confirmed. The government ordered the closure of public buildings and commercial premises to slow down the rate of infections. Some airlines cancelled their flights to the country, and special health checks were instituted for travelers returning from the country. This was, of course,

FROM SPAIN TO MEXICO

much too late. The strain had been active for several months, and had caused infections in the U.S. in January. Within weeks of the Mexican announcement, cases were being reported all over the world, first among travelers returning from Mexico, but soon among the general population. By April, the WHO was warning governments to expect a major outbreak of influenza and pneumonia (see quote), and by June, Margaret Chan had raised the pandemic threat level to maximum.

With no vaccine and only limited supplies of Tamiflu, there was mounting concern, fanned both by the WHO announcement and reports in the more hysterical sectors of the media. Our screens were full of images of people in facemasks from Mexico City to Taiwan, the closures of public buildings, and the immediate quarantine of passengers showing the slightest flu-like symptoms. The pandemic warning was fast turning into a pandemic panic. Governments stockpiled Tamiflu and gave it to anyone considered at risk or showing any flu-like symptoms, and initiated a campaign of mass vaccination as soon as the vaccine became available in bulk in the fall of 2009.

And then suddenly, it was all over: The number of new infections declined rapidly, and with them the deaths. In August 2010 the WHO declared that the H1N1/09 pandemic had entered its post-pandemic phase. Swine flu had infected 1.6 million people (confirmed by testing) and killed a total of 19,633, with the U.S. topping the table with 3,433 deaths, followed by Brazil and India with about 2,000 each. The UK and other major European countries suffered between 300–500 fatalities each. The catastrophe had not happened and both the WHO and national governments were criticized for scaremongering and wasting money (by the very same media outlets that had howled a few months earlier about there being insufficient supplies of Tamiflu). But Chan and the WHO remain unapologetic. Better be safe than sorry, they say, because it is only a matter of time before a really nasty bug does evolve.

THE END OF THE FUTURE: FUTUROLOGY

PREDICTION

Millenarian

Technology

Prophecy

Politics

Military

Natural Disaster

Culture

Economics

Doomsday

Main culprits: Futurologists

What was predicted: TEOTWAWKI—the end of the world as we know it

What actually happened: The world as we know it will come to an end, one day...

It has often been said that, if the human species fails to make a go of it here on Earth, some other species will take over the running. In the sense of developing high intelligence this is not correct. We have, or soon will have, exhausted the necessary physical prerequisites so far as this planet is concerned. With coal gone, oil gone, high-grade metallic ores gone, no species however competent can make the long climb from primitive conditions to high-level technology. This is a one shot affair. If we fail, this planetary system fails so far as intelligence is concerned.

British astronomer Fred Hoyle, quoted in
"The Olduvai Theory: Sliding Towards a
Post-Industrial Stone Age" (1996)

We have almost reached the end of our survey of history's very worst predictions. In the past 49 entries, we have seen the evolution of prediction from those who employed supernatural means to foretell the course of future events—divinely inspired prophets and astrologers—to those who used their expert knowledge in their own fields—political and social science, science and technology, warfare, and culture—to predict future trends and events. As we have seen, no amount of experience has proven any better than scripture, the runes, the crystal ball, or the course of the stars as a guide to the future.

We have also touched briefly in several entries on another type of seer into the future: the science-fiction writer, who uses his or her creativity and intuition to imagine things to come. Although Jules Verne (1828–1905) was uncannily accurate about technological developments in his descriptions of moon shots and submarines, like many sci-fi authors past and present, he places new technology in a world that is socially exactly like his own. The captain of the Nautilus or the men who orbit the Moon are nineteenth-century gentlemen, with a nineteenth-century world view, which is why, though the science may strike us as visionary, Verne's books are at the same time charming, dated period pieces. The inability to conceive of technological change without the accompanying socio-political developments is what makes so many predictions fail.

IN *THE TIME MACHINE*, HUMANITY HAS EVOLVED INTO TWO RACES: THE PEACEFUL, CHILDLIKE ELOI AND THE SINISTER, DEGENERATE MORLOCKS, WHO FEED ON THEM.

A sci-fi writer who looked into the future with much greater prescience than most was H. G. Wells. In his novella, *The Time Machine*, published in 1895, the protagonist travels over 800,000 years into the future to discover that humanity has evolved into two races: the peaceful, childlike Eloi and the sinister, degenerate Morlocks, who feed on them. Going from there into the far future, the time traveler witnesses the end of life on Earth, and then of the planet itself. In his alternate history of the world, *The Shape of Things to Come* (1933), Wells traces the history of humanity from his present in 1933 to 2106.

Unlike the bleak future predicted in *The Time Machine*, *The Shape of Things to Come* presents a utopian view of humanity's fate in the centuries to come, although things do get a lot worse before they get better. Wells predicts a world war as erupting in Europe and the Pacific in 1940—one year out each way. But rather than an outright victory for one side or the other, the war continues until 1950 until both sides collapse economically, bringing the world economy down with them. A plague in 1956–7 wipes out most of humanity and almost destroys civilization. The surviving elite of scientists and engineers, who are the only ones to have access to technology, establish the benevolent "Dictatorship of the Air," which abolishes all religions, imposes English as the world language, and promotes peaceful scientific development. Once its aims are achieved, the dictatorship is disbanded in a bloodless revolution, and human civilization finally achieves its full intellectual and cultural potential.

Since the 1960s, an effort has been made to turn the art of prediction into the science of futurology, with the creation of academic departments and think tanks all vying to predict the future for governments, political parties, the military, and corporations. Although futurologists have developed a number of methodological tools to help them make their forecasts, they have not so far proved to be any more accurate than crystal balls or star charts. While some believe that the application of scientific methods such as probability forecasts, long-range modeling, and statistical analysis will one day enable us to predict the future with a degree of accuracy, others point to chaos theory to claim that the future is basically unpredictable.

- 267 bn bbl
- 110 bn bbl
- 30 bn bbl
- 0

ABYSS
Peak oil theory has been applied to other resources, leading futurologists to predict that industrial civilization will come to an end in 2030. Above: oil reserves by country.

A quick trawl through futurological websites and books throws up far more negative scenarios for humanity's immediate future than positive ones. An example is the Olduvai Theory first proposed by systems engineer Richard Duncan in 1996. The theory posits that our industrial civilization has a lifespan of 100 years, and will last from 1930 to 2030. Duncan defines industrial civilization as the period when per capita energy use rises above 37 percent of its peak value, and ends when it falls below 37 percent. Duncan bases his model on the Hubbert Curve prediction for peak oil (pp. 164–8), and foresees the following stages, all using the imagery of Tanzania's very own Grand Canyon, the Olduvai Gorge: (1) the Olduvai slope (1979–99), when per capita energy use begins to fall; (2) the Olduvai slide (2000–11), when we hit peak oil; and (3) the Olduvai cliff (2012–30), when we run out of oil, and face TEOTWAWKI.

We saw in the entry on peak oil that Hubbert's predictions have been questioned, and in addition, Duncan does not factor in the possible development of alternate energy sources, such as nuclear fusion. But that might be beside the point. There seems to be something inbuilt in many humans that makes them expect the worst in any given situation. After all, a disaster does make a much better story than an optimistic outcome where everything turns out all right in the end. So maybe it is better to fear the worst and be pleasantly surprised when it doesn't happen rather than the other way around.

THE ABSOLUTE END

The end is bound to come one day, of that we're sure—but how? We're currently being told that Earth is warming up, and whether this is a manmade phenomenon or a natural one, temperatures are slowly creeping upward with potentially disastrous consequences for civilization. The long-term trend, however, is that Earth will get a lot colder. In an earlier entry, we examined the 1970s' fears of the coming end of the current interglacial (pp. 199–203). Although it is unlikely to be this century or even this millennium, the next glaciation will come, bringing with it the end of the mild Anthropocene period, and with it the demise of our civilization. Whether humanity survives the next glacial will depend on the extent of the ice coverage. If the ice does not extend past the last glaciation, then part of the temperate zone, the tropics, and the equatorial regions remain habitable, and humanity, much reduced in number, will survive. In the more severe "snowball Earth" scenario, when the ice goes all the way to the Equator, we haven't got an ice cube's hope in hell.

The cold, however, is not the Earth's major worry in the very long-term future. On the cosmological timescale, which runs into billions of years, Earth's fate will be sealed when our star, the Sun, completes the current stage of its stellar life cycle. The Sun is roughly 4.5 billion years old, and is currently halfway in its "main sequence" phase, which has another 5.5 billion years to go. At the end of the main sequence phase, it will expand into a red giant, approximately 250 times its current size, swallowing the inner planets and Earth, turning them into the cosmic equivalent of charcoal briquettes. After a billion years as a red giant, the Sun will shuck off its outer layers, forming a planetary nebula, leaving behind a white dwarf star, which will cool over the next few billion years. However, from the perspective of life on Earth, should it have survived for the next billion years, the end will come much earlier. The Sun's output is increasing by 10 percent every billion years, and this will be sufficient, in a billion years, to boil away the oceans, making life on Earth impossible.

Were humans to have survived and left Earth by this point and be living in other solar systems or galaxies, their existence would still be limited by the lifecycle of the universe itself. According to the Big Bang theory, the universe began in a sudden expansion from a super-dense and super-hot state 13.7 billion years ago and is still expanding. There are several theories about what will happen next: one is the Big Crunch, as the process of expansion is reversed and everything falls back to the super-dense starting point. This could give rise to the Big Bounce—a sort of cosmic yo-yo effect—with new Big Bangs and Big Crunches occurring *ad infinitum*. Alternatives include the Big Rip, when all matter is pulled apart by dark energy, and the Big Freeze, when the expanding universe runs out of gas, stalls, and gradually cools down to absolute zero.

So there we have it; all we need now do is survive global warming and cooling, sea-level rise, World War Three, the next asteroid strike, the possibility of nano-robots turning the world into sludge or intelligent robots taking over, super-volcanic eruptions, pandemic flu, solar flares, the Olduvai Curve, and Armageddon, and in a billion years time, just as the last drop of water evaporates from Earth, we can say smugly, they all got it wrong.

FURTHER READING

There are many excellent general reference works available in printed form or online covering many of the entries featured in this book. Still one of the most authoritative is the *Encyclopaedia Britannica*, available for free at most large public and school libraries, and online at britannica.com as a subscription service. Another reference source that is used by authors and journalists is the ubiquitous Wikipedia (en. wikipedia.org). The content of Wikipedia, however, is user-generated, and is not independently verified. As a result, there are inaccurate or biased articles included in the wiki database (articles identified as having problems or a particular bias are often flagged by the site, but the site itself will not edit or delete articles unless they are proved to be bogus or libelous). Nevertheless, Wikipedia and its associated sites provide a good starting point to find basic information and references on a wide range of topics.

In addition to books and articles, I have included the web addresses of general and specialist sites whenever appropriate. All URLs were correct at the time of writing, but it is the nature of the Internet that these change as sites migrate to new service providers or are taken down. If a website is no longer active or has moved, please conduct a search on the topic in a search engine such as Google.com. The most recent entries have not yet been covered in books, but a great deal of material is available from websites such as the BBC, CNN, major English-language newspapers, and the online archives of magazines such as *The Economist*, *Time*, and *Newsweek*.

The reference materials listed below fall into two categories: In certain instances, they provide detailed accounts of the topics covered in the entries; in others they give the reader a general background on the period, person, or topic. I have tried to include both whenever these were available. When a source listed is strongly biased either for or against the topic under discussion, I have also included a balancing work supporting the opposite point of view. I have also included materials about entries in other media, including videos (most of these are available at Internet sites such as youtube.com) and also film and TV documentaries or dramatizations of the events described in the entries, though often these do not necessarily stick faithfully to the facts, and take Hollywood liberties with storylines and characters.

Sibylline Books

Beard, M., North, J., and Price, S. (1998) *Religions of Rome*, Cambridge: Cambridge University Press

Curnow, T. (2004) *The Oracles of the Ancient World*, London: Duckworth

First Second Coming

The New Testament, Holy Bible, King James Authorized Version

McManners, J. (2001) *The Oxford Illustrated History of Christianity*, New York: Oxford University Press

Maya 2012

Bonewitz, R. (1999) *Maya Prophecy*, London: Piatkus Books

Coe, M. (1992) *Breaking the Maya Code*, London and New York: Thames & Hudson

Grube, N., Eggebrecht, E., and Seidel, M. (2000) *Maya: Divine Kings of the Rain Forest*, Cologne: Köneman

1000 CE

Frassetto, M. (2002) *The Year 1000: Religious and Social Response to the Turning of the First Millennium*, Basingstoke: Palgrave Macmillan

Lacey, R. (1999) *The Year 1000: What Life Was Like at the Turn of the First Millennium*, New York: Little, Brown, and Co

Ragnarök

Byock, J. (Trans.) (2006) *The Prose Edda*, London: Penguin Classics

Crossley-Holland, K. (1996) *The Penguin Book of Norse Myths: Gods of the Vikings*, New York: Penguin

Johannes Stöffler

Niccoli, O. (1990) *Prophecy and People in Renaissance Italy*, Princeton: Princeton Uinversity Press

Thorndike, L. (2003) *History of Magic and Experimental Science*, Part 9, Whitefish, MT: Kessinger Publishing

Mother Shipton

Mother Shipton (1686) *The Strange and Wonderful History of Mother Shipton*, London

Mother Shipton (2010) *The Strange and Wonderful History and Prophecies of Mother Shipton*, London: ECCO

Nostradamus

Abanes R. (1999) *End-Times Visions: The Road to Armageddon*, New York: Four Walls Eight Windows

Leoni, E. (2000) *Nostradamus and his Prophecies*, New York: Bell Publishers

Nostradamus, M. (2006) *The Complete Prophecies of Michel Nostradamus*, Filiquarian Publishing

Wilson, Ian (2003) *Nostradamus: The Evidence*, London: Orion

www.Nostradamus.org

George III

Black, J. (2006) *George III: America's Last King*, New Haven, CT: Yale University Press

Griffiths, S. (2002) *The War for American Independence: From 1760 to the Surrender at Yorktown in 1781*, Champaign, IL: University of Illinois Press

The Madness of King George (1994) dir. Nicholas Hytner

Thomas Malthus

Elwell, F. W. (2001) *A Commentary on Malthus' 1798 Essay on Population as Social Theory*, Pittsburg, PA: Mellon Press

James, P. (1979) *Population Malthus: His Life and Times,* London: Routledge and Kegan Paul.

Joseph Smith

Abanes, R. (2003) *One Nation Under Gods: A History of the Mormon Church*, Emeryville, CA: Thunder's Mouth Press

Tanner, J. and S. (1987) *Mormonism—Shadow or Reality?*, Salt Lake City, UT: Utah Lighthouse Ministry

www.scriptures.lds.org/dc/contents (the official site of the Mormon Church)

Railways

Christopher, J. (2006) *Brunel's Kingdom*, Stroud, Gloucestershire: Tempus Publishing Limited

Wolmar, C. (2008) *Fire and Steam: A New History of the Railways in Britain*, London: Atlantic Books

William Miller

The Old Testament, Holy Bible, King James Authorized Version

Abanes R. (1999) *End-Times Visions: The Road to Armageddon*, New York: Four Walls Eight Windows

Miller, W. (1842) *Evidence from Scripture and history of the second coming of Christ about the year 1843, exhibited in a course of lectures*, ed. by J. Hines. See Lecture III for the full calculation

Karl Marx

Engels, F. and Marx, K. (2010) *The Communist Manifesto*, New York: Simon and Brown

Marx, K. (2008) *Capital: An Abridged Edition*, ed. David McLellan, New York: Oxford University Press

McLellan, D. (2006) *Karl Marx: A Biography*, Basingstoke: Palgrave Macmillan

Telephone

Conrad, D. (2009) *Telephone Tales: History of Telephone People and the Equipment They Worked With*, Indianapolis, IN: Dog Ear Publishing

Fischer, C. (1994) *America Calling: A Social History of the Telephone to 1940*, Berkeley, CA: University of California Press

Shulman, S. (2009) *The Telephone Gambit: Chasing Alexander Graham Bell's Secret*, New York: W. W. Norton & Company

Lightbulb

Nobleman, M. (2000) *The Light Bulb*, Mankato, MN: Capstone Press

Stross, R. (2008) *The Wizard of Menlo Park: How Thomas Alva Edison Invented the Modern World*, New York: Three Rivers Press

Radio

Balk, A. (2005) *The Rise of Radio, from Marconi through the Golden Age*, Jefferson, NC: McFarland & Company

Lindley, D. (2005) *Degrees Kelvin: A Tale of Genius, Invention, and Tragedy*, Washington, DC: Joseph Henry Press

Rude, A. (2008) *Hello, Everybody!: The Dawn of American Radio*, New York: Houghton Mifflin Harcourt

Automobiles

Brinkley, D. (2004) *Wheels for the World: Henry Ford, His Company, and a Century of Progress*, New York: Penguin

Ford, H. (2010) *My Life and Work—An Autobiography of Henry Ford*, Greenbook Publications

"Ford Model T—100 years later" on youtube.com features footage of the Model T and Ford's assembly line.

Glancey, J. (2008) *The Car: A History of the Automobile*, London: Carlton Publishing Group

Airplanes

Grant, R. G. (2008) *Flight: 100 Years of Aviation*, New York: DK Publishing

Kennett, L. (1999) *The First Air War: 1914–1918*, New York: Free Press

Neiberg, M. (2003) *Foch: Supreme Allied Commander in the Great War*, Dulles, VA: Potomac Books Inc.

Titanic

Winocour, J. (2003) *The Story of the Titanic as Told by Its Survivors*, New York: Dover Publications

Ballard, R. D. (2010) *Exploring the Titanic*, Toronto: Madison Press Books

Charles Taze Russell

Abanes R. (1999) *End-Times Visions: The Road to Armageddon*, New York: Four Walls Eight Windows

Zydek, F. (2009) *Charles Taze Russell: His Life and Times: The Man, the Millennium and the Message*, CreateSpace

www.watchtower.org is the official site of the Witnesses

Tanks

Bishop, C. (2004) *The Encyclopedia of Tanks and Armored Fighting Vehicles: From World War I to the Present Day*, Charlotte, NC: Thunder Bay Press

Keegan, J. (2000) *The First World War*, New York: Vintage

Meyer, G. (2006) *A World Undone: The Story of the Great War, 1914 to 1918*, New York: Delacorte Press

Woodrow Wilson

Cooper, J. (2009) *Woodrow Wilson: A Biography*, New York: Knof

Keegan, J. (2000) *The First World War*, New York: Vintage

Meyer, G. (2006) *A World Undone: The Story of the Great War, 1914 to 1918*, New York: Delacorte Press

Talkies

Crafton, D. (1999) *The Talkies: American Cinema's Transition to Sound, 1926–1931*, Berkeley, CA: University of California Press

Nowell-Smith, G. (1999) *The Oxford History of World Cinema*, New York: Oxford University Press

Warner Sperling, C. (2008) *The Brothers Warner*, Warner Sisters

Irving Fisher

Dimand, R. W. and Geanakoplos, J. (Ed.) (2000) *Celebrating Irving Fisher: The Legacy of a Great Economist*, New Jersey: Wiley-Blackwell

Fisher, I. (2006 reprint) *The Money Illusion*, Eigal Meirovich

Albert Einstein

Caldicott, H. (2008) *Nuclear Power Is Not the Answer*, New York: New Press

Herbst, A. and Hopley, G. (2007) *Nuclear Energy Now: Why the Time Has Come for the World's Most Misunderstood Energy Source*, Hoboken, NJ: Wiley

Isaacson, W. (2008) *Einstein: His Life and Universe*, New York: Simon and Schuster

Mahaffey, J. (2010) *Atomic Awakening: A New Look at the History and Future of Nuclear Power*, Cambridge: Pegasus

Leon Trotsky

Kenez, P. (2006) *A History of the Soviet Union From the Beginning to the End*, Cambridge, Cambridge University Press

Trotsky, L. (2008) *History of the Russian Revolution*, Chicago, IL: Haymarket Books

Trotsky, L. (2004) *The Revolution Betrayed*, New York: Dover Books

Neville Chamberlain

Caputi, R. (2000) *Neville Chamberlain and Appeasement*, Selinsgrove, PA: Susquehanna University Press

Gilbert, M. (2004) *The Second World War: A Complete History*, New York: Holt Paperbacks

Smart, N. (2009) *Neville Chamberlain*, New York: Routledge

Adolf Hitler

Gilbert, M. (2004) *The Second World War: A Complete History*, New York: Holt Paperbacks

Hitler, A. (2010) *Mein Kampf*, trans. by Michael Ford, Elite Minds Inc.

Toland, J. (1991) *Adolf Hitler: The Definitive Biography*, New York: Anchor

Toland, J. (2003) *The Last 100 Days: The Tumultuous and Controversial Story of the Final Days of World War II in Europe*, New York: Modern Library

Kamikaze

Gilbert, M. (2004) *The Second World War: A Complete History*, New York: Holt Paperbacks

Inoguchi, R. (1994) *The Divine Wind: Japan's Kamikaze Force in World War II*, Annapolis, MD: US Naval Institute Press

Rielly, R. (2010) *Kamikaze Attacks of World War II: A Complete History of Japanese Suicide Strikes on American Ships, by Aircraft and Other Means*, Jefferson, NC: McFarland

Television

Behlmer, R. (1995) *Memo from Darryl F. Zanuck: The Golden Years at Twentieth Century Fox*, New York: Grove Press

Edgerton, G. (2009) *The Columbia History of American Television*, New York: Columbia University Press

Roman, W. (2008) *From Daytime to Primetime: The History of American Television*, Santa Barbara, CA: Greenwood

Rock'n' Roll

Guralnick, P. (1995) *Last Train to Memphis: The Rise of Elvis Presley*, New York: Back Bay Books

Jorgensen, E. (2000) *Elvis Presley: A Life in Music—The Complete Recording Sessions*, New York: St. Martin's Griffin

Rolling Stone Magazine (1992) *The Rolling Stone Illustrated History of Rock and Roll*, New York: Random House

Atomic Age

Bellows, A. (2006) "The Atomic Automobile," at www.damninteresting.com

Mahaffey, J. (2010) *Atomic Awakening: A New Look at the History and Future of Nuclear Power*, Cambridge: Pegasus

"Alexander M. Lewyt Dead at 79," at *The New York Times* obituaries (www.nytimes.com)

Peak Oil

Deffeyes, K. (2008) *Hubbert's Peak: The Impending World Oil Shortage*, Princeton, NJ: Princeton University Press

Maugeri, L. (2009) "The Crude Truth About Oil Reserves," *Wall Street Journal* online (online/wsj.com)

Space

Barry Johnson, S. (2010) *Space Exploration and Humanity: A Historical Encyclopedia*, Santa Barbara, CA: ABC-CLIO

Murray, C. and Bly Cox, C. (2004) *Apollo*, South Mountain Books

Wolheim, D. (1962) *Lee de Forest: Advancing the Electronic Age*, Encyclopaedia Britannica Press

Mao Zedong

Spence, J. (2006) *Mao Zedong: A Life*, New York: Penguin

Teiwes, F. and Sun, W. (1998) *China's Road to Disaster: Mao, Central Politicians, and Provincial Leaders in the Unfolding of the Great Leap Forward 1955–1959*, Armonk, NY: East Gate Book

The Beatles

The official site of *The Beatles* at www.beatles.com features a collection of articles and videos from the band's early days.

Trynka, P. (2004) *The Beatles: 10 Years That Shook The World*, London: Dorling Kindersley

World War Three

Munton, D. (2006) *The Cuban Missile Crisis: A Concise History*, New York: Oxford University Press

Dr. Strangelove, Or: How I Learned to Stop Worrying and Love the Bomb (1964) dir. George C. Scott

Robots

Asimov, I. (2008) *I, Robot*, New York: Spectra (the movie *I, Robot* (2004) dir. Alex Proyas, is only loosely based on Asimov's novel)

Dick, P. (2006) *Do Androids Dream of Electric Sheep?*, New York:

Del Rey (the movie version is *Blade Runner* (1982) dir. Ridley Scott)

Nocks, L. (2008) *The Robot: The Life Story of a Technology*, Baltimore, MD: The Johns Hopkins University Press

Schaut, S. (2007) *Robots of Westinghouse: 1924–Today*, Schaut

Margaret Thatcher

Lady Thatcher's official website and online archive can be found at margaretthatcher.org.

Berlinski, C. (2010) *There Is No Alternative: Why Margaret Thatcher*, New York: Basic Books

Ice Age

Adler, J. (2006) "Remember Global Cooling," *Newsweek* (www.newsweek.com)

Andersen, R. (2010) "Fire and Ice," at www.businessandmedia.org

Fagan, B. (2009) *The Complete Ice Age: How Climate Change Shaped the World*, London: Thames & Hudson

Personal Computers

www.computerhistory.org is an online museum of computer history with changing exhibits.

Olsen, K. (1982) *Digital Equipment Corporation the First Twenty-Five Years*, New York: Newcomen Society

Rifkin, G. and Harrar, G. (1988) *The Ultimate Entrepreneur—The Story of Ken Olsen and Digital Equipment Corporation*, Chicago: Contemporary Books

The Great Storm of 1987

Michael Fish's original weather forecast from 1987 is available on youtube.com.

Cox, J. (2000) *Weather for Dummies*, Foster City, CA: IDG Books Worldwide

The Rapture

The New Testament, Holy Bible, King James Authorized Version

Abanes R. (1999) *End-Times Visions: The Road to Armageddon*, New York: Four Walls Eight Windows

Lindsey, H. (1970) *The Late Great Planet Earth*, Grand Rapids, MI: Zondervan

Francis Fukuyama

"The End of History?" the essay on which the book is based is available online at www.wesjones.com.

Fukuyama, F. (2006) *The End of History and the Last Man*, New York: Free Press

Suicide Cults

Baigent, M., Leigh, R., and Lincoln, H. (2005) *Holy Blood, Holy Grail*, New York: Delacorte Press

Brown, D. (2004) *The Da Vinci Code*, New York: Doubleday

Daraul, A. (1995) *A History of Secret Societies*, New York: Citadel

Y2K

A good outline of the problem can be found at www.y2ktimebomb.com

Best, B. (2000) "The Y2K Computer Bug—The Yawn of a New Millennium," at www.benbest.com for a good critical view of the Millennium Bug.

Gordon Brown

The "smiling" video is available at youtube.com.

Bellamy Foster, J. and Magdoff, F. (2010) *The Great Financial Crisis: Causes and Consequences*, New York: Monthly Review Press

Keegan, W. (2004) *The Prudence of Mr. Gordon Brown*, Hoboken, NJ: Wiley

H1N1 Pandemic

Barry, J. (2005) *The Great Influenza: The Story of the Deadliest Pandemic in History*, New York: Penguin

www.who.int/csr/disease (Official site of the World Health Organization with information on H1N1 and H5N1 influenza.)

The End of the Future

Cornish, E. (2005) *Futuring: The Exploration of the Future*, Bethesda, MD: World Future Society, (www.wfs.org is the Future Society's website.)

Lombardo, T. (2006) *Contemporary Futurist Thought: Science Fiction, Future Studies, and Theories and Visions of the Future in the Last Century*, Bloomington, IN: AuthorHouse